THE CANADIAN WRITER'S MARKET

Eighth Revised Edition

(1) copyright – call Quebec – matie registered

(2) Call publisher – question list

(1) Burlington

(1) – (2) PaperJacks

Other Books by Adrian Waller

Theatre on a Shoestring

Adrian Waller's Guide to Music

Data for a Candlelit Dinner

The Gamblers

Soulikias: Portrait of an Artist

Writing! An informal, anecdotal guide to the secrets of crafting and selling non-fiction

No Ordinary Hotel: Seventy-five years at the Ritz-Carlton

THE CANADIAN WRITER'S MARKET

Eighth Revised Edition

Adrian Waller

CANADIAN CATALOGUING IN PUBLICATION DATA

Waller, Adrian, 1936–
The Canadian writer's market

8th rev. ed.
Earlier editions by Eileen Goodman.
ISBN 0-7710-8796-9

1. Authorship–Handbooks, manuals, etc. 2. Publishers and publishing–Canada–Directories. 3. Canadian periodicals–Directories. 4. Advertising agencies–Canada–Directories. 4. Advertising agencies–Canada–Directories. 5. Journalism–Study and teaching–Canada–Directories. I. Goodman, Eileen. The Canadian writer's market. II. Title.

PN161.G66 1988 808′.02 C87-095338-9

McClelland and Stewart
The Canadian Publishers
481 University Avenue
Toronto, Ontario
M5G 2E9

Printed and bound in Canada

CONTENTS

INTRODUCTION

You are holding a book containing the names and addresses of more than 1,200 potential buyers for your work – 443 consumer magazines, 427 trade journals, 70 farm publications, 103 daily newspapers listed by province, and 206 Canadian book publishers. And if these numbers suggest that magazine and book publishing is thriving in Canada, so they should. Despite predictions to the contrary, and recent hard times, the industry has never been healthier.

Nearly twenty years ago, when the idea for *The Canadian Writer's Market* was conceived and realized, Canada had a mere 100 consumer magazines, about 150 trade journals, two dozen farm publications, and only 147 book publishers. The industry was soon caught in an upswing, however, and by the mid-1970s, there were 225 consumer magazines in Canada, either sold on our newsstands or delivered to selected households free of charge, and almost as many trade publications distributed in various corners of the workplace and business world. As well, there were fifty-odd farm publications and 160 book publishers.

By 1987, according to *Canadian Advertising Rates & Data* (CARD), which is published monthly by Maclean Hunter Ltd., the number of consumer magazines had grown to 419, with trade journals keeping pace. CARD provides a solid, but only partial survey because it only ever lists publications that accept advertising. Today, there are an increasing number of magazines happy to exist without either advertising or the newsstands. One, by way of example, is Imperial Oil's handsome quarterly journal, *The Review*, which is distributed without charge as a corporate public relations vehicle.

More and more magazines, like *Equinox* and *Reader's Digest*, meanwhile, are sold mainly by subscription; others are kept in business almost entirely by either government grants or funds from specific organizations – *Canadian Geographic*, for instance, published six times a year for members of the Royal Canadian Geographic Society.

Whatever their method of funding or distribution, nearly all of Canada's magazines have now found their way into *The Canadian*

Writer's Market, making it more complete and, consequently, of better service to all writers who fervently seek to sell their words.

This edition is somewhat different from previous ones because it has been taken over by a new author with some new ideas about what it should do, and how. It would be remiss of me, however, if I did not acknowledge Eileen Goodman, a fellow writer who, before her well-earned retirement in the mid-1980s, ushered *The Canadian Writer's Market* into all seven previous editions, always keeping careful note of when magazines were born, when they changed hands, or when they went out of business, and updating the book as frequently as she could.

It was Eileen Goodman, in fact, who originated and refined the original concept of this reference book. She did her job meticulously – long before word processors or memory typewriters – constantly striving to see that what she produced would always be of maximum relevance to writers from coast to coast. With last-minute checking, cross-checking and additions, she sought earnestly to ensure, as I have now, that by the time each edition was published it had not fallen appreciably out of date.

This is a difficult job, at best, because publishing is an extremely transient business, forever moving offices and forever introducing new faces on the way. I have also done my utmost to keep abreast of as many of those changes as possible. For the most part, the revisions I have made are really quite minimal. I hope, nonetheless, that they will prove useful.

First, I have opted not to lump all the magazines together, but to sort them into two main groups: (1) consumer magazines, and (2) business, trade, and professional publications. And to better facilitate a quick and easy reference for writers seeking a suitable market for a good idea, or for those wanting to recycle an article to other buyers, I have narrowed down these two groups of publications even further, according to subject and type:

• Consumer publications now appear in nine sub-groups: general interest; news, opinions, and issues; entertainment, and city and rural; women's and feminist; special interest; sports and outdoors; youth and children's; art, music, and literary; and scholarly.

• Trade publications have been divided into twenty categories according to the professions or trades they serve. These groups range from architecture, business, data processing and electronics, to advertising and the media, office furnishings, transportation, and travel.

Second, to sharpen the book as a marketing tool, I have compiled thumbnail sketches for each consumer magazine to explain – in the limited space available to describe such a large collection – what exactly it is, and what kinds of articles it carries. I have found this necessary because so many magazines have been given names that bear little or no indication of what they really are, who reads them, and, consequently, the kinds of articles or short pieces of fiction they buy.

No one would ever guess, for instance, that a tabloid called *Pandora*, published four times a year in Halifax, is a forum for feminists. Nor would you necessarily think that rather than report on the entertainment world, Winnipeg's *Class Act* gives local high school students fashion news and career-planning tips. And far from being a farm publication, as you might immediately suspect, *Grain* is a spunky little literary publication which, since 1973, has been produced quarterly in Regina by the Saskatchewan Writers' Guild.

I say "publication" quite often throughout this book because, strictly speaking, many of those it lists or mentions are not really magazines as we have come to know them, but news bulletins or tabloid newspapers that feed the needs, sometimes erratically, of a smallish group of loyal readers. Others, however, are very definitely magazines in the truest sense: glossy, highly professional consumer or trade journals that boast respectable circulations and that are distributed regularly, be it weekly, monthly, quarterly, or only twice a year. The word "publication," then, seems to safely cover all listings, large and small.

Much more important to the writer is that all these publications provide opportunities both for established freelancers wanting to break fresh ground and for neophyte writers seeking to have their work published. Each magazine listed accepts outside contributions with varying frequency and for equally varying fees.

Some publications, particularly among the scholarly journals and the literary and arts magazines, admit to not paying their writers at all. Others, such as *Reader's Digest*, *Saturday Night*, and *Equinox*, however, pay fees that are among the highest in North America, and expect high standards of writing and reporting in return.

Except where editors have asked me not to, I have also included telephone numbers with each listing. Writers are always advised, however, to try to sell their work by letter. While it is perfectly acceptable to phone a publication to ask for its contributors' guidelines (which usually say how much it pays for those articles needed for its various editorial departments), business with editors is nearly always more effectively accomplished with a carefully compiled proposal.

Marketing

This vital element of the craft needs some illumination and clarification. Too few beginning writers understand that marketing is as vital an element of their craft as style and subject matter. Without a successful marketing strategy, their words and ideas may never see print.

The professional way to sell a story or a book is to propose it fully in writing so as to eliminate the risks inherent in producing work on speculation. If or when an idea is accepted, the writer and the editor discuss fee, deadline – an *obsession* of the business, by the way – and the preferred writing style for the finished article.

Obviously, writers should always study those magazines for which they would like to write so they can immediately address the question, "What does this particular editor want?" Ultimately, though, they are aiming to satisfy not the editor but the editor's readers, and the only way to find out what *they* like is by reading the kinds of stories they have been fed in the past.

Another sure-fire way of becoming acquainted with a specific group of readers, and getting a feel for what they want, is to take careful note of the type and quality of the advertising that keeps their magazine afloat. In other words, you can only really know what to suggest to an editor after diligently studying his issues – and lots of them – as regularly as you can, in libraries, on the newsstands, or in doctors' offices.

Unquestionably, the hardest writing to sell is the novel. No matter how timely or ingenious a story may be, the effect a piece of fiction ultimately has on readers will depend almost entirely on how well it is constructed and written. Some of this, of course, also applies to non-fiction writing, particularly first-person experience pieces so obviously a part of the writer, and essays that must intelligently set out opinions and arguments. But, whereas the worthiness of most suggestions for magazine articles can be demonstrated aptly in a proposal, the power of the novel really cannot.

Some publishers are able to judge the merits of a piece of fiction from two or three sample chapters accompanied by a synopsis of the remainder of the story. Ideally, these should explain the plot and show the very thing that holds fiction together – the theme. On the basis of this initial work, publishers will give an experienced writer a contract and an advance against royalties to complete the book. Usually, though, they only ever commit themselves to novels submitted by an unknown author after seeing the completed text.

To help sell their work, fiction writers often seek out agents – like the fifteen I have listed later. But, you should remember, agents do not possess magic wands that they can wave to find a market for everything that crosses their desks. On the contrary, they must work extremely hard to sell whatever they can, and their very best acquisitions, usually from good writers, are nearly always the first to find a buyer. So, to make their lives easier, reputable agents only ever handle a work they think will sell so well that it will be financially beneficial for both themselves and their clients.

In some large cities in the United States agents also place magazine articles and essays, but only those written by frequently published authors who are exceptionally well known. In Canada, however, this is not the case. Virtually all articles are sold directly to magazines by authors themselves – with well-crafted proposals.

Not surprisingly, then, the query letter to an editor and the full, detailed proposal or outline that follows it, may well be the most significant piece of work the beginning writer ever undertakes. It not only sells a suggestion, after all, but the writer with it. It should serve to demonstrate to an editor that, beyond any shadow of doubt, the person who conceived the idea and refined it really is the one best able to turn it into a strong, informative piece of writing for a lot of readers to enjoy.

Copyright

Whatever you sell, and by whatever means you choose to do it, one of the most crucial legal elements of the writing craft is copyright. This is nearly always discussed the moment an editor responds favourably to a writer's suggestion.

Put simply, copyright means the sole right to reproduce – or allow others to reproduce – a literary or artistic work. And contrary to popular belief, it begins upon creation rather than publication, and exists until fifty years after the creator's death.

From writers' points of view, it is what they are about to sell when they have agreed upon a fee for their efforts. Or, to put it another way, it is what the magazine or publishing house has actually bought the moment the writer has signed an editorial contract or has cashed the publisher's cheque.

Terms of a copyright agreement may vary greatly in nature or content – a contract, after all, can include whatever conditions one party feels pertinent – but not in principle. Canadian magazines with huge circulations most often buy North American rights – the right to publish an article to be read by an audience scattered across the entire continent. Some large Canadian magazines are content simply to buy Canadian rights, the right to publish a work that will be read only within the country. Some acquire serial rights – the right to publish a work in a sister publication without having to pay extra for it.

A few smaller publications, however, simply buy one-time rights. Under this type of agreement, copyright ownership automatically reverts back to the writer, either immediately upon publication or shortly afterwards, according to the agreement. This leaves the writer legally free to sell the same article in the same words to what is called a "secondary market." If that new market also buys only one-time rights, the same article may then be re-sold to a third magazine without the need for any alteration, then a fourth, and so on down the line.

But there is another element of copyright that must be carefully considered. Most good magazines only ever buy first-time rights because they do not want material that has already been published elsewhere, even though they themselves might plan on buying only one-time rights. In other words, they may indeed want one-time rights, but these must be first-time.

This usually leaves writers with two main options. They can either sell a story several times over to those magazines willing to buy one-time rights, not caring if these are first, second, or even third, or they can take what most experienced freelancers have come to regard as the more lucrative road. That is, they can write a piece for a top fee from a large magazine first, then try selling the same idea to other, smaller, magazines later.

Be careful here, though. While ideas can't ordinarily be copyrighted, the words used to express or explain them can, and are. This is why our copyright laws came into being: to prevent people from taking and using something–in this case words, phrases, expressions, literary structures–that do not belong to them. So if you have sold North American, Canadian, or even World rights to a magazine, remember that before being offered elsewhere, your piece must be totally rewritten and restructured. As it passes from the original buyer to others wanting first-time rights, each text must avoid any of the original word combinations, structures, or "echoes." If, on the other hand, you have sold one-time rights and the copyright has reverted to you, you may send off your article in its original, unaltered form as many times as you wish.

Some magazines–*Reader's Digest*, for example, and Montreal's *Doctor's Review*–buy what are known as "reprint" rights, yet another corner of the maze of copyright. Under this agreement, editors may "pick up" and re-publish articles that have appeared elsewhere so long as they pay the original publishers, and/or the writers, fees for their one-time use. This practice is always restricted to publishers and must never be confused with recycling. It is merely an arrangement made between two magazines, with the copyright laws in mind, which gives the writer a little extra money as a bonus for his or her initial efforts.

Copyright is an extremely complex part of law, and writers are advised to read up on it all they can before negotiating the sales terms of their work, thus putting themselves in a stronger bargaining position. A lot of helpful information can be obtained from the Canadian Copyright Institute, one of the twenty-two writers' organizations listed at the back of this book.

Here, however, are some of the most frequently-posed questions about copyright, with general answers:

Is every piece of written work copyrighted?

No. In Canada, copyright on a work lasts for the life of the author plus fifty years. After that, the work falls into the public domain and may be legally copied at will.

How can I tell who the rightful owner of a copyright is?

In the first few pages of a book or magazine there is a copyright notice. Typically, it will read: Copyright Josephine Blow, 1988; or Joseph P. Blow & Sons, Publishers, 1988. Beneath this will usually appear the publisher's address. Even if the copyright is held in the author's name, it is generally the publisher who has the right–by contract–to authorize reprints of excerpts. If, however, the author has retained these rights exclusively, which may sometimes be the case, he or she can be contacted through the publisher.

How does copyright infringement occur?

Usually through carelessness or ignorance. Few writers, after all, deliberately set out to steal something that doesn't belong to them. They either quote too much of someone else's work without first seeking permission to do so, or use previously written words without making a sufficiently concerted effort to disguise them through thorough rewriting.

What is "too much" of someone else's work?

The answer to this isn't easy. It depends on several factors, principally the quantity and quality of the portion taken and whether its use will detract from the impact and/or the marketability of the original. No one loses sleep if a writer uses a line or two from a book and attributes its source; to reproduce three or four key paragraphs without permission, however–even with *attribution*–could lead to problems. The writer is always advised to contact the copyright holder, quoting the extract(s) he or she wants to use in full, giving a true indication of context, details of format (magazine article, script, or book), and size of audience, and ask for permission to reproduce it. A neophyte writer wanting to use 100 words for *Parallelogramme* probably will not be charged what a "name" writer would be expected to pay for a similar-sized extract in an article for *Equinox*. Many copyright holders, however, do not charge for so few words.

How can I copyright my work?

Often there is no need to. The moment you have written something it is automatically copyrighted. If, however, you feel there is a chance someone may one day say your manuscript is theirs, you may register it for a fee with the Federal Department of Communications' Copyright Office: 50 Victoria Street, 5th Floor, Place du Portage, Tower 1, Hull, Quebec, K1A 0C9. You can also mail your manuscript to yourself in a registered package. This would provide you with a dated receipt, which you would be able to produce when opening the package before a judge, should the manuscript's rightful ownership ever become a legal issue.

If I work for a newspaper, who owns the copyright on my work?

Usually, if you are employed by a company it automatically owns the copyright of everything you write for it in the course of your work. This cannot be reproduced or re-sold in any form without first obtaining permission. Often, newspapers generously allow articles, or portions of them, to be reprinted without charge.

Can a magazine editor steal the idea contained in my story proposal and assign it to someone else to write?

Yes, but the good ones won't. For this reason, it is not necessary to write "copyright" on your proposal. You would be wasting words anyway. Ideas–like titles–are in the public domain and cannot be protected by copyright laws unless part of an invention. And that is yet another branch of copyright law. If you intend to sell movie scripts in Hollywood (in which case you will definitely need an agent to negotiate rights on your behalf), have faith in the people you deal with. Good magazines and publishing houses stay in business because their editors are ethical.

Should I copyright the book I have been contracted to write before sending it to the publisher?

No. All publishers will copyright your work for you, under either their name or yours, depending on the terms of the contract you should already have signed. They will also register it for you, at the National Library in Ottawa, as an original Canadian work.

Libel

Jonathan Swift once complained loudly and logically, in *The Tale of the Tub*, that writers were no longer able to lash out at particular people for particular vices and had to content themselves with general satire on mankind. More than 200 years later, we must all take heed. We must do our best not to make any direct, unfair, or inaccurate allusion to the living that might shed bad light upon their reputations.

Libel suits are notoriously complex – and the traps are wide. Many novelists have the mistaken belief that the use of fictitious names, or a statement saying that any resemblance between the characters in the novel and living persons is purely coincidental, will automatically protect them from the possibility of a libel suit. They are wrong. If the average reader associates a character described in a manuscript with an actual person, and the description reflects unfavourably on his reputation or integrity, there is always the danger of libel.

Fiction writers must always strive to assure that the resemblance really *is* coincidence and most certainly avoid the intention, which may be interpreted by legal minds as a personal attack – and possibly lead to an action.

All writers need to understand enough about Canadian libel laws to protect both themselves and their publishers against court action. This is absolutely necessary since nearly all publishers' contracts provide for indemnification by the author in cases where a person maligned in a manuscript resorts to a suit.

Libel in Canada is mostly covered by civil law and comes under provincial jurisdiction. Its principles are based on the English Common Law for all provinces, except in Quebec where the law stems directly from the French Civil Code. But the principles remain: libel is a printed statement or a picture that exposes a person to hatred, ridicule, or contempt, and imputes to him immorality, crime, or disorderly conduct, or tends to injure him in the pursuit of his profession, office, or trade. In short, anything that might discredit a person may be construed as libellous. And under some circumstances, this can also apply to corporations or their individual members.

If such a statement or picture is printed, the publisher must be prepared to defend his publication on three fronts: truth of the statement; privilege; and fair comment on a matter of public interest.

If the author's statements are accurate and true, there may be no basis for a civil action for libel, but any false or defamatory statement that tends to harm a person's reputation may constitute libel, primarily in Quebec, where even truth is not a sufficient defence.

Privileged reports fall into two classifications: absolute privilege and qualified privilege. If published at the same time as they took place, a fair and accurate report without editorial comment on proceedings heard before a court of justice is absolutely privileged.

Qualified or conditional privilege is enjoyed by reporters while covering proceedings in any government body, whether legislative or administrative, any commission of inquiry or organization whose members represent any public authority in Canada, or municipal council, school board, or board of health meetings.

The defence of qualified privilege extends to the findings or decisions of those Canadian organizations formed to promote the interests of any art, science, religion, or learning; any trade, business, industry, or profession; any game, sport, or pastime to which members of the public are invited as spectators or participants.

Fair and honest comment on matters of public interest is privileged, but any statement of fact must be true to be privileged. An author who comments on current affairs or writes a biography is permitted to express honest opinions or fair criticism of someone's works or accomplishments because this is usually in the public interest and serves to promote a useful purpose. Fair comment extends to criticism of books, magazines, articles, plays, and motion pictures.

Another defence that newspapers and magazines often resort to is mitigation of damages based on a retraction of a statement that was made in error. While this action does not absolve the publication from libel, it nevertheless tends to show that any injury was purely accidental, and this may lessen the amount of the damages levied by the court.

BUT

Simultaneous submissions

There is absolutely nothing wrong with writers sending the same article, proposal, or book manuscript to more than one potential market at the same time. It is their work, after all, so they can do whatever they please with it. But unless they are sending off material simultaneously to those magazine that are happy to buy second, third, or fourth rights, they could be creating problems for themselves when they least want them. 6

The practice can sometimes be unethical. Busy magazines need about a month to assess an idea or a manuscript properly, sometimes more. During this time, several people may be assigned to the job of writing an informed critique explaining to both the writer and the senior editor where the book or article is effective, where it isn't, why, and what revisions may be necessary.

In publishing houses, this work takes considerably longer and is correspondingly more expensive. To be able to judge a promising book proposal or an intriguing "on spec" manuscript of several thousand words usually means that an editor must set aside present work. If she is rushing to complete a book for her spring list, the managing editor or the publisher might have to hire an outside reader to do this extra job instead. Readers are also often hired for their specialized expertise, to judge whether a writer has covered a topic, fact or fiction, properly and accurately. If an idea or manuscript appears tempting, the publisher may recruit market researchers to predict its sales potential. By sending the same material to several houses, the writer may automatically involve them all in the expense of assessing something only one of them would eventually be able to acquire.

Indeed, to established writers, the idea of simultaneous submissions is distasteful. Knowing how busy editors can be, they give them reasonable time to respond – about six weeks on a magazine and as long as three months in a publishing house. If after that they have heard nothing, they fire off a reminder, then turn immediately to other productive work. The publishing business is notorious for its slowness and, unfortunately, this is something all writers have to learn to accept.

Photocopies

Simultaneous submission almost invariably means sending out photocopies of manuscripts, rather than the original. Editors on good magazines often refuse to read photocopies, and for a good reason. They immediately suspect that they have been sent a copy because other copies are in the process of being offered elsewhere. And why should editors bother investing time in something they are not quite sure they will eventually have the chance to buy?

So whatever you may have written, particularly if you are trying to break into a new market with a piece you have crafted on speculation, it is always better to send the original text. There is a strong argument, of course, for keeping originals safe so they won't get lost in the mail. In this case, it is usually wise to explain to an editor that you are sending a photocopy for precisely this purpose, and that the original is available if required.

Word processors

Thanks to modern technology, more and more writers are crafting their poems, articles, and books on personal computers using a word processing program. Most publishers prefer this, not because it saves them a little money, but because it speeds up the production process and helps prevent errors from creeping into the manuscript at the typesetting stage.

During word processing, the initial draft – and all the hundreds of large or small changes that should be inevitable as the work develops – is tapped out on an electronic keyboard and transferred, not onto paper for the moment, but onto a screen for viewing, and onto a disk for storage or safe keeping. The word processor enables the writer to compose words and keep them in files – one file per story or article, perhaps, or one per chapter – then recall them at will. As long as a file has been properly stored, it can be retrieved as many times as the writer wants to make changes.

Word processing enables writers to alter their work limitlessly, without resorting to such traditional and perfectly respectable writers' tools as scissors, stapler, or paste pot. Thus they are spared the drudgery of seemingly endless retyping while striving to make their prose sparkle a little more, or their narrative flow in a smoother, clearer line.

It is amazing technology indeed. All that is required to switch or replace words, polish punctuation, delete sentences, or shift huge blocks of paragraphs to different sections of a growing manuscript, is just a few gentle strokes of a few keys. In other words, writers can now edit, cut, paste, and rebuild their work in the belly of a computer. Once, manuscript typists needed many hours over several days to transform a rough draft into a whistle-clean text. Today, with the final text saved on a disk, clean copy is produced by the writer himself, on his printer, in a matter of minutes.

Some of the more advanced word processing programs contain a spelling checker and a thesaurus. The speller, of course, helps eliminate poor spelling and typographical errors, and the thesaurus gives the writer instant access to a wide choice of synonyms and antonyms. With yet another touch of a key, any word can be selected from the thesaurus to replace one that is no longer wanted in the text.

In recent years, as personal computers have flooded the market, so the consumer has become increasingly confused about what type to buy. Strange as it may seem, the *least* important part of word processing is the computer itself. This – the hardware – is really nothing more than an electronic box with switches, coils, and microchips. It is only as good as whatever program – the software – is inserted into a drive to make it perform in a specific way. Thus, software capabilities must always be foremost in the writer's mind, and he or she is far better off seeking out the most suitable word processing program first, then buying the right computer to accommodate it.

On the surface, this may appear like buying a cart, then searching for the kind of horse able to pull it, and in one sense it is. But the reason is perfectly sound. Just as the market has been flooded with all manner of personal computers, so there have been countless different kinds of software – and more confusion.

Let's look at software. The kind of program you decide to use will ultimately determine the type of hardware you buy to run it. Some powerful word processing programs need equally powerful computers to absorb them, make them run, and still have enough "working" memory. A small, inexpensive computer with, say, 64 kilobytes of memory, it is safe to predict, won't. Nor will a 256K computer. Both types might be fine for a student's essays, or a smallish piece a reporter may want to write for a newspaper, but they will not have sufficient capacity to accommodate a top-notch word processing program. The serious writer would quickly out-grow them, and find them worthless.

Many home computers offered at low prices automatically come with software. There is usually nothing whatsoever wrong with the computer itself – in either power or quality – but all too often the accompanying program, though capable of some basic word processing, will again prove insufficient. The program is likely to be so limited, for example, that it cannot even underline to denote italics. Nor might it contain foreign accents or monetary signs. For a professional-looking manuscript, both these features are absolutely integral.

To be able to store a healthy bank of 2,000-word magazine pieces and have quick and easy access to them, the writer will need a computer with a minimum of 512K. Many busy freelancers have found, however, that it is wiser to spend an extra two hundred dollars or so on a 640K computer. This not only has sufficient power for virtually any word processing program available, but would guarantee more than enough working memory should the computer one day be used for crafting books.

For books, by the way, a powerful computer and software is essential, if only to prevent all the work involved from being cumbersome. Some writers manage to write books on small home computers, but all too often their software restricts them and the computer's capacity is such that they can only get one or two chapters on a single disk. To do the job properly, you will need to be able to store several chapters on one or two disks – without fear of running out of space. If you do, and are left with half of a chapter on one disk, and the other half on another, it will surely create awkward technical problems when the time comes for you to print out your work.

Power, memory, and software capability are one thing. Another aspect of word processing worthy of almost equal consideration is your working speed, which lies largely in using a good keyboard, one with which you feel comfortable.

It is also well to remember that just how quickly a manuscript can be produced does not necessarily depend on how good or expensive your printer is, but how suitable. Here is another chance for writers to save money. Ordinarily, they will never need a costly letter-quality printer – just one capable of providing a clear, draft-quality text in a pleasant, easy-to-read type face.

Both elite and pica typefaces, by the way, are perfectly acceptable for manuscripts, though pica, which is larger and rounder, seems to be preferred. More to the point is that script type faces that resemble italics or Old English should be avoided because they are harder to read. This rule applies to both a word processor *and* a typewriter, electric or otherwise.

Another component of the home computer, and one more integral to comfort than any other, is the screen, which is all too often underestimated or overlooked. Indeed, the profession is full of writers who have spent the past few years wishing they had invested extra money in a high-quality screen, because it would have made their work much less tiring.

Many quite efficient home computers are sold with what are known as "colour" screens. These are fine for games, and for some graphics, imperative. But for a person wanting to master only simple word processing, they are not only superfluous, but unnecessarily expensive. Conversely, other computers come with much cheaper screens that show bulky, disjointed lettering that is difficult and uninviting to read.

Ideally, the writer should aim somewhere between these two extremes. The advice is to get what is called a "high-resolution" screen – preferably one with soft amber or green lettering on a black or grey background. This not only costs a lot less than a colour screen, but helps to reduce eyestrain. Suffice it to say that endlessly watching your work spring to life on a screen you are not comfortable with will make word processing a chore, and certainly not a pleasure.

Finally, before shopping for a word processor, talk to other writers and ascertain what computers and software packages *they* bought, and why. Judge your needs by theirs. All too often, sales clerks will be unable to advise you properly because they have never written professionally. They may not readily know the kind of painstaking self-editing, revising, and polishing that saleable writing entails – or the type of software best suited to the writer's needs.

Manuscripts

It goes without saying that manuscripts that have been poorly typed and are littered with spelling errors look amateurish. Editors don't necessarily expect word-processed texts – just those that are clean and well prepared on white bond letter-size paper, with a covering page bearing a title. If your article is accepted, it is doubtful that the title you gave it will survive. In fact, it usually won't. It is likely to undergo several changes as editors put their heads together to dream up something that suits it better, according to the style of their magazine. When first submitting a piece, then, its title is of little consequence. Your job is to merely call your work *something* so it can be recorded as such when editorial department receives it.

Much more of a priority is other information you must put on the title page – your name, complete address, and telephone number.

Some writers think that if they fold their manuscripts or drive a staple through its top left-hand corner, their chances of seeing it published are jeopardized. They are wrong, of course, because editors are not that fickle. Of infinitely greater consideration to them are such ingredients as uniqueness or importance of subject, and whether it has been properly covered and deftly illustrated with anecdotes. They look, too, for good writing – not so much for clever, or fancy writing, but that which is clear and easy to understand. Editors do find, however, that a neat manuscript is infinitely more inviting to read than an untidy one.

Almost invariably, editors like a manuscript to have a good margin of at least an inch running down the left hand side of each page – sufficient space for their comments to the author in the event that the piece needs to be returned for revision.

Book manuscripts, though, are a little more complex. Each new chapter needs to be denoted as such by starting part way down the page. And for the manuscript to be complete, all pages must be numbered, and have margins about an inch wide. The text will require a title page, too, and others devoted to a full, accurate listing of any permissions the author needed to acquire to be legally entitled to quote from copyrighted works.

The quickest way to impress an editor is to send a *complete* manuscript – including the contents page, the acknowledgements, dedication, introduction or preface for the front of the book, plus any necessary bibliography or appendix for the back—all in one parcel. The surest way to peeve an editor is to make her write or telephone asking for the remainder of the manuscript so she can properly process it in its entirety.

When using a word processor it is always wise to co-ordinate your efforts with those of the publisher so that your disks will not be useless. Many instructions are specific to the type of software used, but some are general: (1) each article or chapter should have its own file; (2) never fill your disks. Always leave room—at least 40K "working space" on each—for the typesetter's format instructions; (3) always make backup disks; (4) never centre or justify the text. This makes it difficult for the publisher to obtain an accurate word count and creates problems for the typesetter during formatting; (5) set your margins so that there are no more than sixty characters per line; (6) never hyphenate a word at the end of a line unless that word has a hyphen anyway; (7) ask the publisher for advice about codes for accents, currency symbols, fractions, footnote or endnote numbers, and use of bold faces and italic faces.

Style

By style, most book and magazine editors mean the conventions of spelling, punctuation, and capitalization. There is, of course, no generally accepted manual for style because it varies from periodical to periodical, publishing house to publishing house, not to mention from fiction to non-fiction, from genre to genre, and from discipline to discipline. Writers should remember, however, that style is an integral part of their craft and, by showing a blatant disregard for it, they can quite inadvertently prejudice an editor against their work.

Writers are expected to observe at least *some* of the basic house rules, and these should be obvious in what has already been published by those magazines and book publishing houses for which they aspire to write. If they are not, the writer is always wise to find out as much as possible about what these rules are, and what stylistic traits—as idiosyncratic as many may appear to be—are preferred.

Canadian newspapers generally follow the Canadian Press style book (which also contains some good tips on reporting, by the way), and magazines tend to develop their own standards and preferences from one authoritative source, or a compilation of many. Book publishers, however, almost always adhere to well-known manuals, of which *Words into Type* (Prentice Hall) and *A Manual of Style* (University of Chicago Press), are among the best known.

Very often, a publishing house has compiled its own guide to house style, and the aspiring writer should never be afraid to ask for a copy.

The word count

The number of words a manuscript contains is another consideration for editors. A large part of their job is to ensure that stories can be fitted into an allotted space. When they order 2,000 words, the manuscript should not be appreciably longer, and preferably 100 words or so less.

For books, the word count is infinitely more crucial because cutting, even merely trimming to a publishable size, is a lot more work than many writers realize. Doing it properly almost always means having to judiciously remove material – a sentence here or a couple of paragraphs there – throughout an entire text and not just from one part of it. The time involved explains why authors lament that they have had potentially good works either rejected out of hand, or returned swiftly to them, for drastic shortening.

Always remember that the real skill in writing is being able to tell a story, fact or fiction, in the shortest number of necessary words. To achieve this, good writers develop keen powers of self-criticism. They are constantly scrutinizing their work for wordiness, clutter, unnecessarily long quotes, or characters that do nothing to enhance the subject of their story, or help the action along. The moment they come upon any of them, they ruthlessly pare away the superfluous material so as to make their text tighter.

They also check regularly to see how many words they are writing. A simple way to count them is to set the left-hand margin of the typewriter or word processor at twenty and the right at seventy-five so that each line of typing will then contain an average of ten words. Twenty-five double-spaced lines on a standard-size page, therefore, will equal roughly 250 words.

Postage

Nearly all magazine and publishing houses, particularly the smaller ones, appreciate writers accompanying unsolicited work with stamped and self-addressed envelopes, so that it can be returned without cost. Postage rates have soared in recent years – they have more than doubled, in fact, since this book was last revised – and so, for any business that relies heavily on our mail system, they now represent a sizeable business expense.

Income tax

In Canada, the Income Tax Act is good to writers, allowing them to deduct legitimate work expenses from their taxable incomes. In return, writers are trusted to show all their earnings, particularly fees that are unsupported by T4, T4A, or T5 slips from magazines and publishing houses that have printed their work.

Basically, writers come under three classifications:

- Salaried employees who supplement incomes by earning a little extra money as occasional freelance writers
- Part-time writers whose major income comes from another job which will almost certainly be cast aside the moment writing becomes more profitable
- Totally self-employed, full-time writers not on any payroll, who are expected to file honest returns mindful that no income taxes have been deducted at source

Writers with other jobs need only attach to their income tax returns a statement summarizing writing income and expenses, and to show whether this extra work resulted in a profit or a loss. Any profit must be added to that taxable income earned from the other job. Losses, however, may be used to reduce it.

Writers living entirely from their craft must keep many more details–a list of all income and from what sources, and receipts and vouchers to support expenses. Maintaining proper financial records serves not only as a reminder of cash that has flowed both in and out, but also helps reduce problems that might be encountered should a tax return be audited.

All writers may reasonably deduct the cost of all stationery, including letterhead, envelopes, typewriter ribbons, pencils, pens, paper clips, even scissors and glue. Telephone costs, particularly long distance calls, are also deductible, as are postage, membership dues in writers' organizations, union dues, accountants' fees, secretarial help, research assistance, subscriptions to newspapers and magazines, reference books, copyright costs, and photocopying charges.

Many writers find that their biggest annual deduction is for their work space. Those who work in an outside office may claim its rent as an expense. If, however, they work at home, they may write off a reasonable portion of their living space. A writer using one room as an office in a six-room apartment, for example, may claim one sixth of the rent plus a sixth of such other expenses as municipal taxes, heating, lighting, minor repairs, and ordinary maintenance.

An area of tax deduction often overlooked is the depreciation of office furniture and equipment. Both may be written off according to a fixed percentage determined by the income tax regulations. A typewriter or word processor can be depreciated by 20 per cent of the total cost each year for five years. The same tax saving may be applied to cameras, tape recorders, filing cabinets, desks, chairs, and telephone answering machines.

Travel is also an allowable expense, whether it is to visit a publisher or gather research for an article. Here the non-fiction writer is at a distinct advantage, because in most cases interviewing people in a different town is absolutely necessary. This could conceivably mean a bus trip from downtown Vancouver to nearby Burnaby, on the one hand, or a flight from Halifax to Istanbul, on the other.

The simple rule is that to be tax deductible, travel *must* relate to work. For the novelist who cannot secure an advance commitment from a publisher, a legitimate business trip may be extremely hard to prove. All is not lost, however. If a visit to Turkey is necessary to gather material that cannot be found elsewhere, it can be claimed as an expense either when the work is published, or written off against royalties the moment they start trickling in.

Car travel, hotels, meals, and entertainment–the drinks you may want to buy a useful contact, the dinner you buy for a person who is figuring prominently in your story, or the pleasant young woman who edited your latest book–are also legitimate writers' expenses. Remember, though, that you cannot claim on your income tax form any expenses that a magazine or publishing house may already have refunded to you. Apart from being illegal, it is dishonest.

American markets

The English-speaking Canadian who has begun to sell with some consistency enjoys a unique geographical advantage over colleague writers overseas. Canada has a southerly neighbour with a population of some 226 million people, most of whom speak English and are thus potential readers of English writing.

The most recent edition of *Writer's Market*, published annually by *Writer's Digest*, lists more than 4,000 paying markets in the U.S.A. for novels, short stories, fillers, plays, gags, verses, even photographs the freelancer may take during travels. This book also gives the names and addresses of editors, and sets out their requirements – what they expect from a manuscript in content and length, and how long it takes them to report back to a writer with a decision on whether or not to publish.

Two monthly magazines are also indispensable to Canadian writers seeking new markets south of the border – *Writer's Digest* itself, published in Cincinnati for practical-minded freelancers, and *The Writer*, published in Boston for those with more literary tastes. These journals not only keep readers informed about markets and trends, but provide both a stimulus and a constant flow of fresh ideas.

Writers aiming for the highest-paying American markets will find a *Writer's Digest* book called *A Complete Guide to Writing and Selling Non-Fiction* particularly valuable.

But books are only a start. The much-repeated rule about studying markets, as you must when writing for Canadian magazines, applies more than ever here because the array of American publications is awesome. And those that at first appear similar most certainly are not on closer examination. Nearly all magazines have their own special character and narrow, specific needs to go with it.

The enormous selection of American magazines, however, in no way diffuses the difficulty in breaking into the huge market they have come to constitute, particularly with a Canadian story. The first point to ask yourself here is, "Why would an American magazine be interested in Canada?" A quick answer to the question is that most really aren't unless they can be *made* to be interested in Canada, or unless the story has a broad appeal to both nations.

Some Canadian stories, of course, may have an obvious and natural tie-in with American events. Most, however, probably won't, and this should help explain why it very hard for a Canadian writer to penetrate the American market, especially with ideas for the consumer magazines.

Most Canadian writers who have consistently sold their work to the U.S.A. can thank those opportunities provided by the vast collection of American trade publications. This is not hard to understand. If Canada is related to the U.S.A. at all, it is by sharing common trade channels, and having similar concerns about world politics and business. The moment American equipment and/or expertise is brought to bear on a Canadian building site, for example, there could legitimately be the makings of a story for an American trade or professional magazine. Sometimes, there may also be a story in how Canada sees, or deals with, problems specific to both countries.

But there is yet another hurdle to cross. Many American trade magazines are so wealthy that they are entirely staff-written. This means that a staff writer will often travel to Canada to cover an American story rooted here, so a manuscript from a Canadian freelancer must be exceptionally strong to win a place.

The odds can be beaten, though. After accepting a few manuscripts from a Canadian contributor, the editor of an American trade magazine might be willing to publish a monthly feature written by a Canadian on the Canadian viewpoint: what his or her country thinks about mutual problems and issues, and what solutions it can offer.

It is well worth trying to secure a foothold in the American market, for purely economic reasons. It is still difficult, after all, for Canadians to make satisfactory livings by writing exclusively for magazines and publishing houses in their own country, which helps explain why most combine crafting poetry, novels, magazine articles, and non-fiction books with other work.

The situation *is* changing, however, and will continue to do so – for the better. The next edition of *The Canadian Writer's Market* promises then, to be bulkier than this one, with even more sales opportunities and contacts for our writers. Let's hope so.

CONSUMER MAGAZINES

Consumer magazines are read by the general public and are sold mostly either on the newsstands or by subscription. An increasing number, however, are controlled-circulation publications delivered to selected homes free of charge. Many, like the Ontario Motor League's *Leisure Ways*, are distributed by various organizations to their members.

Consumer magazines that are supported entirely by advertising can usually afford to pay more for a writer's work, and on submission, than those that are not. In some cases, the fee for a substantial piece of work – a non-fiction article of between 4,000 and 5,000 words – could stretch to more than $2,000, especially if written for well-established or large-circulation magazines like *Saturday Night*, *Equinox*, or *Reader's Digest*.

Several other Canadian periodicals, such as *The Financial Post Moneywise Magazine*, the inflight magazines *Canadian* and *enRoute*, and *Chatelaine*, the country's largest women's journal, pay fees that can often amount to around $1,500. A number of others, which pay about $1,000 for a professionally written full-length magazine piece, usually of around 2,000 words, are *Canadian Business*, *Western Living*, *Canadian Geographic*, and *City and Country Home*.

Magazines with smaller circulations for obvious reasons pay somewhat less, usually between $300 and $800 for an article which could run to 3,000 words. Most of those listed on the following pages fall into this category, the majority still paying by the word, and only on publication.

But all magazines, large and small, are consistently reviewing their fee structures – to make writing more profitable for Canadian contributors.

"Magazines constitute the only national press we possess in Canada," says the *Report of the Special Senate Committee on Mass Media*, published in 1970. "Magazines add a journalistic dimension which no other medium can provide – depth and wholeness and texture, plus the visual impact of graphic design. Magazines, because of their freedom from daily deadlines, can aspire to a level of excellence that is seldom attainable in other media. Magazines, in a different way from any other medium, can help foster in Canadians a sense of themselves."

GENERAL INTEREST

L'actualité
1001 de Maisonneuve Boulevard W., Montreal, Que. H3A 3E1
(514) 845-5141
Contact: Jean Paré, editor
A general-interest monthly produced by and for Quebecers, carrying in-depth features on events and issues affecting life in Quebec. Most stories are pegged in some way to the news.

Alberta Report
17327 - 106A Avenue, Edmonton, Alta. T5S 1M7
(403) 484-8884
Contact: Stephen Hopkins, editor
Covers local, provincial, and national news weekly from a Western point of view – government, business, resources, law, education, religion, arts, sports, medicine, agriculture, and people of Alberta.

Atlantic Advocate, The
P.O. Box 3370, Fredericton, N.B. E3B 5A2
(506) 452-6671
Contact: H.P. Wood, editor
Covers the four Atlantic provinces with articles spotlighting the concerns and achievements of people who live there. Prefers maximum 2,000 words. Buys first Canadian serial rights. Pays on publication. A monthly.

Atlantic Insight
1668 Barrington Street, Halifax, N.S. B3J 2A2
(902) 421-1214
Contact: Ralph Surette, editor
News and views affecting the lives of people living in Atlantic Canada: political, artistic, economic, and business. Also covers trends, sports, entertainment, and recreation. A monthly.

Beaver, The
77 Main Street, Winnipeg, Man. R3C 2R1
(204) 934-1485
Contact: Christopher Dafoe, editor
A market for lively, well-researched, and informative articles on Canadian social history, with a special emphasis on the frontier region of the country, its life and culture. References to the pub-

lisher, the Hudson's Bay Company, and its history, not mandatory. Articles based on unpublished journals or letters are of particular interest. Prefers short features of 800 to 1,500 words, and articles of about 3,000 words. Buys first Canadian serial rights. Pays on acceptance. A quarterly.

Canadian
2802 - 30th Street, Suite 103, Vernon, B.C. V1T 8G7
(604) 549-3131
Contact: Gabriele Scherubl, editor
A monthly inflight magazine for several airlines, including Canadian Airlines International Ltd. Welcomes high-quality contributions from writers and illustrators. Especially interested in profiles of successful entrepreneurs, adventure travel, and people with unusual hobbies. A business or financial component is usually imperative in all articles.

Canadian Geographic
488 Wilbrod Street, Ottawa, Ont. K1N 6M8
(613) 236-7493
Contact: Ross Smith, editor
Describes and illustrates, with good colour photography, all aspects of Canada to make it better known to Canadians. Is interested in geography in its broadest sense, from archeology and climatology to geology and wildlife. Article length: 1,000 to 2,500 words. Buys first Canadian serial rights and pays on publication. Published six times a year by the Royal Canadian Geographical Society.

Canadian Heritage
P.O. Box 1358, Station B, Ottawa, Ont. K1P 5R4
(613) 237-1066
Contact: Tom Pawlick, editor
Explores the relationships of people and cultures with their built environment, through coverage of such subjects as architecture, urban planning, landscape gardening, the archeology of human shelter, and the history of Canadian neighbourhoods, villages, and cities. Published five times a year by The Heritage Canada Foundation.

Canadian West
P.O. Box 3399, Langley, B.C. V3A 4R7
(604) 576-6561
Contact: Garnet Basque, editor
A full-colour adventure and history magazine about the early life and times of British Columbia, Alberta, and the Yukon. Topics include exploration and explorers, extraordinary pioneers who followed, and the tragic fires, shipwrecks, and other disasters they faced while forging the social fabric of western Canada. Published quarterly.

Cape Breton's Magazine
Wreck Cove, Cape Breton Island, N.S. B0C 1H0
(902) 929-2372/929-2001
Contact: Ronald Caplan, editor
Devoted to the history, natural history, and future of Cape Breton. Carries articles conveying the life and variety of the region in its past and present. Published three times a year.

enRoute
2973 Weston Road, Weston, Ont. M9M 2T2
(416) 741-1112
Contact: Caroline Jackson, editor
Air Canada's monthly inflight magazine. Publishes strong Canadian pieces on business trends, unusual hobbies, travel, successful personalities, fashion, and fine dining, aimed at the business flier. Buys first Canadian serial rights. Pays on acceptance.

Envol
252 Route 171 South, St. Etienne, Que. G0S 2L0
(418) 831-5317
Contact: Florian Chassé, editor
Published monthly and distributed among travellers on Quebecair flights, both in Canada and on aircraft the company charters abroad.

Equinox
7 Queen Victoria Road, Camden East, Ont. K0K 1J0
(613) 378-6661
Contact: Barry Estabrook, editor
Canada's world-class magazine of science and geography, serving nearly 200,000 Canadians who desire to discover more about their country and the world around them. Deals with geography in its broadest sense, encompassing biology, astronomy, earth sciences, the arts, architecture, industry, travel, adventure and, of course, the diverse geographical fields: physical, human, urban, political, economic. Buys first Canadian serial rights for non-fiction pieces of 4,000 to 6,000 words. Published six times yearly.

Goodlife Magazine
1300 Yonge Street, Suite 700, Toronto, Ont. M4T 1X3
(416) 961-5002
Contact: Barbara Righton, editor
A monthly, full-colour magazine delivered free to celebrate the good life – wine, food, travel, fashion, trends, home decor, and entertainment. Prefers non-fiction of 2,500 to 3,000 words and pays on acceptance. Buys first Canadian and first North American serial rights.

Graffiti
3510 St. Laurent Boulevard, Montreal, Que. H2X 2V2
(514) 844-8491

Contact: Alistair Sutherland, editor
Carries interviews with politicians, and reviews of music and theatre performances, recordings, cars, motorcycles, and computers. Also prints articles on adventure, fashion, and technology. Published monthly.

Leisure Ways
200 King Street W., P.O. Box 60, Toronto, Ont. M5H 3T4
(416) 596-1412
Contact: Jerry Tutunjian, editor
A Southern Ontario monthly lifestyle magazine financed by the Ontario Motor League. Carries high-quality articles on personalities, interesting places, culture, current events, and ingenious entrepreneurs. Buys first Canadian rights, and pays on acceptance.

Maclean's
777 Bay Street, Toronto, Ont. M5W 1A7
(416) 596-5386
Contact: Kevin Doyle, editor
Canada's most widely acclaimed news magazine with about 2.6 million readers. Examines news events, trends, and issues, all from a Canadian perspective. Has a broad network of bureaus and correspondents in five Canadian cities and thirty-five foreign countries. Staff writers and freelancers contribute to weekly sections on politics, business, entertainment, sports, leisure, science, medicine, and technology. Pays on acceptance for first North American rights.

Newfoundland Lifestyle
197 Water Street, St. John's, Nfld. A1C 6E7
(709) 726-9300
Contact: Adrian Smith, editor
Designed to create a positive image of Newfoundland and Labrador through articles on people and a unique way of life. A bi-monthly.

Northwest Explorer
P.O. Service 9000, Yellowknife, N.W.T. X1A 2R3
(403) 992-1212
Contact: Jake Ootes, editor
This full-colour magazine is published quarterly by Northwest Territorial Airways Ltd., and features articles about Canada's North and the work and lifestyles of people who live there.

Reader's Digest
215 Redfern Avenue, Montreal, Que. H3Z 2V9
(514) 934-0751
Contact: Alexander Farrell, editor
A world-class, monthly mass-interest magazine. The freelancer's most lucrative market. Carries articles on everything from nature, science and politics to drama, self-improvement, and people, important or otherwise. All pieces contain advice, an experience or

philosophy worthy of value to the magazine's more than two million readers. Commissions original articles and adaptations of Canadian subjects. Also buys material previously published in books, magazines, or newspapers.

Review, The
111 St. Clair Avenue W., Toronto, Ont. M5W 1K3
(416) 968-4884
Contact: Kenneth Bagnell, editor
This high-quality current affairs magazine published by Imperial Oil Ltd. carries articles on important facets of Canadian living, profiles on our celebrated institutions, nostalgia, and in-depth pieces on travel and oil exploration. Buys all rights, and pays on acceptance. Published quarterly.

Saturday Night
36 Toronto Street, Suite 1160, Toronto, Ont. M5C 2C5
(416) 368-7237
Contact: John Fraser, editor
An award-winning monthly, which features profiles of the men, women, and institutions that shape and run Canadian society. Its insightful reporting goes far beyond explanations of events and focuses on why things happen, who makes them happen, and how they may affect our future. Publishes high-quality fiction and poetry in about six issues a year.

Sélection
215 Redfern Avenue, Montreal, Que. H3Z 2V9
(514) 934-0751
Contact: Denise Surprenant, editor
This, the French-Canadian edition of *Reader's Digest*, is a high-quality general-interest magazine primarily concerned with a broad spectrum of subjects of concern to Quebecers. A monthly.

Toronto Life Magazine
59 Front Street E., Toronto, Ont. M5E 1B3
(416) 364-3333
Contact: Marq de Villiers, editor
A high-class monthly city magazine which goes far beyond telling readers how Toronto works, lives, and plays. It examines city politics, the power elite, society, business, commerce, sports, and shopping, and is a unique mix of hard-nosed reporting and deft service journalism. Also publishes bi-monthly supplements: *Consumer's Auto Report*, *Toronto Life Great Escapes*, *Toronto Life Homes*, *Toronto Life Epicure*, *Toronto Life Fashion*, and *Men's Fashions*.

Up here, Life in Canada's North
P.O. Box 1350, Yellowknife, N.W.T. X1A 2N9
(403) 920-4652

Contact: Rosemary Allerston, editor
A bi-monthly magazine about Northern travel, wildlife, arts, culture and people who travel the region and cope with harsh winters there.

Western Living
504 Davie Street, Vancouver, B.C. V6B 2G4
(604) 669-7525
Contact: Andrew Scott, editor
A monthly general-interest and lifestyle magazine with a special emphasis on homes. Regular features cover food and cooking, travel, fashion, recreation, arts, and crafts. All stories should have a Western Canadian focus. Preferred length 1,500 to 3,000 words. Buys first Western Canadian serial rights and other rights.

Western Report
17327 - 106A Avenue, Edmonton, Alta. T5S 1M7
(403) 484-8884
Contact: Stephen Hopkins, editor
An expansion of *Alberta Report*: important issues and events from a western perspective. Each weekly edition covers business, resources, law, education, religion, arts, sports, agriculture, medicine, and people in the news.

NEWS, OPINIONS, AND ISSUES

Alternatives
Faculty of Environmental Studies, University of Waterloo, Waterloo, Ont. N2L 3G1
(519) 885-1211
Contact: Linda Norton, editor
Critical analysis, informed comment, and dedicated advocacy on contemporary problems facing our natural and social environments. Published four times yearly.

Briarpatch
2138 McIntyre Street, Regina, Sask. S4P 2R7
(306) 525-2949
Contact: Elizabeth Smillie, editor
A regional magazine providing a window on Saskatchewan. Carries critical articles on the environment, agriculture, native and women's rights, labour, and the arts. Published ten times yearly.

Canadian Dimension
44 Princess Street, Winnipeg, Man. R3B 1K2
(204) 957-1519
Contact: Jim Pringle, editor

Fact and analysis that bring Canada and the world into focus. Carries articles on the labour movement, women's liberation, the fight for peace, native peoples, environmental issues, and popular culture. Published eight times yearly.

Canadian Forum, The
70 The Esplanade, 3rd Floor, Toronto, Ont. M5E 1R2
(416) 364-2431
Contact: John Hutcheson, editor
Tackles a wide range of subjects, including politics, national and international affairs, the arts in Canada, economics, travel, civil liberties, the environment, film, and literature. Carries some high-quality fiction. Published ten times a year.

Canadian Human Rights Advocate
R.R. 1, Maniwaki, Que. J9E 3A8
(819) 449-6072
Contact: Kathleen Ruff, editor
Published ten times yearly to inform on human rights decisions across Canada, equality cases under the Canadian Charter of Rights and Freedoms, issues affecting women, minorities, and the disabled, and the network of resources available to them.

Canadian Public Policy
University of Guelph, MacKinnon Building, Room 039, Guelph, Ont. N1G 2W1
(519) 824-4120
Contact: Rosemary Vandercamp, editor
A quarterly providing a forum of information about economic policy developments affecting all Canadians. Reviews books, articles, and government reports. Accepts submissions up to 5,000 words.

Chinatown News
459 E. Hastings Street, Vancouver, B.C. V6A 1P5
(604) 254-2533
Contact: Roy Mah, editor
Reports important developments locally, provincially, and nationally on issues affecting Canada's Chinese communities. Mostly news, but carries profiles of important figures behind it. Published twice monthly.

City Magazine
72 Cordova Street, Winnipeg, Man. R3N 0Z9
(204) 489-8145
Contact: Rob Ferguson, editor
A quarterly covering urban politics, city planning, public art, architecture, and urban culture. Carries articles on urban design, community development, suburbia, housing, and such social issues as prostitution and slum clearance.

Commonwealth, The
1122 Saskatchewan Drive, Regina, Sask. S4P 0C4
(306) 525-8321
Contact: Ron Thompson, editor
Examines issues and personalities central to Saskatchewan's political scene from a democratic socialist perspective. A bi-weekly.

Content
90 Edgewood Avenue, Unit 126, Toronto, Ont. M4L 3H1
(416) 461-7742
Contact: Dick MacDonald, editor
Canada's only national periodical of news, comment and analysis about journalism. Explores such themes as ethics, the press, politics, the law, word usage, mass media studies, broadcast regulations, and new media technologies. Articles vary in length from 500 to 5,000 words. Pays on or before publication for first Canadian serial rights. Published six times a year.

Democrat, The
517 E. Broadway, Suite 210, Vancouver, B.C. V5T 1X4
(604) 324-2184
Contact: Soren Bech, editor
Federal, provincial, and international political news insofar as it applies to British Columbia's social democrats. Published ten times a year.

International Journal
15 King's College Circle, Toronto, Ont. M5S 2V9
(416) 979-1851
Contact: R.O. Matthews/Charles Pentland, editors
Published quarterly by the Canadian Institute of International Affairs and written by contributors world-wide. Reviews books on international affairs and foreign policy. Pays on publication.

International Perspectives
151 Wellington Street, Suite 302, Ottawa, Ont. K1E 5P9
(613) 238-2628
Contact: Peter Martin, editor
A bi-monthly journal on world affairs written by leading academics, journalists, diplomats, and politicians. Highly specialized.

New Breed
2505 - 11th Avenue, Suite 210, Regina, Sask. S4P 0K6
(306) 525-9501
Contact: Joan Beatty, editor
A newsmonthly dedicated to informing Natives and non-Natives on topics of concern to Saskatchewan's Métis and non-status Indians. Contains interviews, news of events, and articles about Cree and Métis history.

New Directions
P.O. Box 34279, Station D, Vancouver, B.C. V6J 2P2
(604) 738-8991
Contact: Jeannie Kamins, editor
A British Columbian magazine which, in nine yearly issues, reports on and analyses regional concerns, primarily labour problems, women's and multicultural rights, and peace movement activities.

New Internationalist, The
75 Carlton Street, Toronto, Ont. M5A 2K3
(416) 923-9857
Contact: Richard Swift, editor
A monthly magazine which provides information and analysis on the major issues concerning international development.

New Maritimes
Enfield, Hants County, N.S. B0N 1N0
(902) 424-2203
Contact: Scott Milsom, editor
Published ten times a year to explain issues of interest to Maritimers. Covers politics, labour, culture, and history.

NeWest Review
P.O. Box 394, Sub P.O. #6, Saskatoon, Sask. S7N 0W0
(306) 934-1444
Contact: Paul Denham, editor
A cultural magazine of news and opinion on western Canadian social and political issues. Reviews books and theatre, and carries some fiction. Published ten times a year.

Our Times
390 Dufferin Street, Toronto, Ont. M6K 2A3
(416) 531-5762
Contact: Stuart Crombie, editor
Published ten times yearly by a unionized worker-owned co-operative to focus on issues vital and current to today's labour movement. Most articles written by labour activists to be used as educational tools.

Policy Options
P.O. Box 3670, Halifax, N.S. B3T 3K6
Contact: Louis Vagianos, editor
A bilingual public affairs magazine published ten times yearly by the Institute for Research on Public Policy. Contributors usually include leading academics, businessmen, and public servants.

Rites
P.O. Box 65, Station F, Toronto, Ont. M4Y 2L4

Contact: Mary Louise Adams, editor
A lesbian and gay magazine with a feminist bent, and committed to progressive social change. Prints interviews, features, and news stories which explore the issues that concern and affect its readers. Published ten times yearly.

This Magazine
70 The Esplanade, 3rd Floor, Toronto, Ont. M5E 1R2
(416) 364-2431
Contact: Lorraine Filyer, editor
A news and opinion magazine which carries investigative features and commentary on culture, politics, labour, and international affairs. Accepts fiction and non-fiction of 1,000 to 3,000 words. Published six times yearly.

ENTERTAINMENT, AND CITY AND RURAL

Cable TV News
1252 Kingsway, Sudbury, Ont. P3E 2B8
(705) 560-4465
Contact: Betty Killam, editor
Looks behind the entertainment industry scene each week with interviews and personality profiles to complement weekly television program listings.

Calgary Magazine
139 - 17th Avenue S.W., Suite 200, Calgary, Alta. T2S 0A1
(403) 228-5611
Contact: Bob Mercer, editor
A monthly reflecting the interests and concerns of Calgary with factual pieces on the arts, municipal politics, food, fashion, travel, movies, and business. Pays on acceptance for non-fiction of 1,500 to 3,000 words. Buys first Canadian serial rights.

CITIES Magazine
MariMedia Associates, P.O. Box 45, Armdale, N.S. B3L 4J7
(902) 420-0550
Contact: Stephen Kimber, editor
A glossy magazine, published ten times a year for readers in the Halifax/Dartmouth area, which features local personalities and news, and reviews restaurants and current entertainment.

CityScope
1167 Bowness Road N.W., Suite 310, Calgary, Alta. T2N 3J6
(403) 270-2222
Contact: Flemming Nielsen/Brian Humphry, editors

Arts-oriented bi-monthly focusing on cultural events in and around Calgary, and promoting local talent. Also publishes original short stories and poetry.

Edmonton Magazine
10301 - 108th Street, Edmonton, Alta. T5J 1L7
(403) 423-3807
Contact: Bob Mercer, editor
Covers arts, sports, business, food, travel, fashion, and municipal and provincial politics. Also profiles interesting and important Edmontonians. Article lengths vary from 1,500 to 3,000 words. Pays on publication. Buys first Canadian serial rights. A monthly.

en Ville
8270 Mountain Sights Avenue, Suite 201, Montreal, Que. H4P 2B7
(514) 731-9471
Contact: Anthony Ross, editor
A bilingual in-room guest magazine published monthly for the Hotel Association of Greater Montreal. Lists events and activities.

L'Express Rive-Sud
545 Labonté Street, Longueuil, Que. J4H 2R4
(514) 463-0703
Contact: Maurice Giroux, editor
News on business, culture, arts, fashion, home decor, sports, and leisure for executives living on Montreal's south shore. Published monthly in French.

Globe & Mail Broadcast Week, The
444 Front Street W., Toronto, Ont. M5V 2S9
(416) 585-5411
Carries weekly television and radio listings as well as feature articles on entertainment and profiles of TV and radio personalities.

Guelph Magazine
11 Arthur Street N., Guelph, Ont. N1E 4T7
(519) 821-1830
Contact: Mario Maiocco, editor
Full-colour community magazine designed to entertain and inform people aged between twenty-two and forty-eight with articles on business, health, fitness, fashion, entertainment, politics, and the arts. Pays on acceptance. A monthly.

Hamilton Cue Magazine
752 King Street E., Hamilton, Ont. L8M 1A5
(416) 523-5566/823-9855
Contact: John De Roo, editor
Carries full-length feature articles on the people, lifestyles, activities, and concerns of residents of Hamilton and neighbouring

communities. Buys first Canadian serial rights for articles of 3,000 to 6,000 words. A monthly.

Hamilton This Month
1070 Main Street W., Hamilton, Ont. L8S 1B4
(416) 522-6117
Contact: Wayne Narciso, editor
A monthly news and general-interest magazine for Hamilton and its suburbs, focusing on issues, events and concerns – and the personalities behind them. Also covers fashion, interior decor, electronics, automobiles, and restaurants.

Highlights
225 Fairway Road, Kitchener, Ont. N2G 4E5
(519) 894-1630
Contact: Paul Winkler, editor
A full-colour, bi-monthly magazine for the Ontario centres of Kitchener, Waterloo, and Cambridge, and their neighbouring communities. Carries articles about homes, food, fashion, people, and events.

Key to Calgary
118 - 11th Avenue S.E., Room B8, Calgary, Alta. T2G 0X5
(403) 266-5085
Contact: Margaret Haddrick, editor
News of events and attractions for visitors. Also includes restaurant and entertainment reviews, plus shopping guides. Cover stories highlight things to do and see. Buys fiction and non-fiction of 500 to 1,500 words, and pays on publication. A monthly.

Key to Kingston
P.O. Box 1352, Kingston, Ont. K7L 5C6
(613) 549-8442
Contact: Ulrike Bender, editor
News of events and attractions for visitors. Also includes restaurant reviews, shopping guides, and suggestions for area tours. Cover stories highlight things to do and see. Published eight times a year.

Key to Toronto
59 Front Street E., Toronto, Ont. M5E 1B3
(416) 364-3333
Contact: Brian Kendall, editor
For guests in Toronto's hotels. Features articles on theatre, music, art, sports, and city clubs and restaurants. Pays on acceptance for non-fiction of 850 to 2,500 words. Published monthly.

Key to Vancouver
2208 Spruce Street, Vancouver, B.C. V6H 2P3

(604) 736-5586
Contact: Louise Whitney, editor
A monthly visitors' guide incorporating entertainment, shopping, dining, and art gallery listings. Cover stories usually features on West Coast life.

Key to Victoria
2208 Spruce Street, Vancouver, B.C. V6H 2P3
(604) 736-5586
Contact: Janice Strong, editor
A guide for visitors and residents interested in dining, night life, entertainment, and sightseeing. A monthly.

K-W Magazine
11 Arthur Street N., Guelph, Ont. N1E 4T7
(519) 821-1830
Contact: Mario Maiocco, editor
A glossy monthly written to inform an upscale audience aged between twenty-two and forty-eight with special emphasis on community personalities, business, organizations, and events. Regular features include fashion, entertainment, restaurant reviews, business news, and the arts.

Lethbridge Magazine
237 - 12th Street North, P.O. Box 1203, Lethbridge, Alta. T1J 4A4
(403) 327-3200
Contact: Ruth Irene Buchanan, editor
Carries articles about cuisine, wines, travel, fashion, personalities, and community concerns. Published seven times a year.

London Magazine
304 York Street, London, Ont. N6B 1P8
(519) 434-1177
Contact: Douglas Cassan, editor
Covers lifestyles, fashion, politics, art, food, history, business, sports, and entertainment for Londoners and residents of Sarnia and Southwestern Ontario in general. Published six times a year.

Metro Telecaster
2 Second Street, P.O. Box 128, Yarmouth, N.S. B5A 4B1
(902) 742-7111
Contact: Minnie Paddock, editor
Carries short and informative features by local and syndicated writers to complement television listings and news on entertainment and leisure. A weekly.

Montréal ce mois-ci
1844 William Street, Montreal, Que. H3J 1R5
(514) 937-5771

Contact: André Ducharme, editor
Published in French. Contains theatre and restaurant critiques and announces upcoming events of interest to middle and upper income readers. Also features lifestyle articles and reports on fashion, travel, home decor, beauty, and cosmetics. A monthly.

Montreal Magazine
1310 Greene Avenue, Suite 920, Montreal, Que. H3Z 2B5
(514) 933-2555
Contact: Robert Harris, publisher
Contains theatre and restaurant critiques and announces upcoming events of interest to middle and upper income readers. Also features lifestyle articles and reports on fashion, travel, home decor, beauty, and cosmetics. A monthly.

Montreal Mirror
307 Ste. Catherine Street W., Suite 500, Montreal, Que. H2X 2A3
(514) 289-9663
Contact: Martin Siberok, editor
A bi-weekly tabloid which features articles on major issues written from a local perspective and reviews restaurants, films, art shows, books, and new music.

Montreal Scope
1253 McGill College Avenue, Suite 232, Montreal, Que. H3B 2Y5
(514) 933-3333
Contact: Nicolas Evreinow, editor
A monthly, pocket-sized city guide published in English and French. Carries articles on food, entertainment, people, places, and events of interest to residents and visitors.

Newfoundland Herald, The
P.O. Box 2015, St. John's, Nfld. A1C 2G8
(709) 726-7060
Contact: Colleen Shea, editor
A weekly full-colour family magazine focusing on local and international entertainment to provide background to TV listings.

Now
150 Danforth Avenue, Toronto, Ont. M4K 1N1
(416) 461-0871
Contact: Michael Hollet, editor
A weekly news and entertainment magazine for Toronto's young adults. Covers film, music, records, theatre, art galleries, books, fashion, and personalities.

Ottawa Magazine
192 Bank Street, 2nd Floor, Ottawa, Ont. K2P 1W8
(613) 234-7751

Contact: Louis Valenzuela, editor
A monthly news and lifestyle magazine which carries investigative articles on local issues, serious profiles, and stories on lifestyle, film, restaurants, fashion, and gourmet cooking.

Ottawa Newcomer
450 Rideau Street, Suite 200, Ottawa, Ont. K1N 5Z4
(613) 238-4736
Contact: Joanne Butler, editor
Articles on shopping, theatre, sports, real estate, schools, transportation, clubs, and sights of local interest, all aimed at helping Ottawa's newcomers adjust to their surroundings. A monthly.

PASSION Magazine
176 Woolwich Street, P.O. Box 1747, Guelph, Ont. N1H 7A1
(519) 763-5058
Contact: Karen Mantel, editor
Quarterly publication spotlighting dining and entertainment in the Kitchener-Waterloo, Cambridge, and Guelph areas. Buys profiles on regional restaurants and entertainers, entertainment reviews, news, and features.

PrimeTime
5308 Calgary Trail S., Riviera Plaza, Edmonton, Alta. T6H 4J8
(403) 434-7424
Contact: Ruth Kelly, editor
Carries stories on entertainment and the pay-TV industry to complement monthly pay-TV listings. A monthly.

Québec ce mois-ci
1164 Turnbull, Quebec, Que. G1R 2X8
(418) 523-1943
Contact: André Ducharme, editor
Published in French. Contains theatre and restaurant critiques and announces upcoming events of interest to middle and upper income readers. Also features lifestyle articles and reports on fashion, travel, home decor, beauty, and cosmetics. A monthly.

Radio Guide
P.O. Box 320, Station A, Toronto, Ont. M5W 2J4
(416) 365-9510
Contact: Jack McIver, editor
Provides CBC radio schedules, but also carries well-written articles about performers, shows, and the people behind them. Published monthly.

Rocky Mountain Visitor
118 - 11th Avenue S.E., Room B8, Calgary, Alta. T2G 0X5

(403) 266-5085
Contact: Jack Newton, editor
Covers things to do and see for visitors to the Canadian Rockies, particularly in the Banff, Lake Louise, and Canmore areas. Published twice yearly.

Rural Delivery
P.O. Box 1509, Liverpool, N.S. B0T 1K0
(902) 354-5007
Contact: Dirk van Loon, editor
Published ten times a year. A magazine for the Maritime farm family. Carries news on livestock and crop production, and articles on woodlot management, rural culture, and environment.

Starweek Magazine
1 Yonge Street, Toronto, Ont. M5E 1E6
(416) 869-4936
Contact: John Bryden, editor
Carries profiles of top entertainers plus articles on sports, music, videos, and cooking, to complement Toronto-area weekly TV listings. Pays on acceptance for non-fiction of 600 to 800 words. Buys first Canadian serial rights.

Thornhill/Markham/Willowdale Month
P.O. Box 250, Thornhill, Ont. L3T 3N3
(416) 475-1743
Contact: Ellen Chenaux, editor
A community publication containing local news, features, service information, and some fiction.

Thunder Bay Guest/Thunder Bay Guide
1126 Roland Street, Thunder Bay, Ont. P7B 5G5
(807) 623-4424
Contact: Randy Stewart, editor
Provides visitors and tourists with information on what to do and see. Also includes city attractions and guides to shopping and accommodation. A monthly.

Thunder Bay Magazine
1184 Roland Street, Thunder Bay, Ont. P7B 5M4
(807) 623-8545
Contact: John Mallon, editor
News and lifestyle reports for Northwestern Ontarians. Prints articles on business, travel, sports, art, food, history, entertainment, and local issues. Published six times a year.

T.O. Magazine
26 Soho Street, Suite 340, Toronto, Ont. M5T 1Z7

(416) 596-8086
Contact: Barry Rotenberg, editor
Published ten times yearly for Toronto's young adults. Lists upcoming events and carries features on music, films, nightlife, and wining and dining.

Toronto Magazine
444 Front Street W., Toronto, Ont. M5V 2S9
(416) 585-5524
Contact: Ray Mason, editor
A monthly that carries lifestyle articles, personality profiles, some sports stories, and previews upcoming events.

Touring
1425 Mountain Street, Suite 340, Montreal, Que. H3G 1Z3
(514) 842-6005
Contact: Denis Duquet, editor
A Quebec-wide automobile magazine which prints articles on road tests, car maintenance, new technology, plus dining and lifestyle.

TV Guide
50 Holly Street, Toronto, Ont. M4S 3B3
(416) 482-8600
Contact: John Keyes, editor
Carries weekly TV listings and articles on the entertainment industry, children's programming, sports, food, and showbiz personalities. Buys first Canadian serial rights.

TV Hebdo/TV Plus
1001 de Maisonneuve Boulevard W., Suite 1100,
Montreal, Que. H2L 4P9
(514) 527-9601
Contact: Louise Marie Côté, editor
French Canada's guide to TV listings. Carries serious articles on the entertainment industry at large, plus profiles of important television performers. A monthly.

TV Times
150 Bloor Street W., Suite 903, Toronto, Ont. M5S 2Y8
(416) 927-1877
Contact: David Wesley, editor
Carries weekly TV listings, background feature articles, and profiles of current performers.

Upbeat
225 Fairway Road, Kitchener, Ont. N2G 4E5
(519) 894-2231, from Toronto 826-9182
Contact: Don McCurdy, editor

A weekly newspaper supplement. Prints local features and reviews of films, music, and theatre, and interviews with film and television personalities.

V Magazine
200 - 1198 West Pender Street, Vancouver, B.C. V6E 2R9
(604) 684-2644
Contact: Harvey S. Southam/Robert Collison, editors
A city lifestyle magazine distributed monthly through the *Vancouver Sun* to the city's more affluent households. Articles feature local personalities and fashion.

Vancouver Magazine
1205 Richards Street, Vancouver, B.C. V6B 3G3
(604) 685-5371
Contact: Malcolm Parry, editor
A glossy monthly city magazine focusing on current affairs and entertainment. Most issues cover municipal politics, business, media, music, and high society. Also covers upcoming events, wine, and fine dining.

Waterloo Region Magazine
225 Fairway Road, Kitchener, Ont. N2G 4E5
(519) 894-1630, from Toronto 826-9182
Contact: Audrey Wicken, editor
Visitors' information about Waterloo and the surrounding district: shopping, shows, festivals, hotels, and restaurants. A quarterly.

What's On/Voici Ottawa-Hull
450 Rideau Street, Suite 200, Ottawa, Ont. K1N 5Z4
(613) 238-4736
Contact: Joanne Butler, editor
A monthly business visitors' guide published in English and French. Carries some feature articles on interesting aspects of Canada's capital.

What's on in Edmonton
10357 - 109th Street, Suite 208, Edmonton, Alta. T5J 1N3
(403) 420-1041
A monthly visitors' magazine which carries full-length feature articles about important people and events. Also contains shopping and dining reviews.

Windsor This Month
P.O. Box 1029, Station A, Windsor, Ont. N9A 6P4
(519) 966-7411
Contact: Laura Rosenthal, editor
Glossy monthly, reflecting the latest lifestyle trends and interview-

ing local personalities. Also covers fashion, travel, interior design, landscaping, gourmet foods, and entertainment. Accepts material of 2,000 or more words and pays on publication.

Yorkview
570 Hood Road, Unit 27, Markham, Ont. L3R 4G7
(416) 474-1895
Contact: Susan Camenzind, editor
Carries news reflecting the social and business personalities of the city of North York and its surrounding districts.

WOMEN'S AND FEMINIST

Breaking the Silence
P.O. Box 4857, Station E, Ottawa, Ont. K1S 5J1
(613) 233-2691
Contact: Joan Riggs, editor
A quarterly magazine inviting discussion and opinion on women's social welfare needs – support services for survivors of violence, affordable housing, sufficient and good daycare, adequate pensions, and employment.

Broadside
P.O. Box 494, Station P, Toronto, Ont. M5S 2T1
(416) 598-3513
Contact: Philinda Masters, editor
A tabloid newspaper published ten times yearly which features feminist commentary and analysis on everything from erotica to microchips, and Parliament to pornography.

Canadian Living
50 Holly Street, Toronto, Ont. M4S 3B3
(416) 482-8600
Contact: Judy Brandow, editor
A monthly magazine with special emphasis on practical information to help Canadian women better cope with today's changing world as it relates to themselves and their families. Also carries articles on food, beauty, fashion, decorating, crafts, contemporary living, health, and fitness. Prefers original manuscripts of 300 to 2,000 words. Pays on acceptance.

Chatelaine
777 Bay Street, Toronto, Ont. M5W 1A7
(416) 596-5422
Contact: Mildred Istona, editor

High-quality monthly magazine addressing the needs and preferences of women. Covers fashion, beauty, cosmetics, food, home decorating, parenting, travel, and politics. Also publishes short pieces of fiction and profiles interesting women whose successes are examples to others. Accepts short stories and articles of 3,000 to 3,500 words. Buys first North American serial rights. Pays on acceptance.

Châtelaine

1001 de Maisonneuve Boulevard W., Montreal, Que. H3A 2E1
(514) 845-5141
Contact: Francine Monpetit, editor
Published in French as Chatelaine's Quebec sister, with the same editorial philosophy.

Fireweed

P.O. Box 279, Station B, Toronto, Ont. M5T 2W2
(416) 977-8681
Contact: Pamela Godfrey, editor
A quarterly feminist journal of politics and the creative arts, combining analytical articles, fiction, poetry, photos, and drawings. Fiction runs to 3,500 words, articles to 4,000 words.

Flare

777 Bay Street, Toronto, Ont. M5W 1A7
(416) 596-5452
Contact: Bonnie Hurowitz, editor
A national fashion, beauty, and lifestyle magazine aimed monthly at working women aged between eighteen and thirty-four. Covers health, sex, relationships, recreation, travel, and home decorating. Also buys fiction up to 5,000 words through an annual contest. Pays on acceptance for first Canadian serial rights. Ten issues a year.

Healthsharing

101 Niagara Street, Suite 200A, Toronto, Ont. M5V 1C3
(416) 862-1791
Contact: Connie Clement, editor
A quarterly magazine about women's health issues. Examines personal and political health, physical, mental, and social issues from a feminist perspective.

HERizons

478 River Street, Suite 200, Winnipeg, Man. R3L 0C8
(204) 477-1730
Contact: Debbie Holmberg-Schwartz, editor
Published eight times yearly to cover issues in the forefront of Canada's women's movement: economic security, prostitution, abor-

tion, lesbian rights, violence against women, pornography, reproductive health, and midwifery. Also contains news from feminist presses world-wide.

Homemaker's
2300 Yonge Street, Toronto, Ont. M4P 1E4
(416) 482-8260
Contact: Mebbie Black, editor
Published ten times a year, it is directed at women between twenty-five and fifty-four with children at home. Feature articles, which average about 3,000 words, deal with issues of particular concern to women, their families and communities. There is a strong emphasis on relationships. Also published in French as *Madame au Foyer.* Buys first North American serial rights, and pays on acceptance.

Images
50 Holly Street, Toronto, Ont. M4S 3B3
(416) 482-9399
Contact: Charlotte Empey, editor
A blend of articles on beauty, health, and fitness for today's young working woman. Also reports on nutrition, diet, and career development. Published six times a year.

Kinesis
400A W. 5th Street, Vancouver, B.C. V5Y 1J8
(604) 873-1427
Contact: Jan Degrass, editor
A newsmagazine for feminists. Covers victories, defeats, activism, commitments of women in Canada and abroad. Also covers music, dance, literature, film, and the visual arts from a feminist perspective. Published ten times a year.

Northern Woman Journal
69 North Court Street, Thunder Bay, Ont. P7A 4T7
(807) 345-7802
Contact: Carolyn Greenwood, editor
Published quarterly since 1973, provides information and analysis on such women's concerns as health, violence, employment, law reform, daycare, and isolation at home and in the workforce.

Pandora
5533 Black Street, Halifax, N.S. B3K 1P7
(902) 455-1287
Contact: Betty-Ann Lloyd, editor
A quarterly tabloid which analyses feminist concerns and experiences, particularly in the Maritimes.

Verve
1450 Don Mills Road, Don Mills, Ont. M3B 2X7
(416) 445-6641
Contact: Ylva Van Buuren/Jim Adair, editors
Designed for Canadian women who have made health and fitness integral parts of their busy, active lifestyles. Carries articles on food and nutrition, medical awareness and healthcare, exercise and sports, personal care, and beauty. Published eight times a year.

Vitality
P.O. Box 99, Debert, N.S. B0M 1G0
Contact: Mary Magill, editor
A quarterly feminist journal focusing on health issues and related topics from a personal and political viewpoint. Carries articles on physical, mental, emotional, and environmental health insofar as they affect women.

Vivre
225 Roy Street E., Montreal, Que. H2W 2N6
(514) 282-9600
Contact: Louis-Jean D'Amour, editor
A monthly stressing good health, beauty, and well-being to women aged between twenty-five and forty-nine. Published in French.

Women and Environments
Centre for Urban & Community Studies, University of Toronto, 455 Spadina Avenue, Room 426, Toronto, Ont. M5S 2G8
(416) 978-4478
Contact: Judith Kjellberg, editor
A feminist magazine exploring women's relationships to their various environments and focusing on women's needs in housing, the work place, urban centres, neighbourhoods, and other natural and built environments. Published three times yearly.

Women's Education des Femmes
47 Main Street, Toronto, Ont. M4E 2V6
(416) 699-1909
Contact: Aisla Thomson, editor
The bilingual quarterly journal of the Canadian Congress for Learning Opportunities for Women. Feature articles cover such diverse issues as non-sexist education, women in science, government job strategy and its impact on women, and the childcare needs of women learners.

You Magazine
37 Hanna Avenue, Toronto, Ont. M6K 1X4
(416) 537-2604
Contact: Bettie Bradley, editor

A quarterly magazine of beauty, fashion, and fitness tips. Special emphasis on skincare and the use of cosmetics.

SPECIAL INTEREST

Alive

4728 Byrne Road, P.O. Box 67333, Burnaby, B.C. V5W 3T1
(604) 438-1919
Contact: Rebecca Clarkes, editor
A magazine for health-conscious Canadians featuring how-to articles of 600 to 800 words by health professionals and personalities. Also carries short book reviews. Pays on publication. Published eight times a year.

Annals of Sainte Anne de Beaupré

Basilica of Sainte Anne, Sainte Anne de Beaupré, Que. G0A 3C0
Contact: Roch Achard, editor
Monthly general-interest religion magazine. Buys fiction and articles with a Roman Catholic dimension. Pays on acceptance for North American serial rights.

Arrival

1256 W. Pender Street, Suite 201, Vancouver, B.C. V6E 2S8
Contact: Douglas Keough, editor
Buys strong travel articles with commercial orientation, and pays on publication. A monthly.

ATV Canada Buyer's Guide

2077 Dundas Street E., Suite 202, Mississauga, Ont. L4X 1M2
(416) 624-8218
Contact: Reg Fife, editor
Covers the virtues of all-terrain vehicles for personal and commercial use.

Au Masculin

7568 St. Denis Street, Montreal, Que. H2R 2E6
(514) 270-9823
Contact: Jacques Cimon, editor
Published in French. A monthly magazine for high-achieving men with tastes for fashion, nightlife, and physical fitness.

Best Wishes

37 Hanna Avenue, Toronto, Ont. M6K 1X4
(416) 530-4226
Contact: Kathy Fremes, editor
Published by Family Communications Inc., and designed to meet

the needs of pregnant women. Articles on pregnancy, birth, and looking after baby, written mostly by healthcare professionals. Pays on publication. A quarterly.

Books in Canada
366 Adelaide Street E., Suite 432, Toronto, Ont. M5A 3X9
(416) 363-5426
Contact: Michael Smith, editor
A national magazine, founded in 1971, about the world of books and related cultural fields. Carries reviews by some of the country's best known writers and critics. Buys first Canadian serial rights and pays on publication. Nine issues yearly.

Camera Canada
22 Abbeville Road, Scarborough, Ont. M1H 1Y3
(416) 864-1920
Contact: Günter Ott, editor
Published quarterly by the National Association for Photographic Art. Showcases the work of up-and-coming photographers through their portfolios and biographical information.

Canada à la carte
366 Denison Street, Markham, Ont. L3R 2B2
(416) 475-8811
Contact: Julia Aitken, editor
A monthly about food, wine, arts, entertainment, and the restaurant scene in various Canadian cities.

Canada Quilts
P.O. Box 326, Grimsby, Ont. L3M 4G5
(416) 945-9290
Contact: Marilynn Holowachuk, editor
Twenty-four pages of news, ideas, and patterns and colour photographs relating to quilting. Published five times yearly.

Canada's Original Bridal Buyers' Guide
1360 Danforth Avenue, Suite 1406, Scarborough, Ont. M1J 1G4
(416) 264-3535
Contact: Randy Crane, editor
A wedding planning guide featuring articles on trends, ethnic customs, etiquette, and honeymoon attractions. Published four times a year.

Canadian Biker
P.O. Box 4122, Station A, Victoria, B.C. V8X 3X4
(604) 384-0333
Contact: Len Creed, editor
Carries a variety of articles and columns for sport and touring motorcycle enthusiasts. Published eight times a year.

Canadian Churchman
600 Jarvis Street, Toronto, Ont. M4Y 2J6
(416) 924-9192
Contact: Jerrold Hames, editor
National publication of the Anglican Church of Canada. Contains reports of current news events and human interest features from across Canada and abroad, always with an Anglican perspective. Prefers newspaper style. Payment by arrangement. A monthly.

Canadian Coin News
P.O. Box 12000, Bracebridge, Ont. P0B 1C0
(705) 687-6691
A semi-monthly publication for collectors of Canadian and British Commonwealth coins. Pays on publication for first Canadian serial rights.

Canadian Do-It-Yourself Magazine
2000 Ellesmere Road, Unit 1, Scarborough, Ont. M1H 2W4
(416) 438-1153
Contact: Michael McVean, editor
A monthly for home hobbyists, carrying articles about maintenance, primarily woodworking, interior decorating, landscaping, and gardening. Article length 1,500 words. Buys first Canadian serial rights, and pays on acceptance.

Canadian Guider
50 Merton Street, Toronto, Ont. M4S 1A3
(416) 487-5281
Contact: Marita Robinson, editor
Published five times a year by Girl Guides of Canada and serving 230,000 members aged between six and seventeen, and 40,000 Guide leaders.

Canadian House & Home
491 Eglinton Avenue, Suite 305, Toronto, Ont. M5N 1A8
(416) 484-0256
Contact: Elaine Sills, editor
Focuses on creative home decoration and design with how-to articles and pictorial essays. Published six times a year.

Canadian Jewish Outlook
6184 Ash Street, Suite 3, Vancouver, B.C. V5Z 3G9
(604) 324-5101
Contact: Ben Chud/Henry Rosenthal, editors
An Anglo-Jewish magazine with a left-wing perspective on world events. Focuses on issues affecting Israel and world Jewry. Published ten times a year.

Canadian Lawyer Magazine
56 The Esplanade, Suite 401, Toronto, Ont. M5E 1A7

(416) 368-7746
Contact: Kim Lockhart, editor
Written for and about Canada's legal world with profiles of controversial and successful lawyers who mirror trends and developments in their profession. Article length 1,500 to 3,000 words. Pays on acceptance for first Canadian serial rights. Nine issues yearly.

Canadian Leader, The
P.O. Box 5112, Station F, Ottawa, Ont. K2C 3H4
(613) 224-5131
Contact: Garth Johnson, editor
A national magazine officially acknowledged by Boy Scouts of Canada for adult leaders of youth organizations. Buys first Canadian serial rights. Published six times a year.

Canadian Living's Food Magazine
50 Holly Street, Toronto, Ont. M4S 3B3
(416) 482-8600
Contact: Judy Brandow, editor
Published six times yearly with regular features on microwave menus, calorie-reduced cooking, and international cuisine.

Canadian Materials
151 Sparks Street, Suite 902, Ottawa, Ont. K1P 5E3
(613) 232-9625
Contact: Laurie Bowes, editor
Published six times yearly to evaluate books, magazines, films, games, and educational kits that have been produced for young children and teenagers.

Canadian MoneySaver
P.O. Box 370, Bath, Ont. K0H 1G0
(613) 353-7448
Contact: Dale Ennis, editor
A national consumer finance magazine offering articles on such current topics as personal finance, investment techniques, retirement planning, consumer purchases, small business practice, and discount service. Published nine times yearly.

Canadian Stamp News
P.O. Box 10000, Bracebridge, Ont. P0B 1C0
(705) 645-8733
Contact: John Dinner, editor
Semi-monthly publication serving Canadian philatelists and those around the world who collect Canadian stamps. Buys first Canadian serial rights. Pays on publication.

Canadian Ultralight News
P.O. Box 563, Station B, Ottawa, Ont. K1P 5P7
(613) 236-4901

Contact: W.N. Peppler, editor
A tabloid serving Canada's ultralight movement in Canadian aviation, covering news, personalities, and events pertaining to this new and growing sport.

Canadian Workshop Magazine
130 Spy Court, Markham, Ont. L3R 5H6
(416) 475-8440
Contact: Bob Pennycook, editor
A how-to publication for the avid do-it-yourselfer, with information on a variety of home projects from laying floors and cleaning furnaces to renovating basements and making kitchen cabinets. Article lengths vary from 1,500 to 5,000 words. Pays on publication. A monthly.

Canadian Zionist
1310 Greene Avenue, Suite 800, Montreal, Que. H3Z 2B2
(514) 934-0804
A magazine focusing on the political and socio-economic scene in Israel. Promotes Hebrew and Jewish cultural studies and travel to the Middle East. Article length 2,000 to 2,500 words. Pays on publication. Seven issues a year.

Carmag
287 Macpherson Avenue, Suite 303, Toronto, Ont. M4V 1A4
(416) 928-1096
Contact: Ed Belitsky, editor
Carries consumer-oriented car care articles and evaluates the latest in automobiles and accessories. A bi-monthly.

Century Home
21 Dorset Street E., Port Hope, Ont. L1A 1E2
(416) 885-2928
Contact: J. Rumgay, editor
A magazine for lovers of vintage homes. Carries articles about decorating, furnishings, art, crafts, architecture, restoration, renovation, gardens, and country fare. Published six times a year.

C'est Pour Quand?
2260 des Patriotes, Ste-Rose, Laval, Que. H7L 3K8
(514) 622-0091
Contact: Manon Lemoyne, editor
Published eight times a year in French and aimed at expectant mothers. Carries articles on breast feeding, nutrition, husband-wife relations, and pregnancy discomforts.

City & Country Home
777 Bay Street, Toronto, Ont. M5W 1A7
(416) 596-5900

Contact: Anita Draycott, editor
A monthly upscale lifestyle magazine concentrating on fine interior design in Canadian homes and residences. Publishes articles on collecting, art and antiques, heritage buildings, gardens, shopping, travel, cuisine, fashion. Also profiles interesting up-and-coming designers.

Communicating Together
350 Rumsey Road, Toronto, Ont. M4G 1R8
(416) 424-3806
Contact: Ann Kennedy, editor
Published quarterly by the Blissymbolics Communication Institute as a forum for those interested in the experiences, the systems, and the technology relating to non-speaking people.

Companion of Saint Francis and Saint Anthony
P.O. Box 535, Station F, Toronto, Ont. M4A 2L8
Contact: Friar Philip Kelly, editor
A monthly general-interest magazine aimed at the Roman Catholic family. Prefers strong human-interest feature articles about coping with "physical and emotional ills." Buys all rights with reprint permission. Pays on acceptance.

Computing Now!
1300 Don Mills Road, Don Mills, Ont. M3B 3M8
(416) 445-5600
Contact: Steve Rimmer, editor
Helps users of personal and small business micro-computers to better understand computer technology. Also includes market surveys, industry news, and product reviews. A monthly.

Condominium Magazine, The
25 Overlea Boulevard, Suite 501, Toronto, Ont. M4H 1B1
(416) 429-4600
Contact: Monique Persh, editor
A monthly magazine addressing the issues affecting both managers and residents of Canada's condominiums.

Connexions
427 Bloor Street W., Toronto, Ont. M5S 1X7
(416) 960-3903
Contact: Ulli Diemer, editor
A quarterly digest of Canadian groups and resources moving for social change and justice. Carries articles on new publications, films, teaching materials, projects, and organizations.

Country Estate Magazine
7 Labatt Avenue, Toronto, Ont. M5A 3P2
(416) 368-3483

Contact: Michael Pembry, editor
A lifestyle magazine for upscale country dwellers who maintain the sophisticated tastes of the urbanite. Prints regular articles on gardening, art, antiques, cuisine, and wines, plus home renovation and swimming pool maintenance. Buys first Canadian serial rights and pays on publication. A quarterly.

CraftNews
346 Dundas Street W., Toronto, Ont. M5T 1G5
(416) 977-3551
Contact: Susan Eckenwalder, editor
Published eight times yearly for serious hobbyists and professional craftspeople. Covers events and developments in education, and reviews books and exhibitions. Also includes a calendar of shows, conferences, workshops, and lectures.

Cycle Canada
411 Richmond Street E., Suite 102, Toronto, Ont. M5A 3S5
(416) 362-7966
Contact: John Cooper, editor
A monthly written for Canadian motorcycle enthusiasts: product tests and evaluations, technical information, and how-to maintenance articles, plus profiles of personalities in the world of biking. Buys first North American serial rights, and pays on acceptance.

Deaf Canadian Magazine, The
P.O. Box 1291, Edmonton, Alta. T5J 2M8
Contact: David Burnett, editor
Buys cartoons, articles, short stories, and poetry related to the deaf. Pays on publication for first Canadian serial rights. A monthly.

Décormag
11450 Albert Hudon Street, Montreal North, Que. H1G 3J9
(514) 327-4464
Contact: Nicole Charest, editor
A decor magazine published monthly in French, carrying articles on art and antiques, architecture, and home entertaining. Each issue highlights a well-known person in his or her own environment. Pays on publication. Also publishes an English edition. Eleven issues a year.

Destinations
444 Front Street W., Toronto, Ont. M5V 2S9
(416) 368-7237
Contact: Jack McIvor, editor
A quarterly travel and leisure magazine. Carries articles on travel, hiking, scuba diving, sailing, golf, mountain climbing, and holidays that cater to such specific hobbies as wine and art collecting, and wildlife photography.

Diesel Magazine
70 Otonabee Drive, Kitchener, Ont. N2C 1L6
(519) 894-4000
Contact: John McBain, editor
Consumer information on small high-speed diesel engines in passenger cars, light trucks, and boats. Promotes diesel power and reports on service facilities and new products, including fuels and lubricants. Article length 1,500 words. Buys all rights and pays on publication. Six issues a year.

Discovery
302 Merton Street, Toronto, Ont. M4S 1A9
(416) 484-1771
Contact: Mary Schmieder, editor
Canada's only national lifestyle magazine for people aged fifty-five and up. Carries articles on travel, financial planning, gardening, photography, food and nutrition, crafts and hobbies, antiques, fitness, and health. Published ten times a year.

Dogs in Canada
43 Railside Road, Don Mills, Ont. M3A 3L9
(416) 441-3228
Contact: Elizabeth Dunn, editor
A monthly magazine first published by The Canadian Kennel Club in 1889. Geared toward the dog breeder and exhibitor. An extra issue is broadened to appeal to all dog-owners with articles on animal health and training.

Easy Living
13281 Comber Way, Surrey, B.C. V3W 5V8
(604) 591-5101
Contact: Trudy Lancelyn, editor
Distributed to homes and businesses in suburban areas of Victoria and British Columbia's lower mainland – restaurant listings, home improvement articles, and features on beauty, lifestyles, and travel. A monthly.

ECHEC +
P.O. Box 640, Station C, Montreal, Que. H2L 4L5
(514) 844-5104
Contact: Louis Morin, editor
A chess magazine, published six times a year in French, carrying game strategies, news of international events, and questions to an internationally known Grand Master.

Elder Statesman, The
1201 W. Pender Street, Suite 301, Vancouver, B.C. V6E 2V2
(604) 683-1344
Contact: Gerald Kidd, editor
A monthly magazine for middle-aged, West Coast Canadians, pub-

lishing articles on travel, health, nutrition, finances, and life after retirement.

Electronics Today
1300 Don Mills Road, Don Mills, Ont. M3B 3M8
(416) 445-5600
Contact: William Markwick, editor
A monthly how-to publication featuring technical articles about electronics and home computing for both the amateur and the professional. Buys all rights, and pays on publication.

Enterprise
1441 Creekside Drive, Vancouver, B.C. V6J 4S7
(604) 734-2511
Contact: David Morton, editor
A magazine for members, staff, and directors of British Columbia's credit unions and other co-operatively owned businesses in the province. Carries articles on business technology, how to reduce financial risk, and economic trends. Published five times a year.

Family Health
10468 Mayfield Road, Suite 214, Edmonton, Alta. T5P 4P4
(403) 489-5160
Contact: Dr. P. Sackman, editor
Prints articles, mostly by health professionals, on nutrition, skin-care, parenting, sexuality, sports and fitness, and addiction. Also profiles common illnesses and diseases. Published six times a year.

Financial Post Moneywise Magazine, The
777 Bay Street, Toronto, Ont. M5W 1A7
(416) 596-5658
Contact: Paul Rush, editor
World-class monthly personal finance magazine, with articles written mostly by experts or seasoned journalists – how people make money, spend it, and sometimes lose it. Publication is aimed at professionals and managers. Buys first Canadian serial rights and sometimes other rights. Pays on acceptance.

Forum
60 Mobile Drive, Toronto, Ont. M4A 2P3
(416) 751-8300
Contact: Paul Brandon, editor
A magazine of news, views, adventure, and personal experiences. Distributed four times yearly to more than 36,000 Ontario high school teachers. Published by the Ontario Secondary School Teachers' Federation.

Freemason, The
385 The West Mall, Suite 257, Etobicoke, Ont. M9C 1E7
(416) 622-8827

Contact: Stephen Maizels, editor
Provides national coverage of Canadian masonic events. Published four times a year.

Good Health
801 York Mills Road, Suite 201, Don Mills, Ont. M3B 1X7
(416) 444-4952
Contact: Ed Mounsey, editor
National magazine for Canadian women pursuing good health and fitness. Regular articles cover diet, nutrition, exercise, weight control, beauty, cooking, and medical advances. Published six times a year.

GlobeHopper, The
619 Huron Street, Toronto, Ont. M5R 2R8
(416) 960-0944
Contact: Joanna Ebbutt, editor
Articles spotlight unusual and popular destinations for avid travellers. Published four times a year.

Hands Magazine
P.O. Box 340, Station L, Toronto, Ont. M6E 4Z2
(416) 657-8521
Contact: Isobel Warren, editor
Showcases Canadian craft designs, motifs, and methods, six times a year. Emphasis is on "how-to" stories of up to 1,500 words. Pays on acceptance. Buys first Canadian serial rights.

Harrowsmith
7 Queen Victoria Road, Camden East, Ont. K0K 1J0
(613) 378-6661
Contact: James Lawrence, editor
A bi-monthly magazine for a highly thoughtful, critical audience interested in self-reliance. Subject areas most frequently covered: country life, food gardening, solar and wind energy, folk arts, ecology, small-stock husbandry, owner-builder architecture, and alternative lifestyles. Also accepts fiction of 2,000 to 3,500 words, and pays on acceptance. Buys first North American serial and anthology rights.

Hi-Rise Magazine
95 Leeward Glenway, Unit 121, Don Mills, Ont. M3C 2Z6
(416) 424-1393
Contact: Valerie Dunn, editor
A magazine mirroring the concerns of high-rise dwellers. Carries self-help articles about indoor gardening, plus regular features on food, travel, sports, hobbies, and money. Published ten times a year.

Humanist in Canada
P.O. Box 2007, Station D, Ottawa, Ont. K1P 5W3

(613) 283-7210
Contact: Donald Page, editor
A quarterly magazine "which promotes a moral life within an atheist perspective." Carries articles on anti-nuclear education, the problems of technology, and other social issues.

Influence
250 The Esplanade, 5th Floor, Toronto, Ont. M5A 1J2
(416) 365-9366
Contact: Ernest Hillen, managing editor
Aimed at men aged between twenty-five and forty-nine who have a post-secondary education and earn more than $35,000 a year. Each issue highlights "Men of Influence," and covers travel, fitness, cars, career enhancement, and personal finance. Buys first Canadian serial rights, and pays on acceptance. Published seven times yearly.

Jonathan
1310 Greene Avenue, Suite 710, Montreal, Que. H3Z 2B2
(514) 934-0772
Contact: Esther Mouyal, editor
A Jewish French-language magazine published eight times a year and serving as a forum for the exchange of ideas and information between people of different cultural backgrounds. Quebecers who have travelled Israel are encouraged to submit pieces on their experiences.

Kerby News for Seniors
10022 - 103rd Street, Edmonton, Alta. T5J 0X2
(403) 429-3258
Contact: Mollie Good, editor
A monthly publication dealing with the concerns of Southern Alberta's senior citizens.

KIN Magazine
P.O. Box KIN, Cambridge, Ont. N3H 5C6
(519) 653-1920
Contact: David Brown, editor
Published five times a year by The Association of Kinsmen Clubs, and circulated to members Canada-wide.

Legion
359 Kent Street, Suite 504, Ottawa, Ont. K2P 0R6
(613) 235-8741
Contact: Mac Johnston, editor
A general-interest monthly magazine for Canada's war veterans and their families. Carries news, views, and opinions, and serious articles affecting the daily life of an aging society – pensions, health, immigration, and justice. Also buys memoirs and nostalgia, humorous or serious. Accepts articles up to 1,500 words.

Let's Know Our Neighbours
2100 St. Marc Street, Suite 1801, Montreal, Que. H3H 2G6
(514) 989-1443/935-8725
Contact: J. Noel Parenteau, editor
Prints articles that promote travel and cultural events between Canada and the United States. Includes guides to hotels, restaurants, concerts, art galleries, events, and shopping. A quarterly.

Lifestyles 5746
84 Advance Road, Toronto, Ont. M8Z 2T7
(416) 232-3600
Contact: Suzanne Winkler, editor
A national magazine publihed six times a year for Jewish readers. Carries articles home decorating, fashion, cooking, travel, and finance. Profiles prominent Jewish business leaders.

Log Home Guide for Builders & Buyers
1 Pacific Avenue, Ste-Anne-de-Bellevue, Que. H9X 1C5
(514) 457-2045, or (615) 487-2256
Contact: Allan Muir, editor
Quarterly magazine for people who long to own a log home. Carries articles about building, space conservation, energy efficiency, and tools and equipment. Buys one-time rights, and pays on publication.

Mon Bébé
2260 des Patriotes, Ste-Rose, Laval, Que. H7L 3K8
(514) 622-0091
Contact: Manon Lemoyne, editor
An established childcare magazine published twice yearly in French, for Quebec's new mothers.

Monarchy Canada
3050 Yonge Street, Suite 206, Toronto, Ont. M4N 2K4
(416) 482-4157
Contact: Arthur Bousfield, editor
A quarterly magazine that looks at the Monarchy from a Canadian historical perspective and carries articles on constitutional, social, and political affairs. Also reviews books, and profiles personalities associated with the Monarchy. Pays on publication.

Moving To . . .
1939 Leslie Street, Don Mills, Ont. M3B 2M3
(416) 441-1168
Contact: Ronald Wood, editor
A series of seventeen separate editions serving nine major Canadian cities, and eight in the United States, designed to help people relocate in unfamiliar communities. Articles cover shopping, dining, education, and transportation. All editions are monthlies.

Muse
280 Metcalfe Street, Ottawa, Ont. K2P 1R7
(613) 233-5653
Contact: Raymond Bendall, editor
A national, bilingual quarterly about heritage museums, art galleries, and historical sights. Written for museum and gallery professionals and students of art history, fine arts, and museum and Canadian studies. Published four times a year.

New Mother
777 Bay Street, Toronto, Ont. M5W 1A7
(416) 596-5422 A quarterly reference magazine for new mothers. As part of *Chatelaine*, it carries articles addressing most areas of first-year baby care, from breast-feeding to choosing clothing and furnishings. All editorial material is checked by a team of pediatric specialists. Also published in French as *Mère Nouvelle* with *Châtelaine*.

News for Seniors
10022 - 103rd Street, Edmonton, Alta. T5J 0X2
(403) 429-3258
Contact: Irene Ramsell, editor
Mirrors the concerns and needs of senior citizens in Central and Southern Alberta. Carries articles on pensions, health, personal finance, and retirement as a second career. A monthly.

Ontario Amateur, The
P.O. Box 246, Port Credit Postal Station,
Mississauga, Ont. L5G 4L8
(416) 489-5373
Contact: Ray Pellowe, editor
A monthly magazine for Ontario's radio enthusiasts. Carries articles on antennae, electronic equipment, repeaters, and satellites. Also spotlights amateur radio clubs.

Ontario Craft
346 Dundas Street W., Toronto, Ont. M5T 1G5
(416) 977-3551
Contact: Susan Eckenwalder, editor
A quarterly magazine covering the contemporary craft movement. Profiles interesting craftspeople and reviews their work. Also buys good photographs.

Ontario Living
2300 Yonge Street, Toronto, Ont. M4P 1E4
(416) 482-8260
Contact: Liz Primeau, editor
Focuses on all aspects of urban home ownership in Southern Ontario, mostly decorating, renovation, and home entertainment. A monthly.

Orah Magazine
1310 Greene Avenue, Suite 900, Montreal, Que. H3Z 2B8
(514) 937-9431
Contact: Lily Frank, editor
Published monthly by Hadassah-WIZO Organization of Canada to report on aspects of life in Israel and on themes of Canadian Jewish concern, particularly women's and children's rights.

Our Family
P.O. Box 249, Department E, Battleford, Sask. S0M 0E0
Contact: Albert Lalonde, editor
Monthly religious magazine of general interest. Buys photo stories and photo essays on personalities, events, and human/religious themes. Also publishes some fiction. Preferred length 1,000 to 3,000 words. Rights purchases vary with article. Pays on acceptance.

Pacific Tribune
2681 E. Hastings Street, Vancouver, B.C. V5K 1Z5
(604) 251-1186
Contact: Sean Griffin, editor
A weekly news and opinion tabloid focusing on British Columbia's labour movement, its members, and its administrators.

Papyrus
3100 Keele Street, Downsview, Ont. M3M 2H4
(416) 633-6317
Contact: Jack McEwan, editor
News of Ramses Shrine clubs and units throughout central Ontario, as well as articles on activities and progress on the national and international level. Published six times yearly.

Peace Magazine
10 Trinity Square, Toronto, Ont. M5C 1B1
(416) 533-7581
Contact: Janet Daley, editor
A quarterly magazine providing interviews, commentary, and topical features that pertain to nuclear disarmament.

Pentecostal Testimony, The
10 Overlea Boulevard, Toronto, Ont. M4H 1A5
Contact: Robert Skinner, editor
Buys articles with a conservative theological viewpoint on all contemporary issues, events on the church calendar, Christmas, and Pentecost. A monthly.

Perception
55 Parkdale Avenue, P.O. Box 3505, Station C,
Ottawa, Ont. K1Y 4G1
(613) 728-1865
Contact: Robert Bisson, editor

Published by the Canadian Council on Social Development – a bilingual publication providing analysis and insight into Canada's economic and social policies and programs. Article lengths varies from 750 to 2,000 words. Buys first Canadian serial rights, and pays on publication. Five issues a year.

Pets Magazine
1300 Don Mills Road, Don Mills, Ont. M3B 3M8
(416) 445-5600
Contact: Halvor Moorshead, editor
A monthly magazine of advice, help, and guidance for Canadian pet owners.

Phoenix Rising
P.O. Box 7251, Station A, Toronto, Ont. M5W 1X9
(416) 699-3194
Contact: Donald Weitz, editor
A quarterly published by a self-help group of former psychiatric patients. Each issue carries personal accounts of psychiatric abuses, letters, and news of feminist and legal issues.

Photo Life
130 Spy Court, Markham, Ont. L3R 5H6
(416) 475-8440
Contact: Norm Rosen, editor
Caters to the interests of Canadian photographers, both amateur and seasoned professional. Covers film and video techniques, and provides information on new equipment and supplies. A monthly.

Photo Sélection
2026 Persico Street, P.O. Box 383, Sillery, Que. G1T 2R5
(418) 687-3550
Contact: Yolande Racine, editor
Written for Quebec photographers, amateur and professional. Contains photo stories, offbeat media shots, and advice from experienced photographers. Published six times a year.

Plan Canada
R.R. 3, Belfast, P.E.I. C0A 1A0
(902) 659-2888
Contact: John Curry, editor
A magazine for people interested in the land development of Canada. Carries articles, columns, and book reviews on land use planning, urban design, economic development in the community, and environmental planning. Published ten times a year.

Probe Post
12 Madison Avenue, Toronto, Ont. M5R 2S1
(416) 926-1647

Contact: Gail Richardson, editor
Published four times a year by the Pollution Probe Foundation. Prints features and analytical articles on such environmental issues as acid rain, toxic waste, water quality, food additives, and pesticides.

Protect Yourself
5199 Sherbrooke Street E., Suite 2580, Montreal, Que. H1T 3X1
(514) 873-7771
Contact: David Clerk, editor
A popular magazine, published by Quebec's Consumer Protection Office, which tests and rates products with safety, reliability, and value for money in mind. A monthly. Also published in French as *Protegez-vous*.

Québec Science
P.O. Box 250, Sillery, Que. G1T 2R1
(418) 657-3551
Contact: Jean-Pierre Rogel, editor
Deals with the broad spectrum of science and its impact on current affairs, particularly in French Canada. A monthly.

Quill & Quire
56 The Esplanade, Suite 213, Toronto, Ont. M5E 1A7
(416) 364-3333
Contact: Ann Vanderhoof, editor
Monthly journal of the Canadian book trade. Prints news, reviews, lists of recently published and upcoming books, plus profiles of authors, distributors, and publishing houses.

Real Estate News
1883 Yonge Street, Toronto, Ont. M4S 1Y7
(416) 481-6151
Contact: Leslie Ironstone, editor
A weekly self-help guide for Toronto home buyers, with stories on home-ownership tips, market trends, mortages, and property insurance.

Recipes Only/Bien Manger
17 Isabella Street, Toronto, Ont. M4Y 1M7
(416) 960-3688
Contact: Carroll Allen, editor
Celebrates food and its preparation, and provides a forum for Canadians to share their recipes with each other. Published six times a year.

Rehabilitation Digest
1 Yonge Street, Suite 2110, Toronto, Ont. M5E 1E5
(416) 862-0340

Contact: Heather Ney, editor
News, views, and articles on rehabilitation medicine for professionals and the disabled themselves. A forum in which physiotherapists, counsellors, consumer advocates, and others concerned with rehabilitation can share knowledge and experience. Published quarterly.

Report on Business Magazine
444 Front Street W., Toronto, Ont. M5V 2S9
(416) 585-5129
Contact: Margaret Wente
A high-quality monthly magazine covering the national business scene and international developments affecting Canada. Carries profiles of important business and political personalities, book reviews, regular columns on personal finance, and national opinion.

Reward
12228 - 55th Street, Edmonton, Alta. T5W 3R4
(403) 474-6430
Contact: Dean Barts, publisher
A monthly magazine for salespeople. Carries interviews with those successful in sales plus articles on such topics as motivation, training, time management, stress reduction, and staff hiring.

Select Homes Magazine
1450 Don Mills Road, Don Mills, Ont. M3B 2X7
(416) 445-6641
Contact: Michael McVean, editor
Western Office:
2000 W. 12th Avenue, Vancouver, B.C. V6J 2G2
(604) 731-7727
Contact: Pam Withers, editor
Canada's largest homeowners' publication, with a 175,000 circulation. Published eight times yearly, carrying articles on interiors renovation and maintenance. Also covers news on new energy techniques and products, plus information on mortgages and insurance. Well known for its how-to pieces on woodworking, construction, and ingenious space-saving ideas and devices. Pays half on acceptance, half on publication. Buys first Canadian serial rights.

Sentinel, The
94 Sheppard Avenue W., Willowdale, Ont. M2N 1M5
(416) 223-1690
Contact: Norman Ritchie, editor
The Loyal Orange Association's official publication, containing news of national and international current events of interest to members of the organization.

Social Worker, The/Travailleur Social, Le
55 Parkdale Avenue, Ottawa, Ont. K1Y 1E5

(613) 728-1865, extension 24
Contact: Sherri Torjman, editor
A quarterly forum in which social workers and researchers share their knowledge, skills and information with the general public. Published in English and French.

Sound & Vision
250 The Esplanade, 5th Floor, Toronto, Ont. M5A 1J2
(416) 365-9366
Contact: Alan Lofft, editor
A magazine that helps audio, video, cellular phone, and personal computer consumers stay informed about new products. Published six times a year.

Stereo Guide
6 Byng Avenue, Brampton, Ont. L6Y 1L1
(416) 451-8395
Contact: Maurice Holtham, editor
A popularly-written bi-monthly for sound system buyers. Carries product reports and profiles of new equipment. Pays on acceptance.

Studio Magazine, The
215 Carlingview Drive, Unit 102, Rexdale, Ont. M9W 5X8
Contact: B.J. Murray, editor
Buys factual articles with appeal to professional designers, illustrators, and photographers. Pays on publication. Published seven times a year.

Today's Bride
335 Lesmill Road, Don Mills, Ont. M3B 2V1
(416) 441-3030
Contact: Susan Johnston, editor
Complete how-to advice on planning and co-ordinating the formal wedding. A quarterly.

Today's Health
273 Richmond Street W., Toronto, Ont. M5V 1X1
(416) 593-5127
Contact: Heather Howie, editor
Covers all aspects of good health including diet, nutrition, fitness, personal hygiene, and preventative medicine. Also carries short articles on Canadian and international medical research, health-care products, and leisure activities. Published six times yearly.

Today's Parent
273 Richmond Street W., Suite 200, Toronto, Ont. M5V 1X1
(416) 596-8680
Contact: Nancy Lagan, editor
A self-help magazine published six times a year for parents of

children and teens. Carries articles about education, health, day-care, and shared responsibility in the family.

Toronto Life Fashion Magazine
59 Front Street E., Toronto, Ont. M5E 1B3
(416) 364-3333
Contact: John MacKay, editor
A supplement to *Toronto Life*. Carries articles on clothes, fitness, health, beauty, and other fashion-related topics. Article length up to 3,000 words. Pays on acceptance for first Canadian serial rights. Six issues a year.

Toronto Parent
P.O. Box 670, Station F, Toronto, Ont. M4Y 2N6
(416) 967-4550
Contact: John Ball, editor
Bi-monthly regional magazine for parents and professionals in the childcare field. Features articles on bringing up children, and profiles major organizations available to those with problems.

Touring and Travel
480 University Avenue, Suite 1100, Toronto, Ont. M5G 1V2
(416) 598-8830
Contact: Paul Ross, editor
Self-help and entertainment articles of interest to Canadians travelling in North America or abroad. Published five times a year.

United Church Observer, The
85 St. Clair Avenue E., Toronto, Ont. M4T 1M8
(416) 960-8500
Contact: Hugh McCullum, editor
Published monthly for members of the United Church of Canada, but with an independent editorial policy. Prints serious articles on major issues, all with a Christian perspective. Also covers the religious dimension of art, literature, and theatre. Lengths vary from 800 to 2,000 words. Pays on publication, and buys first Canadian serial rights.

Video Scene
542 Mt. Pleasant Road, Suite 203, Toronto, Ont. M4S 2M7
(416) 482-1696
Contact: Forbes Calder, editor
Keeps Canadians informed about recent developments in the video industry and all related fields. Reviews the latest tapes, recordings, and personal computers. Published six times a year.

Videomania
1314 Britannia Road E., Mississauga, Ont. L4W 1C8
(416) 673-1033

Contact: Salah Bachir, editor
Canada's largest monthly video magazine, containing test reports, news of new products, and technical how-to articles. Also includes interviews with prominent cinema personalities, both on and off the screen, and reviews of new movies available on video cassette. Buys first Canadian serial rights and other rights. Pays on publication.

Videotex World
55 Town Centre Court, 5th Floor, Scarborough, Ont. M1P 4X5
(416) 296-4435
Contact: Diane Matthews, editor
A quarterly glossy magazine for serious investigators of interactive information technologies in business, education, training, marketing, and government.

Vitamin Supplement, The
260 S.W. Marine Drive, Vancouver, B.C. V5X 2R5
(604) 325-7311
Contact: B.H. Lyman, editor
Written for Canadians who want to improve their quality of life through diet, preventative medicine, exercise, and dietary supplements. Prints articles on health news, sports, nutritional consultation, vitamins, and cooking. A quarterly.

Wedding Bells
22 O'Meara Street, Ottawa, Ont. K1Y 4N6
(613) 722-6006
Contact: Crys Blundell, editor
A fat, glossy magazine with editions in Calgary, Edmonton, Hamilton, London, Ottawa, Montreal, Toronto, Vancouver, and Winnipeg. Directed towards brides and grooms and their families, and offering information about every aspect of wedding planning.

Wildflower
35 Bauer Crescent, Unionville, Ont. L3R 4H3
(416) 296-3105
Contact: James French, editor
A quarterly devoted to the conservation, cultivation, and study of wildflowers and other flora. Contains book reviews, notices of coming events, and plant sources. Published in cooperation with the Canadian Wildflower Society.

Wine Tidings
5165 Sherbrooke Street W., Suite 414, Montreal, Que. H4A 1T6
(514) 481-5892
Contact: Barbara Leslie, editor
A magazine published eight times yearly for discerning wine lovers. Reports on price trends and vintages, offers recipes, and

profiles well-known wine cellars. Also compares wines and grape types, and reviews developments in the Canadian wine industry. Lengths vary from 800 to 3,000 words. Buys first serial rights, and pays on publication.

World of Wheels
4035 Wilson Avenue, Suite 100, Montreal, Que. H4A 2V1
(514) 487-3770
Contact: Len Coates, editor
A quarterly magazine for car and motorcycle owners. Contains maintenance tips and information, and evaluates and compares the latest vehicles.

Your Money
56 The Esplanade, Suite 208, Toronto, Ont. M5E 1A7
(416) 364-4266
Contact: Penny Williams, editor
A glossy personal finance magazine published eight times yearly, which aims to help readers earn more, invest more wisely, save more, and get the greatest value for their money. Each issue includes a variety of lifestyle features, and stories on investment, law, and financially successful people.

SPORTS AND OUTDOORS

Alberta Wild Rose Quarter Horse Journal
P.O. Box 550, Nanton, Alta. T0L 1R0
(403) 237-5230
Contact: Liz Zacher, editor
Covers developments in the quarter horse markets, showmanship trends, major sales, and official notices of the Alberta Quarter Horse Association. A monthly.

Angler & Hunter
P.O. Box 1541, Peterborough, Ont. K9J 7H7
(705) 748-3891
Contact: David Golden, editor
Carries news of the 55,000 member Ontario Federation of Anglers & Hunters, plus where-to-go articles and updated reports on Ontario's natural resources. Prefers articles of 1,500 to 2,000 words, and pays on publication. Buys first Canadian serial rights. Published ten times yearly.

Athletics
1220 Sheppard Avenue, Willowdale, Ont. M2K 2X1
(416) 495-4053

Contact: Cecil Smith, editor
Established in 1876 as Canada's first athletics magazine for families. Carries self-help articles on diet, training, and nutrition. Published nine times yearly.

Atlantic Salmon Journal, The
1435 St. Alexandre Street, Suite 1030, Montreal, Que. H3A 2G4
(514) 842-8059
Contact: Joanne Eidinger, editor
A quarterly published by the Atlantic Salmon Federation for serious anglers who fly-fish. Carries articles on researching salmon and on where to catch them. Article lengths vary from 800 to 3,000 words. Buys first Canadian serial rights, and pays on acceptance.

Auto Sport Canada
3045 Universal Drive, Mississauga, Ont. L4X 2E2
Contact: Peter Chapman, editor
Buys general-interest articles pertaining to the automotive and motor sport fields–road tests and personality profiles. Occasionally publishes fiction. Buys first Canadian serial rights. A monthly.

BC Fishing Guides
1132 Hamilton Street, Suite 202, Vancouver, B.C. V6B 2S2
(604) 687-1581
Contact: Henry Frew, editor
Annual guides to both fresh and salt water fishing. Contains maps and directions to British Columbia's best fishing spots. Pays on acceptance for first Canadian serial rights.

BC Outdoors
1132 Hamilton Street, Suite 202, Vancouver, B.C. V6B 2S2
(604) 687-1581
Contact: Henry Frew, editor
Carries articles on outdoor recreation and conservation: wildlife, camping, hunting, sports shooting, and salt and fresh water fishing. Maximum article length 2,000 words. Pays on acceptance. Ten issues a year.

BC Sport Fishing
909 Jackson Crescent, New Westminster, B.C. V3L 4S1
(604) 521-4901
Contact: Rikk Taylor, editor
Published six times a year for sportsmen looking for the best fishing opportunities in major British Columbia resort areas.

Beautiful British Columbia
Tourism British Columbia, Department of Travel Industry, Parliament Buildings, Victoria, B.C. V8W 2Z
Contact: Bryan McGill, editor

A quarterly general-interest travel magazine with a Western Canada focus. Buys strong photo essays and adventure pieces. Pays on acceptance for first Canadian serial rights.

Birdfinding in Canada
P.O. Box 519, Kleinberg, Ont. L0J 1C0
(416) 832-1357
Contact: G. Bennett, editor
Published six times a year for everyone interested in wild birds from the casual observer to the ornithologist. Carries news and important reference material.

Boating News
26 Coal Harbour Wharf, 566 Cardero Street,
Vancouver, B.C. V6G 2W6
(604) 684-1643
Contact: Don Tyrell, editor
A monthly tabloid carrying local and international boating news across North America and Europe.

Bowbender
P.O. Box 912, Carstairs, Alta. T0M 0N0
(403) 337-3023
Contact: Kathleen Windsor, editor
A quarterly magazine written by archers for archers. Contains regular articles on photography, wildlife, outdoor cooking, and archery equipment. Published for members of the Canadian Field Archery Association.

Camping Canada
3414 Park Avenue, Suite 221, Montreal, Que. H2X 2H5
(514) 282-0191
Contact: Reg Fife, editor
Carries articles on travel and routes, and gives technical information on the latest motor homes, wide-body vans, trailers, and trailer homes. Accepts articles of 1,500 to 3,000 words. Buys first Canadian serial rights. Six issues a year.

Canadian Boating
5200 Dixie Road, Suite 204, Mississauga, Ont. L4W 1E4
(416) 625-5277
Contact: Gary Arthurs, editor
Carries articles on power boating, family boating, racing, navigational techniques, and profiles important people in boating. Pays on publication. Published eight times yearly.

Canadian Fisherman and Ocean Science
6725 Darlington Avenue, Suite 200, Montreal, Que. H3S 2J7
Contact: Keith Fredericks, editor

Buys articles on the business element of fishing and oceanography. Pays on publication. Published monthly.

Canadian Horse, The
7240 Woodbine Avenue, Suite 210, Markham, Ont. L3R 1A4
(416) 475-7722
Contact: H. Weston, editor
News, views, and opinions from the North American thoroughbred scene. Accepts 1,000- to 2,500-word articles on personalities and owners, as well as anecdotes on racing. Buys all rights, and pays on publication. Published ten times a year.

Canadian Rodeo News
2116 - 27th Avenue N.E., Suite 223, Calgary, Alta. T2E 7A6
(403) 250-7292
Contact: Dwayne Erickson, editor
A monthly tabloid of news, views, and opinions from the North American rodeo circuit. Also accepts articles related to the West or to Western heritage. Pays on acceptance.

Canadian Skater
333 River Road, Ottawa, Ont. K1L 8H9
Contact: Teresa Moore, editor
Official quarterly publication of the Canadian Figure Skating Association. Interested in exclusive features and photo stories on leading amateur figure skaters and on the figure skating scene across Canada and around the world. Regular departments include technical articles, competitions, clubs, carnivals, personalities (including former champions), and a children's section. Welcomes on-spec contributions. Pays on publication.

Canadian Sportsman, The
25 Townline Road, P.O. Box 603, Tillsonburg, Ont. N4G 4J1
(519) 842-4824
Contact: Gary Foerster, editor
Carries features and news mostly about harness racing in Canada. A weekly.

Canadian Yachting
777 Bay Street, Toronto, Ont. M5W 1A7
(416) 596-5019
Contact: John Morris, editor
Written for boating enthusiasts – both power and sail – in Eastern Canada. Reviews latest equipment and carries how-to articles and features on all aspects of yachting. Buys first North American serial rights, and pays on acceptance. A monthly.

Champion
333 River Road, Ottawa, Ont. K1L 8H9

(613) 748-5601
Contact: David Stubbs, editor
A quarterly focusing on issues important to the Canadian amateur sports community. Carries articles on sports medicine, marketing, and medal-winning performances by Canadians at home and abroad.

Coaching Review
333 River Road, Ottawa, Ont. K1L 8H9
(613) 748-5624
Contact: Steve Newman, editor
Published six times yearly by the Coaching Association of Canada. Covers more than forty sports from the coach's point of view with articles on sports nutrition, medicine, psychology, administration, and coaching techniques. Buys first Canadian and first North American serial rights. Pays on publication.

Corinthian HORSE SPORT in Canada, The
225 Industrial Parkway S., P.O. Box 670, Aurora, Ont. L4G 4J9
(416) 727-0107
Contact: Susan Jane Anstey, editor
An authoritative monthly equestrian publication which features articles on horse care, riding techniques, breeding, animal health, and the industry at large. Also covers the activities of the Canadian Equestrian Team.

Diver Magazine
8051 River Road, Richmond, B.C. V6X 1X8
(604) 273-4333
Contact: Neil McDaniel, editor
A magazine published nine times a year for North American sport divers. Carries regular articles on travel destinations and snorkeling, and scuba and deep-water diving. Also covers marine life and underwater photography. Article lengths range from 500 to 2,500 words. Buys first Canadian serial rights, and pays on publication.

Eastern Seasons
P.O. Box 102, St. John's, Nfld. A1C 5H5
(709) 753-8802
Contact: Ken Harvey, editor
A glossy quarterly which promotes the outdoors with articles on fishing, camping, wilderness travel, and wildlife.

Equinews
R.R. 7, Site 13, Comp. 106, Vernon, B.C. V1T 7Z3
(604) 545-9896
Contact: Dr. Jan White, editor
An all-breed, all-discipline monthly magazine formerly called *Hoof Beats*. Covers equine events world wide with special emphasis on

Western Canada. Official publication of the Horse Council of British Columbia.

Explore
P.O. Box 2197, Canmore, Alta. T0L 0M0
(403) 335-6622
Contact: Al Gordon, editor
Published six times a year for people who enjoy self-propelled outdoor recreational activities such as hiking, bicycling, paddling, and skiing. Articles cover adventure, travel, equipment evaluations, new products, and environmental issues.

Gam On Yachting
366 Adelaide Street E., Suite 443, Toronto, Ont. M5A 1N4
(416) 363-6495
Contact: Rick Walsh, editor
A magazine for the racing and cruising sailor with how-to articles, upcoming events, harbour profiles, book reviews, safety information, and humour. Special issues coincide with Canadian boat shows. Published ten times a year.

Gardening & Leisure Living
109 Vanderhoof Avenue, Toronto, Ont. M4G 2H7
(416) 422-1454
Contact: Norman Williamson, editor
Carries how-to and when-to articles for Ontario's gardeners, as well as do-it-yourself articles and news of new products. Published six times a year.

Hockey News, The
85 Scarsdale Road, Suite 100, Don Mills, Ont. M3B 2R2
(416) 445-5702
Contact: Bob McKenzie, editor
A weekly covering all levels of hockey, from the minor, college, and amateur to the international professional teams, and those in the NHL. Also contains opinions and interesting statistics, and reports on promotions, trades, and controversies.

Horse Sense Magazine
P.O. Box 269, Elora, Ont. N0B 1S0
(519) 846-5369
Contact: James Barton, editor
Articles deal with the people, places, and events prominent in Canada's equestrian field. Published six times a year.

Horses All
P.O. Box 550, Nanton, Alta. T0L 1R0
(403) 646-2271
Contact: Jacki French, editor

Carries stories about Canadian horses and their owners, with a special section devoted to young riders. A monthly.

Island Grower, The
7007 Richview Drive, R.R. 4, Sooke, B.C. V0S 1N0
Contact: Phyllis Kusch, editor
A magazine for gardeners in southern mainland B.C. Carries articles on organic gardening, pest control, as well as book reviews and gardeners' experiences. Published eleven times a year.

Landmarks
511 King Street, Toronto, Ont. M7A 1W3
Contact: Karen Heiber, editor
A quarterly magazine about Ontario's natural resources, covering all aspects of mining, forestry, hunting, fishing, parks, waterways, and wildlife.

Lottery & Gaming Review
261 Queen Street S., Mississauga, Ont. L5M 1L9
(416) 821-7900
Contact: H. Linden, editor
A monthly for the serious game player, containing articles and editorials on strategy for lotteries, casino games, contests, and sweepstakes.

Mon Jardin
110 Cremazie Boulevard W., Suite 422, Montreal, Que. H2P 1B9
(514) 382-4350
Contact: Lucie Dumoulin, editor
Carries articles about Quebec gardens, with how-to articles and news of new products. Published quarterly in French.

Motoneigiste Canadien
3414 Park Avenue, Suite 221, Montreal, Que. H2X 2H5
(514) 282-0191
Contact: Jean-Guy Langlois, editor
A twice-yearly snowmobiling magazine for French Canadians. Carries articles about resorts, trails, adventure, and upcoming events.

Mountain News
1615 W. 4th Street, Vancouver, B.C. V6J 1L8
(604) 732-1351
Contact: Dave Milligan, editor
Published five times yearly to encourage and inform 40,000 readers about hiking, biking, and wise use of the natural terrain.

Nature Canada
75 Albert Street, Suite 203, Ottawa, Ont. K1P 6G1
(613) 238-6154

Contact: Judy Lord, editor
A quarterly published by the Canadian Nature Federation and focusing on all aspects of Canadian wildlife, from butterflies and beluga whales to wildflowers and Halley's Comet. Also carries how-to stories on outdoor recreation and tales of life in the field. Features vary from 500 to 5,000 words. Pays on publication.

OHA Hockey News
222 Argyle Avenue, Delhi, Ont. N4B 2Y2
(519) 582-2510
Contact: Don Glendinning, editor
Published four times a year for the Ontario Hockey Association, with player profiles, league standings, and news.

Oldtimers' Hockey News
P.O. Box 951, Peterborough, Ont. K9J 7A5
(705) 743-2679
Contact: Dave Tatham, editor
Aimed at adult hockey players, and containing fitness features, viewpoints, letters, and editorials. A monthly.

On Court
1200 Sheppard Avenue E., Suite 503, Willowdale, Ont. M2K 2S5
(416) 497-1370
Contact: Tom Tebbutt, editor
Published eight times a year for active racquet-sports players. Most stories about tennis, but many articles explain badminton, racquetball, and squash.

Ontario Out of Doors
777 Bay Street, Toronto, Ont. M5W 1A7
(416) 596-5022
Contact: Burton Myers, editor
A magazine for Ontario's hunters and fishermen. Carries how-to and where-to articles, and covers boating, firearms, and backroad touring. Prefers articles of 1,000 to 2,000 words, and pays on acceptance. Buys first Canadian serial rights. Published ten times a year.

Ontario Quarter Horse News
P.O. Box 96, Acton, Ont. L7J 2M3
(519) 853-1090
Contact: Barbara Lennox, editor
News and events about Ontario's quarterhorse industry – shows, sales, breeding, and personalities involved. Published ten times a year.

Ontario Tennis
1220 Sheppard Avenue E., Willowdale, Ont. M2K 2X1
(416) 495-4215

Contact: Peter Lindsay, editor
A tabloid published six times yearly with news, views, and opinions from members of the Ontario Tennis Association.

Outdoor Canada
801 York Mills Road, Suite 301, Don Mills, Ont. M3B 1X7
(416) 443-8888
Contact: Sheila Kaighin, editor
A magazine published eight times yearly dedicated to the use and conservation of Canada's outdoors. Carries articles on fishing, boating, hunting, cross-country skiing, canoeing, hiking, outdoor photography, and camping. Invites on-spec submissions. Pays on publication.

Pacific Yachting
1132 Hamilton Street, Suite 202, Vancouver, B.C. V6B 2S2
(604) 687-1581
Contact: Paul Burkhart, editor
Written for Canada's sailboat and powerboat owners. Carries racing reports, adventure, and articles on coastal and offshore cruising, powerboat handling, and the latest technical information. Buys first North American serial rights, and pays on publication. A monthly.

Plongée, La
4545 Pierre de Coubertin, P.O. Box 1000, Station M, Montreal, Que. H1V 3R2
(514) 252-3009
Contact: Tristan Léonard, editor
Published in French six times yearly to promote underwater sports in Quebec and inform readers of new diving techniques, equipment, and products.

Pocket Pro Golf Magazine
2 St. Clair Avenue E., Suite 202, Toronto, Ont. M4T 2T5
(416) 961-8647
Contact: Bruce Longhurst, editor
Carries instructional and entertaining reading for golfers. Published twenty-two times a year.

Port Hole, The
26 Golden Gate Court, Scarborough, Ont. M1P 3A5
(416) 293-2438/1-800-268-3579
Contact: Neville Barnett, editor
Published quarterly by Canadian Power and Sail Squadrons to promote safe boating. Carries stories on new products and equipment as well as on issues affecting pleasure sailing.

Power Boating Ontario
2077 Dundas Street E., Suite 202, Mississauga, Ont. L4X 1M2

(416) 624-8218
Contact: Jean-Guy Langlois, editor
Carries stories on powerboat performance and evaluates new equipment and boating techniques. Also covers waterskiing. Published five times a year.

Quebec Yachting & Voile
465 Saint-Jean Street, Suite 903, Montreal, Que. H2Y 3S4
(514) 842-6491
Contact: Claude Beauchamp, editor
Published ten times a year in French for Quebec's sailors and boaters. Carries articles on boat and engine tests, navigation techniques, and the latest races and events.

Sailing Canada
95 Berkeley Street, Toronto, Ont. M5A 2W8
(416) 366-3538
Contact: Richard Holmes, editor
Reflects the ideas and interests of Canadian sailors. Carries articles on navigation, sail trim, chartering, boat building, electronics, and weather. Prefers articles of 2,000 to 3,500 words, and pays on publication. Buys first Canadian serial rights. Published six times a year.

Saskatchewan Ski Journal
413 Hilliard Street E., Saskatoon, Sask. S7J 0E7
(306) 653-2765
Contact: Dennis Adkin, editor
Provides detailed skiing information to families in Saskatchewan, and carries articles on equipment, clothing, and the sport in general. Published six times a year.

Scope Camping News
P.O. Box 39, Hyde Park, Ont. N0M 1Z0
(519) 471-9109
Contact: Harold Merton, editor
A quarterly national camping magazine which caters to both the beginning and experienced camper with stories on clubs, sites, and equipment.

Score Magazine
287 MacPherson Avenue, Toronto, Ont. M4V 1A4
(416) 928-2909
Contact: Lisa Leighton, editor
A national golf magazine published quarterly with four regional editions. Profiles prominent golfers and golfing personalities, and reviews courses, clubs, and equipment. Also carries articles on travel and international competitions.

Seasons
355 Lesmill Road, Don Mills, Ont. M3B 2W8
(416) 532-6855
Contact: Gail Muir, editor
A quarterly nature and outdoors magazine published by the Federation of Ontario Naturalists and designed to enhance feelings and knowledge about the natural world. Most articles are on nature and ecology, where to go, and what to look for.

Ski Canada
777 Bay Street, Toronto, Ont. M5W 1A7
(416) 596-5018
Contact: Clive Hobson, editor
Published monthly during the ski season to contain a balanced mixture of entertainment and information for both the experienced skier and the beginner. Tests equipment and new products, and offers articles on instruction, ski resorts, competitions, fashion, and prominent people in the business. Also carries fiction and humour. Article lengths vary from 600 to 4,000 words.

Ski Quebec
9851 Parkway Boulevard, Montreal, Que. H1J 1P3
(514) 353-4747
Contact: Claude André Lavergne, editor
Written exclusively for Quebec skiers and distributed five times during the ski season.

Ski-Runner
P.O. Box 32, Station R, Toronto, Ont. M4G 3Z3
(705) 445-1890
Contact: Art Benson/Fran Wood, editors
Published quarterly by the Toronto Ski Club to feature articles on local, national and international ski racing, fashion, and travel of interest to alpine and cross-country skiers.

Snow Goer
130 Spy Court, Markham, Ont. L3R 5H6
(416) 475-8440
Contact: Norm Rosen, editor
Published quarterly to keep Canadian snowmobiling families informed on new products, events, and activities.

Snowmobile Canada
3414 Park Avenue, Suite 221, Montreal, Que. H2X 2H5
(514) 282-0191
Contact: Reg Fife, editor
Published twice a year to promote snowmobiling in Canada with articles on adventure, where to go, what to see, fashion, trails, new products, and wildlife. Buys first Canadian serial rights, and pays on publication.

Snowmobile Sports
1255 Yonge Street, Suite 105, Toronto, Ont. M4T 1W6
(416) 922-7197
Contact: Rob Johnson, editor
Published twice a year for the active snowmobiling family. Covers trail rides, resort packages, and new products. Carries a winter snowmobile fashion section.

Soccer News
1220 Sheppard Avenue E., Willowdale, Ont. M2K 2X1
(416) 495-4251
Contact: Ed Bernacki, editor
Canada's pre-eminent soccer magazine, published six times a year for players, coaches, and spectators, with news and views on how to play and referee the game better. Also lists tournaments and results and reports on the World Cup.

Sports Journal, The
3505 - 14th Street S.W., Calgary, Alta. T2T 3W2
(403) 287-2060
Contact: Barry Whetstone, editor
A monthly sports magazine covering football, hockey, and baseball in both the American and National leagues. Buys first Canadian serial rights and other rights. Pays on publication.

Squash Life
1220 Sheppard Avenue E., Willowdale, Ont. M2X 2X1
(416) 495-4140
Contact: Jan Atkinson, editor
Official publication of Squash Ontario, distributed five times yearly. Carries news, views, and opinions on events, tournaments, clinics, and leagues.

Standardbred, The
P.O. Box 150, Acton, Ont. L7J 2M3
(519) 853-1090
Contact: Barbara Lennox, editor
Covers news and developments on the Canadian harness-racing scene from coast to coast. Readers are owners, trainers, drivers, and breeders. Carries articles on sales results, market analysis, training reports, and animal health. A quarterly.

Take Five
1715 Idylwyld Drive N., Saskatoon, Sask. S7L 1B4
(306) 652-9878
Contact: Susan Warwick, editor
A Saskatchewan monthly sports and recreation magazine aimed at helping readers enjoy the outdoors.

Vie et Camping
3414 Park Avenue, Suite 221, Montreal, Que. H2X 2H5
(514) 282-0191
Contact: Jean-Guy Langlois, editor
Published in French twice yearly to keep vehicle enthusiasts informed with articles on travel and routes. Also carries how-to technical pieces and reviews the latest wide-body vans, trailers, and campers.

Western Sportsman
P.O. Box 737, Regina, Sask. S4P 3A8
(306) 352-8384
Contact: Rick Bates, editor
Provides residents of Alberta and Saskatchewan with news and feature articles on hunting, fishing, wildlife, camping, and other outdoor activities such as backpacking and canoeing. Accepts articles up to 2,500 words, and pays on publication. Buys first Canadian serial rights. A quarterly

Windsport
550 Bronte Road, Oakville, Ont. L6J 4Z3
(416) 827-5462
Contact: Steve Jarrett, editor
Devoted to windsurfing. Carries articles on travel and adventure, and gives consumer tips and buyers' guides to the latest equipment. Also buys interviews of prominent windsporters. Published seven times a year.

YOUTH AND CHILDREN'S

Ahoy, The Children's Magazine
P.O. Box 5074, Armdale, N.S. B3L 4M7
Contact: Dana Philip Doiron, editor
Buys fiction, articles, and poetry for children aged between eight and twelve. Pays on publication for North American rights. Published bi-monthly.

Canada and the World
777 Bay Street, Toronto, Ont. M5W 1A7
(416) 596-5836
Contact: Rupert Taylor, editor
A publication for high school students enrolled in social studies courses, and used as a classroom teaching aid to help them understand Canada and the world in which they live. Carries articles on politics, economics, science, and environmental and social issues.

Buys all rights, and pays on acceptance. Published nine times a year.

Class Act
1835 Sargent Avenue, Winnipeg, Man. R3H 0E3
(204) 775-8681
Contact: Guy Ruchon, editor
Carries articles on career planning, entertainment, sports, movies, fashion, and lifestyle – all for Greater Winnipeg high school students. A monthly.

Chickadee
56 The Esplanade, Suite 304, Toronto, Ont. M5E 1A7
(416) 868-6001
Contact: Diane Davy, editor
A magazine which offers three- to nine-year-olds a bright, lively look at the world around them, with a focus on nature. Each issue contains photographs, stories, games, puzzles, crafts, and ideas for classroom projects. Ten issues a year.

Hibou
300 Arran Avenue, St. Lambert, Quebec J4R 1K5
(514) 875-0327
Contact: Luc Payette, editor
The French sister magazine to *OWL*. Published ten times a year with articles on science and nature for eight- to twelve-year-olds.

High School Trend
10022 - 103rd Street, Edmonton, Alta. T5J 0X2
(403) 429-3258
Contact: Denis Burns, editor
Designed to foster the positive aspects of student life in Alberta. Articles mostly cover entertainment, sports, and fashion. Also prints fiction. A monthly.

JAM (Just About Me)
56 The Esplanade, Suite 202, Toronto, Ont. M5E 1A7
(416) 364-5938
Contact: Ulla Colgrass, editor
A monthly magazine for ten- to fifteen-year-olds with articles on peer pressure, divorce, and planning for the future, as well as columns on fashion, film, and music.

OWL
56 The Esplanade, Suite 304, Toronto, Ont. M5E 1A7
(416) 868-6001
Contact: Kathy Farris, editor
A discovery magazine for eight- to twelve-year-olds. Sparks

children's curiosity in the world around them and encourages them to become involved in caring for the environment. Ten issues yearly.

Teen Generation
621B Mt. Pleasant Road, Toronto, Ont. M4S 2M5
(416) 487-3204
Contact: Stoney McCart/Donna Douglas, editors
A magazine for Canadian teenagers, carrying articles on fashion, sports, fitness, nutrition, careers, as well as profiles of people of importance to teens. Also prints fiction. Buys first Canadian serial rights, and pays on acceptance.

ART, MUSIC, AND LITERARY

Antigonish Review, The
St. Francis Xavier University, P.O. Box 135,
Antigonish, N.S. B2G 1C0
(902) 867-3962
Contact: George Sanderson, editor
A creative literary quarterly featuring poetry, fiction, and critical articles from Canada and abroad. Buys first Canadian serial rights.

Art Post
238 Davenport Road, Suite 29, Toronto, Ont. M5R 1J6
(416) 364-5541
Contact: Pat Fleisher, editor
Features art gallery reviews, museum previews, and profiles of artists, dealers, and collectors. Also comments on controversial issues in the arts. Published six times yearly.

ArtsAtlantic
P.O. Box 848, Charlottetown, P.E.I. C1A 7L9
(902) 566-2464, extension 138
Contact: J.H. Sherman, editor
Features and reports quarterly on Atlantic Canada's fine arts: cinema, video, artisanship, performance, and literature.

Arts in formation
161 Gower Street, St. John's, Nfld. A1C 1P7
(709) 739-7190
Contact: Joan Sullivan, editor
Devoted to covering the arts in Newfoundland and Labrador six times yearly. Each issues contains interviews, reviews, articles, features, and forums focusing on artists, art organizations, and related social and political issues.

Arts West
6028 - 5th Street S.E., Calgary, Alta. T2H 1L4
Contact: Carolyn Leier, editor
Buys strong articles on all elements of the arts from across Canada. Articles vary from 750 to 3,000 words. Buys first Canadian serial rights, and pays on publication. Published ten times a year.

Artviews
439 Wellington Street W., 3rd Floor, Toronto, Ont. M5V 1E7
(416) 591-8883
Contact: Rachel Rafelman, editor
A quarterly magazine for artists, members of the art community, and Canadians interested in keeping informed about the visual arts.

Border Crossings
160 Princess Street, Suite 301, Winnipeg, Man. R3B 1K9
(204) 942-5778
Contact: Meeka Walsh, editor
A quarterly review featuring articles, book reviews, artists' profiles, and interviews covering the full range of the contemporary arts in Manitoba and the West.

Border/lines
31 Madison Avenue, Toronto, Ont. M5R 2S2
(416) 967-9469
Contact: Alex Wilson, editor
A quarterly magazine featuring articles, reviews, and visual pieces on the theory and practice of culture and communications.

Brick
P.O. Box 537, Station Q, Toronto, Ont. M4T 2M5
Contact: Linda Spalding, editor
Reviews Canadian and international literature and features essays, interviews with writers, and excerpts from journals. Published three times a year.

C Magazine
P.O. Box 5, Station B, Toronto, Ont. M5T 2T2
(416) 977-0850
Contact: Richard Rhodes, editor
Carries criticism on contemporary art worldwide. Largely pictorial. A quarterly.

Canadian Antiquer
P.O. Box 70, Station Q, Toronto, Ont. M4T 2P1
(416) 964-1454
Contact: Donald Owen, editor
A Canada-wide monthly newspaper devoted to antiques and collec-

tibles. Lists shows, sales, flea markets, auctions, and carries experts' reports on antiques.

Canadian Art
56 The Esplanade, Toronto, Ont. M5E 1A7
(416) 364-3333
Contact: Susan Walker, editor
A colourful quarterly containing news, reviews, profiles, and feature articles. Written for the gallery-goer, art collector, artist, and general reader.

Canadian Author and Bookman
24 Ryerson Avenue, Toronto, Ont. M5T 2P3
(416) 364-4203
Contact: Anne Osborne, editor
A quarterly national writers' magazine which features Canadian writing. Carries profiles and interviews with people who influence Canadian literature.

Canadian Collector
27 Carlton Street, Suite 406, Toronto, Ont. M5B 1L2
(416) 977-0770
Contact: Marian Hahn Bradshaw, editor
A bi-monthly publication devoted to the fine antiques and decorative arts that influence and reflect Canada's rich cultural heritage. Carries articles on restoration, auctions, collecting, and market trends.

Canadian Fiction Magazine
P.O. Box 946, Station F, Toronto, Ont. M4Y 2N9
Contact: Geoffrey Hancock, editor
A quarterly dedicated to new Canadian fiction, including translations from French and other languages spoken in Canada. Also buys book reviews, interviews, manifestos, graphics, and some photographs. Pays on publication. Buys first North American serial rights.

Canadian Library Journal
151 Sparks Street, Ottawa, Ont. K1P 5E3
(613) 232-9625
Contact: Laurie Bowes, editor
Provides a forum for the discussion, analysis, and evaluation of librarianship issues. A bi-monthly.

Canadian Literature
University of British Columbia, 209 West Mall, Suite 223.
Vancouver, B.C. V6T 1W5
(604) 228-2780
Contact: W.H. New, editor

A quarterly devoted to studying all aspects of Canadian writing: fiction, non-fiction, poetry, and drama. Buys first Canadian serial rights, and pays on publication.

Canadian Musician
832 Mt. Pleasant Road, Toronto, Ont. M4P 2L3
(416) 485-8284
Contact: Ted Burley, editor
A bi-monthly publication written for professional and amateur musicians, as well as serious music enthusiasts and industry personnel. Accepts articles of 2,000 to 3,000 words. Buys all rights, and pays on acceptance.

Canadian Print & Portfolio
3152 Dundas Street W., Toronto, Ont. M6P 2A1
(416) 767-4032
Contact: Deborah Grund, editor
A quarterly magazine about print-making, photography, letter-press, and paper-making.

Canadian Theatre Review
University of Toronto Press, 63A St. George Street,
Toronto, Ont. M5S 1A6
(416) 978-6678
Contact: Angela Fritsch, editor
Serves both the practising and scholarly theatre communities. Publishes playscripts, essays of concern to theatre professionals, and interviews playwrights, actors, directors, and designers. A quarterly.

Capilano Review, The
2055 Purcell Way, North Vancouver, B.C. V7J 3H5
(604) 986-1911
Contact: Dorothy Jantzen, editor
A quarterly review which features poetry, prose, and visual materials by innovative writers and artists. Buys first Canadian serial rights, and pays on publication.

Cerebus
P.O. Box 1674, Station C, Kitchener, Ont. N2G 4R2
(519) 576-0610
Contact: Karen McKiel, editor
A long-running comic book, sold by subscription, which deals with slapstick, politics, religion, and romance. A monthly.

CineACTION!
40 Alexander Street, Apartment 705, Toronto, Ont. M4Y 1B5
(416) 964-3534
Contact: Anthony Irwin, editor

A quarterly film magazine which explores neglected and unconventional cinema, both mainstream and independent productions, from a feminist and socialist perspective.

Cinema Canada
834 Bloomfield Avenue, Montreal, Que. H2V 3S6
(514) 272-5354
Contact: Jean-Pierre Tadros/Connie Tadros, editors
Features film industry production news, reviews on new releases, and interviews with prominent film makers. Also carries articles on Canadian cinema – past, present, and future. Pays on publication. A monthly.

Coda Magazine
P.O. Box 87, Station J, Toronto, Ont. M4J 4X8
(416) 593-7230
Contact: Bill Smith, editor
A jazz magazine published six times yearly with articles, essays, personality profiles, and reviews.

Continuo Magazine
6 Dartnell Avenue, Toronto, Ont. M5R 3A4
(416) 964-0819
Contact: Matthew Redsell, editor
A magazine published eleven times yearly for lovers of Renaissance and Baroque music. Articles are mostly about performance, practice, and noted makers of harpsichords, flutes, oboes, and the many stringed instruments of these two musical periods.

Cross-Canada Writers' Quarterly
P.O. Box 277, Station F, Toronto, Ont. M4Y 1T1
(416) 690-0917
Contact: Ted Plantos, editor
A quarterly dedicated to fine literary journalism. Also carries poetry and some fiction, and lists literary writers' markets.

CV/II
University of Manitoba, P.O. Box 32, University Centre, Winnipeg, Man. R3T 9Z9
(204) 474-9610
Contact: Jane Casey, editor
A quarterly publication from the University of Manitoba. Analyses Canadian poetry via interviews with poets and articles about their work. Buys first Canadian serial rights.

Dalhousie Review
Dalhousie University, Sir James Dunn Building, Suite 314, Halifax, N.S. B3H 3J5
(902) 424-2541

Contact: Dr. A.E. Kennedy, editor
Carries news, reviews, and criticism of Canadian arts and literature and the political issues affecting them. Preferred article length 4,000 to 5,000 words. Pays on publication for first Canadian serial rights. A quarterly.

Dance in Canada
38 Charles Street E., Toronto, Ont. M4Y 1T1
(416) 921-5169
Contact: Steve Dymond, editor
A glossy quarterly covering Canadian dance through personality profiles, articles, and reviews. Read by dance students, dance teachers, performers, and audiences. Buys first Canadian serial rights, and pays on publication.

Dandelion
922 - 9th Avenue S.E., Calgary, Alta. T2G 0S4
(403) 265-0524
Contact: Cecilia Frey, editor
Publishes poetry and fiction from writers Canada-wide, plus interviews and articles about the Canadian literary scene.

Descant
P.O. Box 314, Station P, Toronto, Ont. M5S 2S8
(416) 489-6198
Contact: Karen Mulhallen, editor
A quarterly literary magazine which publishes poetry, prose, fiction, interviews, travel pieces, letters, photographs, engravings, art, and literary criticism.

Ellipse
University of Sherbrooke, P.O. Box 10, Sherbrooke, Que. J1K 2R1
(819) 821-7277
Contact: Joseph Bonenfant, editor
Dedicated to Canadian poetry. Each issue feature two poets – one French, one English – and assesses their work. Published twice yearly.

Event
Douglas College, P.O. Box 2503, New Westminster, B.C. V3L 5B2
(604) 520-5400
Contact: Vye Flindall, editor
Presents Canadian and international writers and artists through their fiction, poetry, drama, and reviews of their work. Published twice yearly.

Exile
P.O. Box 67, Station B, Toronto, Ont. M5T 2C0
Contact: Barry Callaghan, editor

A quarterly journal devoted entirely to unique fiction, poetry, drama, painting, and drawing from Canada and abroad. Buys first Canadian serial rights and other rights. Pays sometimes on acceptance, sometimes on publication.

Fiddlehead, The
University of New Brunswick, P.O. Box 4400, Old Arts Building, Room 317, Fredericton, N.B. E3B 5H1
(506) 454-3591
Contact: Michael Taylor, editor
A quarterly which publishes fine poetry, prose, and art work, primarily from the Atlantic region.

Fine Arts & Auction Review
2227 Granville Street, Vancouver, B.C. V6H 31
(604) 734-4944
Contact: Anthony Westbridge, editor
Covers the national and international antiques and fine art auction market scene with previews, interviews, analysis, and industry-related articles.

FUSE Magazine
489 College Street, 5th Floor, Toronto, Ont. M6G 1A5
(416) 928-0914
Contact: Jocelyn Grills, editor
Published five times yearly to cover all aspects of contemporary culture, from independent production to mass media. Also carries articles on women's issues, minority politics, labour struggles, economic and policy analysis, plus reviews of video, film, art, television, music, performance, theatre, and books.

Germination
428 Yale Avenue, Riverview, N.B. E1B 2B5
(506) 386-1687
Contact: Allan Cooper, editor
A journal about poetry and prose for poets. Published twice yearly.

Grain
P.O. Box 1154, Regina, Sask. S4P 3B4
Contact: Brenda Richies, editor
A literary quarterly, first published by the Saskatchewan Writers' Guild in 1973, of national and international scope. Prints high-quality literary and visual art, and offers constructive how-to articles about writing. Pays on publication.

Impulse
471 Richmond Street W., Toronto, Ont. M5V 1X9
(416) 368-7511

Contact: Eldon Garnet, editor
Published four times yearly to include unique Canadian fiction and international fiction in translation. Also interviews film makers, philosophers, architects, and other culture producers.

Insight on Collectables
P.O. Box 130, Durham, Ont. N0C 1R0
(519) 369-5155
Contact: Jim Heyens, editor
A monthly, in newspaper format, which provides information on collector plates, figurines, limited edition lithographs, and new products. Also interviews Canadian artists and artisans.

Inter
629 St. Jean Street, Quebec, Que. G1R 1P7
(418) 529-9680
Contact: Alain-Martin Richard, editor
A Quebec-based quarterly, published in French, about cultural phenomena, mostly visual arts, writing, performance, music, and cinema.

Journal of Canadian Art History
Concordia University, 1395 Dorchester Boulevard W.,
Room VA 422, Montreal, Que. H3G 2M5
(514) 848-4699
Contact: Don Andrus, editor
A journal published twice yearly and devoted to scholarly articles on the history of Canadian art, architecture, photography, and the decorative arts.

Last Issue
815 - 1st Street S.W., Suite 604, Calgary, Alta. T2P 1N3
(403) 263-3232
Contact: Heather Elton, editor
Publishes an eclectic mix of visual art, fiction, commentary, satire, poetry, interview, and essay twice yearly.

Live! Le Journal Rock
P.O. Box 281, Laval-des-Rapides, Que. H7N 3J9
(514) 687-1428
Contact: Marie-France Remillard, editor
Published in French to focus on the rock music world. Carries interviews with top international artists and reviews of new albums, videos, and concerts.

Malahat Review, The
University of Victoria, P.O. Box 1700, Victoria, B.C. V8W 2Y2
(604) 721-8524

Contact: Constance Rooke, editor
A distinguished, award-winning quarterly dedicated to publishing some of Canada's best poets and short story writers.

Matrix
P.O. Box 510, Lennoxville, Que. J1M 1Z6
(819) 564-3653
Contact: Philip Lanthier, editor
Publishes new Quebec writers and carries interviews with those already established, twice yearly. Pays on publication. Buys first Canadian serial rights.

Museum Quarterly
38 Charles Street E., Toronto, Ont. M4Y 1T1
(416) 923-3868
Contact: Betty-Ann Jordan, editor
A quarterly about Canadian museums, galleries, historic sites, science centres, and zoos. Looks at both the philosophy and practice of museum work – collecting, exhibiting, conserving, and funding.

Music Magazine
56 The Esplanade, Suite 202, Toronto, Ont. M5E 1A7
(416) 364-5938
Contact: Ulla Colgrass, editor
Presents, five times yearly, the world of Canadians performing classical music at home and abroad. Also reviews books, recordings, videos, and concerts.

Musicworks
1087 Queen Street W., Toronto, Ont. M6J 1H3
(416) 533-0192
Contact: Sibylle Preuschat, editor
Quarterly magazine distributed with audio-visual backup – cassettes and videos to illustrate articles and interviews on a broad spectrum of music.

New Quarterly, The
University of Waterloo, English Language Proficiency Program, Waterloo, Ont. N2L 3G1
(519) 885-1211
Contact: Mary Merikle, editor
Publishes poetry, short fiction, and excerpts from novels, but encourages "new voices and directions" in Canadian writing. Four issues a year.

Noovo Masheen
1 Cooper Street, Suite 506, Ottawa, Ont. K1R 5H9
(613) 237-3178
Contact: James Whittall, editor

Published twice a year to "revitalize Canadian poetry," and interview established poets.

Northward Journal
7 Aurora Street, Kapuskasing, Ont. P5N 1J6
(705) 335-2988
Contact: John Flood, editor
A quarterly of Northern arts, featuring reviews of artists, galleries, exhibitions, and books. Pays on publication. Buys one-time rights.

Open Letter
104 Lydhurst Avenue, Toronto, Ont. M5R 2Z7
(416) 922-9912
Contact: Frank Davey, editor
A magazine published three times a year to provoke theoretical and critical exploration of contemporary and experimental Canadian writing.

Opera Canada
366 Adelaide Street E., Suite 433, Toronto, Ont. M5A 3X9
(416) 363-0395
Contact: Ruby Mercer, editor
Devoted for more than twenty-five years to Canadian opera and its followers. Reviews performances and interviews our best singers and conductors. Pays on publication. A quarterly.

Ovo
307 St. Catherine Street W., Suite 300, Montreal, Que. H2X 2A3
(514) 849-6253
Contact: Jorge Guerra, editor
A photographic quarterly which deals with a broad spectrum of social concerns.

Parachute
4060 St. Laurent Boulevard, Suite 501, Montreal, Que. H2W 1Y9
(514) 842-9805
Contact: Chantal Pontbriand, editor
A bilingual quarterly which offers readers in-depth articles on the theory and practice of art today – interviews with artists, and articles on music, cinema, photography, theatre, dance, and video. Pays on publication. Buys first Canadian serial rights.

Parallelogramme
183 Bathurst Street, 1st Floor, Toronto, Ont. M5T 2R7
(416) 869-3854
Contact: Tanya Mars, editor
Published five times a year to cover developments in contemporary art, including painting, sculpture, installations, video, new music, dance, and performance.

Performing Arts in Canada
52 Avenue Road, 2nd Floor, Toronto, Ont. M5R 2G2
(416) 921-2601/921-5188
Contact: Mary Ann Pathy, editor
A quarterly magazine which explores the issues and trends affecting performing arts in Canada, primarily theatre, dance, opera, ballet, and film. Also carries profiles on individual performers, companies, and troupes. Prefers articles of 1,200 to 1,800 words. Pays on publication.

Photo Communique
P.O. Box 129, Station M, Toronto, Ont. M6S 4T2
(416) 868-1443
Contact: Gail Fisher-Taylor, editor
A quality magazine which explores the way photography touches every aspect of our lives and culture. Reproduces fine photographs and carries insightful interviews, book reviews, current news, and opinions. A quarterly.

Playboard
7560 Lawrence Drive, Burnaby, B.C. V5A 1T6
(604) 420-6115
Contact: John Friesen/Stephen Mitchell, editors
A lively arts magazine which gives concert- and theatre-goers behind-the-scenes articles and interviews with key performers. A monthly.

Poetry Canada Review
307 Coxwell Avenue, Toronto, Ont. M4L 3B5
(416) 694-3348
Contact: David Lawson, editor
A fifty-page quarterly tabloid which publishes about 100 poems each issue, some by our best poets, others by new writers.

Poetry Toronto
217 Northward Drive, Willowdale, Ont. M2M 2K5
(416) 222-4690
Contact: Maria Jacobs, editor
A monthly which features works by as many as eight poets each issue. Also profiles poets, reviews books, and lists workshops and poetry readings throughout the Toronto area.

Pop Rock
3646 St. Germain Boulevard, Montreal, Que. H1W 2V5
(514) 521-3262
Contact: G. Giguère, editor
Publishes news, interviews, and stories about artists at local, national, and international levels. Also reviews records, videos, and some films. Published six times a year.

Prairie Fire
100 Arthur Street, Winnipeg, Man. R3B 1H3
(204) 943-9066
Contact: Andris Taskans, editor
A quarterly which publishes poetry, fiction, essays, plays, interviews, reviews, and criticism.

Prairie Journal of Canadian Literature, The
P.O. Box 997, Station G, Calgary, Alta. T3A 3G2
(403) 284-6052
Contact: A. Burke, editor
An eclectic magazine which publishes poetry, fiction, critical articles, one-act plays, and reviews of recent releases from the Prairie presses. Published twice yearly.

PRISM International
University of British Columbia, 1866 Main Mall, Room E462, Vancouver, B.C. V6T 1W5
(604) 228-2514
Contact: Dianne Maguire, editor
A quarterly magazine which emphasizes contemporary Canadian literature and publishes works by leading authors, poets, and dramatists.

Quarry
P.O. Box 1061, Kingston, Ont. K7L 4Y5
(613) 544-5400
Contact: Bob Hilderly, editor
For more than thirty years this magazine, published six times yearly, has been publishing new, innovative poetry, essays, and fiction by young, emerging Canadian writers.

Québec Rock
3510 St. Laurent Boulevard, Suite 404, Montreal, Que. H2X 2V2
(514) 844-8491
Contact: Patrick Emiroglu, editor
Carries reviews and reports, mostly on Quebec's music scene. A monthly.

Raddle Moon, The
9060 Ardmore Drive, Sidney, B.C. V8L 3S1
(604) 656-4045
Contact: Susan Clark, editor
An international review which prints previously untranslated writing – short stories and poetry – from Spain, Sweden, Chile, India, Japan, and Mexico, among many other countries. Published twice a year.

Rampike
95 Rivercrest Road, Toronto, Ont. M6S 4H7

Contact: Karl Jirgens, editor
Features poetry, fiction, one-act plays, and cinema and video scripts from around the world. Published twice yearly.

Rock Express
37 Madison Avenue, Toronto, Ont. M5R 2S2
(416) 964-6626
Contact: Keith Sharp, editor
Covers and promotes the pop, rock, and contemporary music scene in Canada. Also carries a stereo information guide and sections on movies, videos and musical instruments. A monthly.

Room of One's Own
P.O. Box 46160, Station G, Vancouver, B.C. V6R 4G5
Contact: Robin Bellamy, editor
Solicits fine writing and editing from Canada's best women authors, both well-known and unknown. A quarterly.

Rotunda
100 Queen's Park, Toronto, Ont. M5S 2C8
(416) 586-5581
Contact: Sandra Shaul, editor
A quarterly magazine, published by the Royal Ontario Museum, which carries authoritative pieces on art, archeology, the earth and life sciences, astronomy, and museology.

Rubicon
McGill University, 853 Sherbrooke Street W.,
Montreal, Que. H3A 2T6
(514) 286-0652
Contact: Peter O'Brien, editor
A semi-annual journal of contemporary writing – mostly poetry and short stories – and visual art.

Soul Survivor
436 Queen Street W., Toronto, Ont. M5V 2A8
(416) 591-1282
Contact: Mary Koppel, editor
A quarterly magazine devoted to rhythm and blues from the 1960s. Reviews performances and profiles performers.

Studies in Canadian Literature
University of New Brunswick, English Department,
Fredericton, N.B. E3B 5A5
(506) 453-4598
Contact: Barrie Davies, editor
Publishes, semi-annually, notes, essays, and commentaries on all aspects of Canadian writing in French and English. Contributors are both established scholars and cogent new critics. Buys first Canadian serial rights.

Theatre History in Canada
214 College Street, Toronto, Ont. M5T 2Z9
(416) 586-7980
Contact: Richard Plant, editor
Focuses, twice a year, on all aspects of the history of both English- and French-language theatre in Canada. Also publishes book reviews and articles on companies and people who have contributed to theatre and criticism.

Toronto South Asian Review, The
P.O. Box 6996, Station A, Toronto, Ont. M5W 1X7
Contact: Nurjehan Aziz, editor
Publishes poetry, fiction, drama, and criticism from the Indian subcontinent, in English and in translation, three times yearly.

Vanguard
40 E. Cordova Street, Vancouver, B.C. V6A 1K2
(604) 685-6032
Contact: Russell Keziere, editor
Focuses on the visual arts in Canada. Carries reviews on exhibitions at commercial galleries, artist-run centres, and public museums. Places emphasis on graphic design. Published six times yearly.

Vie des Arts
373 St. Paul Street W., Montreal, Que. H2Y 2A7
(514) 282-0205
Contact: Andre Paradis, editor
A high-quality quarterly magazine, published in French, concerned mainly with plastic arts, photography, video, architecture, archeology, ceramics, performances, collections, and music.

WAG Magazine
176 Woolwich Street, P.O. Box 1747, Guelph, Ont. N1H 7A1
(519) 763-5058
Contact: Karen Mantel, editor
Scheduled to debut in mid-1988, this publication will be dedicated to the preservation of humorous writing.

WAVES
79 Denham Drive, Richmond Hill, Ont. L4C 6H9
(416) 889-6703
Contact: Bernice Lever, editor
Publishes three times a year both new and known Canadian writers of short fiction, poetry, reviews, interviews, and literary articles.

West Coast Review
Simon Fraser University, Department of English,
Burnaby, B.C. V5A 1S6

(604) 291-4287
Contact: Frederic Candelaria, editor
A quarterly creative arts magazine focusing mostly on West Coasters and featuring contemporary poetry, short fiction, drama, and photography. Pays on acceptance.

Wildlife Collectables Journal, The
P.O. Box 130, Durham, Ont. N0G 1R0
(519) 369-5155
Contact: Catherine MacFabe, editor
Concentrates on articles about collectables with wildlife themes – stamps, figurines, original prints, collector plates, original art, and antique souvenirs. Also carries stories on native Canadian animals, conservation efforts, artists, and wildlife art collectables in North America. A monthly.

Writing
P.O. Box 69609, Station K, Vancouver, B.C. V5K 4W7
(604) 732-1013
Contact: Colin Browne, editor
A quarterly magazine of experimental poetry and official journal of the Kootenay School of Writing.

SCHOLARLY

Telephone numbers and contact names have been purposely omitted. Too many of these magazines function on the other side of university or college switchboards and are edited not by one person, but by an ever-changing committee of professors and/or graduate students.

Acadiensis
University of New Brunswick, Campus House,
Fredericton, N.B. E3B 5A3
Includes original academic research, review articles, documents, notes, and a running bibliography compiled by librarians in the four Maritime provinces. Published twice yearly.

Arctic
University of Calgary, The Arctic Institute of North America,
2500 University Drive N.W., Calgary, Alta. T2N 1N4
Publishes papers from all areas of Arctic scholarship dealing with the polar and sub-polar regions of the world. Manuscripts are original works and have undergone intensive peer review. A quarterly.

Atlantis
Mount Saint Vincent University, 166 Bedford Highway,
Halifax, N.S. B3M 2J6
Encourages original interdisciplinary scholarship on women's issues, in both English and French. Published twice yearly by the Institute for the Study of Women at Mount Saint Vincent University.

B.C. Studies
University of British Columbia, 2029 West Mall,
Vancouver, B.C. V6W 1W5
An award-winning quarterly journal focusing on all aspects of human history in British Columbia. Articles cover a wide range of subjects including resource management, politics, anthropology, literature, economics, archeology, and history.

Canadian Children's Literature
P.O. Box 335, Guelph, Ont. N1H 6K5
Offers in-depth criticism of Canadian literature for young people. Scholarly articles and reviews are supplemented by graphics, photographs, and interviews with authors of children's books. A quarterly.

Canadian Ethnic Studies
University of Calgary, 2500 University Drive N.W.,
Calgary, Alta. T2N 1N4
An interdisciplinary journal devoted to the study of ethnicity, immigration, inter-group relations, and the history and cultural life of ethnic groups in Canada. Published three times yearly.

Canadian Historical Review
University of Toronto Press, Journals Department,
5201 Dufferin Street, Downsview, Ont. M3H 5T8
Covers, as it has for nearly seventy years, a broad spectrum of Canada's history in lively articles, comprehensive reviews, authoritative research, and extensive bibliographies of recent historical publications. A quarterly.

Canadian Journal of Education
14 Henderson Avenue, Ottawa, Ont. K1N 7P1
Constitutes the chief means of scholarly communication among members and among the diverse constituent sub-disciplines of the field of education – education psychology, curriculum studies, sociology, administration, and comparative education. Articles are abstracted in English, French, Spanish, and German. A quarterly.

Canadian Journal of Philosophy
University of Calgary Press, University of Calgary,

2500 University Drive N.W., Calgary, Alta. T2N 1N4
A leading Canadian philosophical journal which investigates and contributes to the scholarship, teaching, and research of the country's major philosophers. A quarterly.

Canadian Journal of Political & Social Theory
Concordia University, 7141 Sherbrooke Street W., Montreal, Que. H4B 1M8
A serial publication on key themes in contemporary theory, culture, and society. Two issues yearly.

Canadian Modern Language Review, The
237 Hellems Avenue, Welland, Ont. L3B 3B8
Publishes literary, linguistic, and pedagogical articles, book reviews, current advertisements, and other material of interest to teachers of French, German, Italian, Russian, Spanish, Ukrainian, and English as a second language, at all levels of instruction. A quarterly first published in 1944.

Canadian Poetry
University of Western Ontario, Department of English, London, Ont. N6A 3K7
A scholarly and critical journal devoted to the study of poetry from all periods and regions of Canada. Also prints articles, reviews, and documents. Published twice yearly since 1976.

Canadian Public Administration
897 Bay Street, Toronto, Ont. M5S 1Z7
A refereed journal which examines structures, processes, and outcomes of public policy and public management related to executive, legislative, judicial, and quasi-judicial functions in municipal, provincial, and federal spheres of government. A quarterly.

Canadian Review of Sociology and Anthropology
Concordia University, 1455 de Maisonneuve Boulevard W., Room G-323, Montreal, Que. H3G 1M8
Official quarterly journal of the Canadian Sociology and Anthropology Association. Presents scholarship and research findings, mostly in research notes, rejoinders, book reviews, and review essays.

Canadian Woman Studies Journal
York University, Founders College, Room 204, 4700 Keele Street, Downsview, Ont. M3J 1P3
A quarterly which makes accessible current writing and research on a wide variety of feminist topics. Welcomes creative writing, experimental articles, and essays, as well as book, art, and film reviews.

ENVIRONMENTS
University of Waterloo, Faculty of Environmental Studies,

Waterloo, Ont. N2L 3G1
An interdisciplinary journal for scholars and practitioners who aim to integrate the fields of environment, development, and design. Published three times yearly.

Essays on Canadian Writing
307 Coxwell Avenue, Toronto, Ont. M4L 3B5
Devoted to criticism of Canadian writers and their works. Concentrates on essays that deal with contemporary authors and current critical approaches. Publishes bibliographies, interviews, and full-length book reviews of fiction, poetry, and criticism. Appears three times yearly. Author retains all rights.

Grail: An Ecumenical Journal
University of St. Jerome's College, Waterloo, Ont. N2L 3G3
A quarterly multidisciplinary journal inspired by Vatican II's urgings for investigation of the human condition in modern scholarship.

Journal of Canadian Studies
Trent University, Champlain College, Peterborough, Ont. K9J 7B8
Publishes a variety of scholarly articles, critical comment, and book reviews pertaining to Canadian history, politics, the economy, education, literature and the arts, public policy, communications, anthropology, and sociology. Accepts articles between 3,000 and 10,000 words. A quarterly.

Labour/Le Travail
Memorial University, Department of History,
St. John's, Nfld. A1C 5S7
An interdisciplinary, historical journal concerned with work, workers, and the labour movement. Includes articles, book notes, archival notes, and an annual bibliography of Canadian labour studies. Published twice yearly.

Material History Bulletin
National Museums of Canada, Publishing Services,
Ottawa, Ont. K1A 0M8
Encourages new methods and new forms of evidence in studying history from a variety of research fields: history, folk culture, geography, anthropology, historical archeology, artistry, and history of technology and of architecture. Appears twice yearly.

Modern Drama
University of Toronto Press, Journals Department,
5201 Dufferin Street, Downsview, Ont. M3H 5T8
Focuses exclusively on world drama from 1850 to the present. Carries bibliographies, essays, and interviews with famous theatrical creators, critics, and scholars. A quarterly.

Pacific Affairs
University of British Columbia, 2029 West Mall,
Vancouver, B.C. V6T 1W5
A source of scholarly insight into the social, cultural, political, and economic issues of the Pacific region. Carries articles, review articles, and research notes contributed by authors throughout the world. Also reviews books – about sixty each issue. A quarterly published since 1928.

Provincial Essays
P.O. Box 844, Station P, Toronto, Ont. M5S 2Z2
Contains a series of monographs and symposia that address the need for source material and basic scholarship on Canadian visual culture of the recent past. Published twice yearly.

Queen's Quarterly
Queen's University, Kingston, Ont. K7L 3N6
A distinctive and authoritative university-based review, first published in 1895, which features scholarly articles of wide general interest. Has a Canadian focus and an international outlook. Carries articles on politics, history, science, the humanities, and arts and letters, plus regular music and science columns, original poetry, fiction, and extensive book reviews. Pays on publication for first Canadian serial rights. A quarterly.

RACAR: Revue d'art canadienne/Canadian Art Review
P.O. Box 68, Ahuntsic Station, Montreal, Que. H3L 3N5
Presents articles and documentation on art, and architecture and the decorative arts, all with an historical point of view. Official publications of the Universities Art Association of Canada. Contributions are published in English and French. Appears twice yearly.

Renaissance Universal Journal
904 Sandford Drive, Burlington, Ont. L7T 3G6
Examines obstacles to society-building and suggests solutions. Proposes that human progress is hampered by poverty, socio-exploitation, political subjugation, economic colonization, war, and distributive injustice, and offers neo-humanist thought as a pathway to a clearer understanding of mankind's life goals. A quarterly.

Resources for Feminist Research/Documentation sur la Recherche Feministe
252 Bloor Street W., Toronto, Ont. M5W 1V6
(416) 923-6641
Contact: Mary Louise Adams, editor
A quarterly journal of feminist scholarship containing papers, abstracts, reviews, reports of work in progress, and bibliographies.

Scholarly Publishing
University of Toronto Press, 5201 Dufferin Street,
Downsview, Ont. M3H 5T8

Concerned with the "pleasures and perils" of publishing. Coverage ranges from the classic concerns of manuscript editing and list building to such contemporary issues as on-demand publishing and computer applications. Also explores the "delicate balance" of author-editor relations, and the intricacies of production and budgeting. Carries articles with a unique blend of philosphical analysis and practical advice. Buys first serial rights. Published quarterly since 1971.

Studies in Political Economy: A Socialist Review
P.O. Box 4729, Station E, Ottawa, Ont. K1S 5H9
Offers a multidisplinary approach to contemporary and historical issues. Presents original research and theoretical work with a socialist perspective by prominent Canadian and international authors. Covers key debates in public policy, workers' history, feminism, the labour movement, international affairs, economics, and the peace movement. Published three times yearly.

Theatrum: A Theatre Journal
69 Niagara Street, Toronto, Ont. M5V 1C3
Aimed at the theatrical community, both patrons and practitioners alike, as a forum for the working professional to discuss his/her craft. Provides a place for discussion and exposure in "an art form that is becoming increasingly more exciting and complex." A quarterly.

University of Ottawa Quarterly
603 Cumberland Street, Ottawa, Ont. K1N 6N5
A bilingual journal, founded in 1931, which publishes scholarly articles in the humanities and social sciences. Editorial content in international and interdisciplinary in character. Includes literary criticism, scholarly analysis, research findings, edited or translated original texts, and regular book reviews in English or French. A quarterly.

Urban History Review
University of Winnipeg, Institute of Urban Studies,
515 Portage Avenue, Winnipeg, Man. R3B 2E9
A bilingual interdisciplinary and refereed journal which presents lively articles covering such topics as architecture, heritage, urbanization, housing, and planning, all in a generously illustrated format. Regular features include in-depth articles, research notes, two annual bibliographies covering Canadian and international publications, comprehensive book reviews, and notes and comments on conferences, urban policy, and publications. Published three times yearly.

TRADE, BUSINESS, AND PROFESSIONAL PUBLICATIONS

These publications comprise part of the writer's market that is all too often ignored. Yet it can be lucrative. Trade, business, and professional journals rarely pay more than $500 for a story of about 2,500 words, and usually only about $150. The pieces they require, however, invariably have considerably fewer sources than are necessary for consumer magazine articles and can, therefore, often be completed in only a day or two, sometimes after research and interviews conducted solely by telephone.

The secret to making reasonable money from these magazines and tabloids is to work frequently for as many of them as possible, always bearing in mind that they usually want a lot of technical detail that will inform readers already well acquainted with the specific fields they serve.

In general, magazines in each of the following categories carry pieces about new products, inventions and developments, unusual marketing and promotion ideas, innovative management techniques, and important people and events specific to their industry.

Canada's largest publishers of trade magazines are: Maclean Hunter Ltd., 777 Bay Street, Toronto, Ont. M5W 1A7; Sanford Evans Publishing Ltd., 1077 St. James Street, P.O. Box 6900, Winnipeg, Man. R3C 3B1; Southam Business Publications Ltd., 1450 Don Mills Road, Don Mills, Ont. M3B 2X7; Wadham Publications Ltd., 109 Vanderhoof Avenue, Suite 101, Toronto, Ont. M4G 2J2.

ARCHITECTURE AND LANDSCAPING

Canadian Architect, The
1450 Don Mills Road, Don Mills, Ont. M3B 2X7
(416) 445-6641
Contact: Robert Gretton, editor

Construction Canada
1 St. Clair Avenue W., Suite 1206, Toronto, Ont. M4V 1K6
(416) 924-4020
Contact: Cliff Fowke, editor

Section a
570 Wellington Street, Toronto, Ont. M5V 2X5
(416) 861-0231
Contact: Odile Henault, editor

Gardenland
43 Glen Road, Hamilton, Ont. L8S 3M6
(416) 528-1496
Contact: Gwen Stupple, editor

Greenmaster, The
698 Weston Road, Suite 32, Toronto, Ont. M6N 3R3
(416) 767-0387
Contact: Mary Gurney, editor

Landscape Ontario
1293 Matheson Boulevard, Mississauga, Ont. L4W 1R1
(416) 629-1184
Contact: Jim Bradley, editor

Landscape Trades
1293 Matheson Boulevard, Mississauga, Ont. L4W 1R1
(416) 629-1184
Contact: Jim Bradley, editor

Nursery Trades B.C.
15290 - 103A Avenue, Suite 101A, Surrey, B.C. V3R 7A2
(604) 585-2225
Contact: J.F. Crocco, editor

Prairie Landscape Magazine
10215 - 176th Street, Edmonton, Alta. T5S 1M1
(403) 489-1991
Contact: Jane McIntosh, editor

AUTOMOBILE AND ACCESSORIES
(See also Transportation)

L'Automobile
109 Vanderhoof Avenue, Suite 101, Toronto, Ont. M4G 2J2

(416) 425-9021
Contact: Jean-Marie Germain

Autoparts Distributor
287 MacPherson Avenue, Toronto, Ont. M4V 1A4
(416) 928-1096
Contact: Ed Belitsky, editor

Bodyshop
109 Vanderhoof Avenue, Suite 101, Toronto, Ont. M4G 2J2
(416) 425-9021
Contact: Brian Harper, editor

Canadian Auto Review
777 Bay Street, Toronto, Ont. M5W 1A7
(416) 596-5784
Contact: Richard Jacobs, editor

Canadian Automotive Fleet
95 Barber Greene Road, Don Mills, Ont. M3C 3E9
(416) 449-2252
Contact: John Arnone, editor

Canadian Automotive Trade
777 Bay Street, Toronto, Ont. M5W 1A7
(416) 596-5784
Contact: Richard Jacobs, editor

Canadian Autoparts Marketing
777 Bay Street, Toronto, Ont. M5W 1A7
(416) 596-5784
Contact: Richard Jacobs, editor

Driver Owner
777 Bay Street, Toronto, Ont. M5W 1A7
(416) 596-5929
Contact: David Thompson, editor

Jobber News
109 Vanderhoof Avenue, Suite 101, Toronto, Ont. M4G 2J2
(416) 425-9021
Contact: Bob Blans, editor

Motor in Canada
1077 St. James Street, P.O. Box 6900, Winnipeg, Man. R3C 3B1
(204) 775-0201
Contact: James Buchok, editor

Service Station & Garage Management
109 Vanderhoof Avenue, Suite 101, Toronto, Ont. M4G 2J2

(416) 425-9021
Contact: Gary Kenez, editor

BUILDING, ENGINEERING, AND HEAVY CONSTRUCTION

Alberta Construction
10010 - 105th Street, Suite 304, Edmonton, Alta. T5J 1C4
(403) 428-6164
Contact: Aaron Bushkowsky, editor

B.C. Professional Engineer, The
1201 Melville Street, Vancouver, B.C. V6E 2X9
(604) 685-3241
Contact: Mike Painter, editor

Bâtiment
777 Bay Street, Toronto, Ont. M5W 1A7
(416) 596-5762
Contact: Marc Castro, editor

Building Guide
280 Yorkland Boulevard, Willowdale, Ont. M2J 4Z6
(416) 494-4990
Contact: Paul Lebel, editor

Building Renovation
777 Bay Street, Toronto, Ont. M5W 1A7
(416) 596-5760
Contact: John Fennell, editor

Canadian Building
777 Bay Street, Toronto, Ont. M5W 1A7
(416) 596-5762
Contact: John Fennell, editor

Canadian Construction Record
1450 Don Mills Road, Don Mills, Ont. M3B 2X7
(416) 445-6641
Contact: Tim Tolton, editor

Canadian Consulting Engineer
1450 Don Mills Road, Don Mills, Ont. M3B 2X7
(416) 445-6641
Contact: Louanne Smrke, editor

Canadian Surveyor
P.O. Box 5378, Station F, Ottawa, Ont. K2C 3J1

(613) 224-9851/993-5745
Contact: Neil Grant, editor

Construction Alberta News Ltd.
3324 Parsons Road, Edmonton, Alta. T6N 1B5
(403) 463-9715
Contact: Don Coates, editor

Canadian Construction Record
1450 Don Mills Road, Don Mills, Ont. M3B 2X7
(416) 445-6641
Contact: Gene Lethbridge, editor

Construction Sightlines
124 W. 8th Street, North Vancouver, B.C. V7M 3H2
(604) 985-8711
Contact: John Doyle, editor

Daily Commercial News and Construction Record
280 Yorkland Boulevard, North York, Ont. M2J 4Z6
(416) 494-4990
Contact: Scott Button, editor

Engineering Digest
111 Peter Street, Suite 411, Toronto, Ont. M5V 2W2
(416) 596-1624
Contact: Werner Meyfarth, editor

Engineering Dimensions
1155 Yonge Street, Toronto, Ont. M4T 2Y5
(416) 961-1100
Contact: Mary Curtis, editor

Génie-Construction
310 Victoria Avenue, Suite 201, Westmount, Que. H3Z 2M9
(514) 487-2302
Contact: G. Fortin, editor

Heavy Construction News
777 Bay Street, Toronto, Ont. M5W 1A7
(416) 596-5848
Contact: Russ Noble, editor

L'Ingénieur
P.O. Box 6980, Station A, Montreal, Que. H3C 3L4
(514) 340-4765
Contact: Henri Kélada, editor

Journal of Commerce
2000 W. 12th Avenue, Vancouver, B.C. V6J 2G2

(604) 731-1171
Contact: Stefan Koehl, editor

Journal Constructo
2441 des Iles Boulevard, Entrelacs, Que. J0T 2E0
(514) 228-2541, 1-800-363-3674
Contact: Johanne Rouleau, editor

Machinerie Lourde
921 du Séminaire Boulevard N., Suite 110, St-Jean-sur-Richelieu, Que. J3A 1B6
(514) 481-7387
Contact: Georges Duval, editor

Mart, Le
6841 St. Hubert Street, Suite 201, Montreal, Que. H2S 2M7
(514) 273-7261
Contact: Camil Charland, editor

Northpoint
1043 McNicholl Avenue, Scarborough, Ont. M1W 3W6
(416) 491-9025
Contact: William Mates, editor

Ontario Land Surveyor, The
1043 McNicholl Avenue, Scarborough, Ont. M1W 3W6
(416) 491-9020
Contact: Bryan Davies, editor

Ontario Technologist, The
40 Orchard View Boulevard, Suite 253, Toronto, Ont. M4R 2G1
(416) 488-1175
Contact: Ruth Klein, editor

Pegg, The
1 Thornton Court, Suite 1010, Edmonton, Alta. T5J 2E7
(403) 426-3990
Contact: Lyn Brown, editor

Plan
2020 University Street, 14th Floor, Montreal, Que. H3A 2A5
(514) 845-6141
Contact: Charles Allain, editor

Project Magazine
Clark Hall, Queen's Univesity, Kingston, Ont. K7L 3N6
(613) 547-3079
Contact: Sharon Peters, editor

Québec Construction
465 St. Jean Street, Suite 903, Montreal, Que. H2Y 3S4
(514) 842-6491

Reporter
Published for the Lumber and Building Materials Association of Ontario 4500 Sheppard Avenue E., Scarborough, Ont. M1S 3R6
(416) 298-1731
Contact: Paul Laurin, editor

Toronto Construction News
720 Spadina Avenue, Suite 419, Toronto, Ont. M5S 2T9
(416) 961-1028
Contact: Robert Bradford, editor

BUSINESS, COMMERCE, BANKING, CIVIC, CONTROL SYSTEMS, PENSIONS, INSURANCE, AND CONVENTIONS

Access
1450 Don Mills Road, Don Mills, Ont. M3B 2X7
(416) 445-6641
Contact: Bill Knapp, editor

Action Canada France
360 St. François Xavier Street, Montreal, Que. H2Y 2S8
(514) 281-1246
Contact: B. Namy, editor

Affaires, Le Magazine
465 St. Jean Street, Suite 903, Montreal, Que. H2Y 3S4
(514) 842-6491
Contact: Michel Lefèvre, editor

B.C. Agent, The
P.O. Box 35070, Station E, Vancouver, B.C. V6M 4G1
(604) 687-8003
Contact: Patrick Durrant, editor

BC Business Magazine
550 Burrard Street, Suite 200, Vancouver, B.C. V6C 2J6
(604) 669-1721
Contact: Richard Murray, editor

Benefits Canada
777 Bay Street, Toronto, Ont. M5W 1A7
(416) 596-5958
Contact: John Milne, editor

Business & Finance in Ontario
205 Rivera Drive, Unit 1, Markham, Ont. L3R 2L6

(416) 477-7757
Contact: Jack Mills, editor

Business & Professional Woman
95 Leeward Glenway, Unit 121, Don Mills, Ont. M3C 2Z6
(416) 424-1393
Contact: Valerie Dunn, editor

Business Quarterly
University of Western Ontario, Neville House,
1393 Western Road, London, Ont. N6A 5B9
(519) 679-3204
Contact: Doreen Sanders, editor

Business Review
100 Sutherland Avenue, Winnipeg, Man. R2W 3C7
(204) 947-0222
Contact: Will Oliver, editor

CA Magazine
Published by The Canadian Institute of Chartered Accountants
150 Bloor Street W., Toronto, Ont. M5S 2Y2
(416) 962-1242
Contact: Nelson Luscombe, editor

CGA Magazine
Published by the
Certified General Accountants Association of Canada
1176 W. Georgia Street, Suite 704, Vancouver, B.C. V6E 4A2
(604) 669-3555
Contact: Len Webster, editor

CCI, Canadian Controls and Instrumentation
1450 Don Mills Road, Don Mills, Ont. M3B 2X7
(416) 445-6641
Contact: Leslie Burt, editor

Calgary Commerce
517 Centre Street S., Calgary, Alta. T2G 2C4
(403) 263-7435
Contact: Jean Andryiszuyr, editor

Canadian Associations Canadiennes
815 Danforth Avenue, Suite 403, Toronto, Ont. M4J 1L2
(416) 465-4621
Contact: Colin McLaren, editor

Canadian Banker
2 First Canadian Place, P.O. Box 348, Toronto, Ont. M5X 1E1

(416) 362-6092
Contact: Brian O'Brien, editor (English edition)
Jacques Hébert, editor (French edition)

Canadian Business
70 The Esplanade, Toronto, Ont. M5E 1R2
(416) 364-4266
Contact: Charles Davies, editor

Canadian Business Journal
1492 Wallace Road, P.O. Box 306, Oakville, Ont. L6J 5A2
(416) 825-2229
Contact: Don Wall, editor

Canadian Business Life
1 St. John's Road, Toronto, Ont. M6P 4C7
(416) 766-5744
Contact: Darryl Simmons, editor

Canadian Export World
501 Oakdale Road, Downsview, Ont. M3N 1W7
(416) 746-7360
Contact: R.S. Brown, editor

Canadian Insurance
366 Adelaide Street E., Suite 323, Toronto, Ont. M5A 3X9
(416) 864-0453
Contact: Michael Steeler, editor

Canadian Manager, The
2175 Sheppard Avenue E., Suite 110, Willowdale, Ont. M2J 1W8
(416) 493-0155
Contact: Ruth Max, editor

Canadian Secretary
777 Bay Street, Toronto, Ont. M5W 1A7
(416) 596-5251
Contact: Tom Kelly, editor

Canadian Underwriter
109 Vanderhoof Avenue, Suite 101, Toronto, Ont. M4G 2J2
(416) 425-9021
Contact: Larry Welsh, editor

Civic Public Works
777 Bay Street, Toronto, Ont. M5W 1A7
(416) 596-5252
Contact: Cliff Allum, editor

Commerce News
10123 - 99th Street, Suite 600, Edmonton, Alta. T5J 3G9
(403) 426-4620
Contact: Karen Belsher, editor

Commercial News
5251 Duke Street, Suite 400, Halifax, N.S. B3J 1P3
(902) 422-6447
Contact: J.P. Mason, editor

Conventions & Meetings Canada
72 Wellington Street W., Suite 207, Markham, Ont. L3P 1A8
(416) 471-1550
Contact: James Nuttall, editor

Edmonton Commerce & Industry Report on Business
11802 - 124th Street, Suite 214, Edmonton, Alta. T5L 0M3
(403) 454-5540
Contact: Doug Homersham, editor

Exchange
225 Fairway Road, Kitchener, Ont. N2G 4E5
(519) 894-1630, Toronto (416) 826-9182
Contact: Alan Howell, editor

Equity
1198 W. Pender Street, Suite 200, Vancouver, B.C. V6E 2R9
(604) 684-1414
Contact: Harvey Southam, editor

Finance
381 Notre Dame Street W., Suite 200, Montreal, Que. H2Y 1V2
(514) 284-0339
Contact: Jacques Forget, editor

Financial Post, The
777 Bay Street, Toronto, Ont. M5W 1A7
(416) 596-5632
Contact: Neville Nankivell, editor

Financial Times of Canada
920 Yonge Street, Suite 500, Toronto, Ont. M4W 3L5
(416) 922-1133
Contact: Terence Corcoran, editor

Gestion
674 Place Publique, Suite 215, Laval, Que. H7X 1G1

(514) 689-2982
Contact: Pierre Lesage, editor

Greater Winnipeg Business
1835 Sargent Avenue, 2nd Floor, Winnipeg, Man. R3H 0E2
(204) 775-8681
Contact: Guy Rochon, editor

Growth Digest
9847 - 44th Avenue, Edmonton, Alta. T6E 5E3
(403) 437-0592
Contact: Larry Anderson, editor

HR Professional
Published by The Personnel Association of Canada
2 Bloor Street W., Suite 601, Toronto, Ont. M4W 3E2
(416) 923-2324
Contact: Ruta Lovett, editor

Inter-National
322 King Street W., 4th Floor, Toronto, Ont. M5V 1J2
(416) 591-1551
Contact: Howard Gerring, editor

Invest Canada
8 Pailton Crescent, Toronto, Ont. M4S 2H8
(416) 483-9649
Contact: A.J. Kirby, editor

Italcommerce
2045 Stanley Street, Suite 1414, Montreal, Que. H3A 2V4
(514) 844-4249
Contact: Aldo Pier-Federici, editor

Italy Canada Trade
901 Lawrence Avenue, Suite 306, Toronto, Ont. M6A 1C3
(416) 789-7169/789-7160
Contact: Antonio Valeri, editor

LUAC Forum
Published by The Life Underwriters' Association of Canada
41 Lesmill Road, Don Mills, Ont. M3B 2T3
(416) 444-5251
Contact: Elizabeth Chong, editor

Magazine MBA
Published for Master of Business Administration graduates
1800 Bercy Street, Suite 100-D, Montreal, Que. H2K 4K5

(514) 526-3753
Contact: Denis Gauthier, editor

Manitoba Business
330 Graham Avenue, Suite 874, Winnipeg, Man. R3C 4A5
(204) 944-1441
Contact: Roger Newman, editor

Meetings and Incentive Travel
777 Bay Street, Toronto, Ont. M5W 1A7
(416) 596-5810
Contact: Patrick Dineen, editor

Metropolitan Toronto Business Journal
3 First Canadian Place, P.O. Box 60, Toronto, Ont. M5X 1C1
(416) 366-7139/366-6811
Contact: Alan Morntz, editor

Mid-Canada Commerce
100 Sutherland Avenue, Winnipeg, Man. R2W 3C7
(204) 947-0222
Contact: Will Oliver, editor

Mississauga Business
2065 Dundas Street E., Suite 205, Mississauga, Ont. L4X 2W1
(416) 625-7070
Contact: Bill Dzugan, editor

News and Views
1133 Melville Street, Vancouver, B.C. V6E 4E5
(604) 681-3264
Contact: Deborah Folka-Slater, editor

Northern Ontario Business
158 Elgin Street, Sudbury, Ont. P3E 3N5
(705) 673-5705
Contact: Ted Thaler, editor

Office Management & Automation
2 Lansing Square, Suite 703, Willowdale, Ont. M2J 5A1
(416) 497-9562
Contact: Gordon Campbell, editor

Ontario Business
205 Riviera Drive, Unit 1, Markham, Ont. L3R 5J8
(416) 427-7757
Contact: John Fergus, editor

Ottawa Business Life
192 Bank Street, Ottawa, Ont. K2P 1W8
(613) 234-7751
Contact: Louis Valenzuela, editor

Pensions-Benefits and Business Insurance
109 Vanderhoof Avenue, Suite 101, Toronto, Ont. M4G 2J2
(416) 425-9021
Contact: Peter Beeching, editor

Plan Canada
Curry & Associates, R.R. 3, Belfast, P.E.I. C0A 1A0
(902) 659-2888
Contact: John Curry, editor

Regards/la revue de l'assurance
300 Léo Pariseau Street, Suite 801, Montreal, Que. H2W 2N1
(514) 842-2591
Contact: Sophie Brzozowska-Lavigne, editor

Revue Commerce
465 St. Jean Street, Suite 908, Montreal, Que. H2Y 2R6
(514) 844-1511
Contact: Michel Lord, editor

Revue Municipale, La
6841 St. Hubert Street, Suite 201, Montreal, Que. H2S 2M7
(514) 273-7261
Contact: Marc Plourde, editor

Saskatchewan Business
438 Victoria Avenue E., Regina, Sask. S4N 0N7
(306) 949-6666
Contact: Paul Martin, editor

Science & Technologie
P.O. Box 1800, Côte-des-Neiges Station, Montreal, Que. H3S 2R1
(514) 288-1373
Contact: Bernard Lévy, editor

Small Business, The Magazine for Independent Companies
777 Bay Street, Toronto, Ont. M5W 1A7
(416) 596-5924
Contact: Donald Rumball, editor

Successful Executive
1450 Don Mills Road, Don Mills, Ont. M3B 2X7
(416) 445-6641
Contact: Patricia Anderson, editor

Toronto Secretary's Efficiency Guide
186 Main Street, Unionville, Ont. L3R 2H3
(416) 477-2922
Contact: Derek Suchard, editor

Trade and Commerce
1077 St. James Street, Winnipeg, Man. R3C 3B1
(204) 775-0201
Contact: George Mitchell, editor

Trader's Post
3 First Canadian Place, P.O. Box 60, Toronto, Ont. M5X 1C1
(416) 368-1681
Contact: Merideth Wilson, editor

Toronto Business Magazine
186 Main Street, Unionville, Ont. L3R 2H3
(416) 477-2977
Contact: Derek Suchard, editor

Travelling on Business
310 Dupont Street, Toronto, Ont. M5R 1V9
(416) 968-7252
Contact: Edith Baxter, editor

Western Commerce & Industry
945 King Edward Street, Winnipeg, Man. R3H 0P8
(204) 775-0387
Contact: Gren Yeo, editor

Western Municipal Product News
1224 - 53rd Avenue N.E., Suite 158, Calgary, Alta. T2E 7E2
(403) 275-9468
Contact: Gerry Skinner, editor

Western Ontario Business
P.O. Box 7400, Station E, London, Ont. N5Y 4X3
(519) 472-7601
Contact: Herb Shoveller, editor

CHEMICALS AND PHARMACEUTICALS

Canadian Chemical News/L'Actualité Chimique Canadienne
151 Slater Street, Suite 906, Ottawa, Ont. K1P 5H3
(613) 233-5623
Contact: Anne Alper, editor

Canadian Journal of Hospital Pharmacy
123 Edward Street, Suite 303, Toronto, Ont. M5G 1E2
(416) 979-2049
Contact: Susan Tremblay, editor

Canadian Pharmaceutical Journal
1815 Alta Vista Drive, Suite 101, Ottawa, Ont. K1G 3Y6
(613) 523-7877
Contact: Jean-Guy Cyr, editor

Canadian Process Equipment & Control News
745 Mt. Pleasant Road, Toronto, Ont. M4S 2N5
(416) 481-6483
Contact: Vince Sharp, editor

Drug Merchandising
777 Bay Street, Toronto, Ont. M5E 1A7
(416) 596-5950
Contact: Vil Meere, editor

Pharmacien, Le
1001 de Maisonneuve Boulevard W., Suite 1000,
Montreal, Que. H3A 3E1
(514) 845-5141
Contact: Xavier de Lusigny, editor

Pharmacy Practice
5915 Airport Road, Suite 701, Mississauga, Ont. L4V 1T1
(416) 673-2500
Contact: Ian Corks, editor

Process Industries Canada
1450 Don Mills Road, Don Mills, Ont. M3B 2X7
(416) 445-6641
Contact: Leslie Burt, editor

Québec Pharmacie
5115 St. Denis Street, Montreal, Que. H2J 2M1
(514) 273-0644
Contact: Paul-Emile Payette, editor

CLOTHES, JEWELLERY, AND GIFTS

Bijou
2950 Masson Street E., Suite 207, Montreal, Que. H1Y 1X4
(514) 728-1155
Contact: Lise Petitpas, editor

Canadian Apparel Manufacturer
1 Pacifique Street, Ste-Anne-de-Bellevue, Que. H9X 1C5
(514) 457-2347
Contact: Fred Dafoe, editor

Canadian Ceramics Quarterly
2175 Sheppard Avenue E., Suite 110, Willowdale, Ont. M2J 1W8
(416) 491-3556
Contact: Ruth Max, editor

Canadian Footwear Journal
1 Pacifique Street, Ste-Anne-de-Bellevue, Que. H9X 1C5
(514) 457-2347
Contact: Keith Pearson, editor

Canadian Jeweller
777 Bay Street, Toronto, Ont. M5W 1A7
(416) 596-5733
Contact: Simon Hally, editor

Canadian Textile Journal
1 Pacifique Street, Ste-Anne-de-Bellevue, Que. H9X 1C5
(514) 457-2347
Contact: Fred Dafoe, editor

Children's Apparel Merchandising Aids (CAMA)
8270 Mountain Sights Avenue, Suite 101, Montreal, Que. H4P 2B7
(514) 731-7774
Contact: Anthony Ross, editor

Elan
1620 Pine Avenue W., Montreal, Que. H3G 1B4
(514) 931-7322
Contact: Eileen Collyer, editor

Footwear Forum
85 Scarsdale Road, Suite 307, Don Mills, Ont. M3B 2R2
(416) 447-7263
Contact: Pat Machearn, editor

Fur Trade Journal
Oak Street, Bewdley, Ont. K0L 1E0
(416) 797-2281
Contact: Charlotte Clay, editor

Fur Trade Journal of Canada
176 Woolwich Street, P.O. Box 1747, Guelph, Ont. N1H 7A1
(519) 763-5058
Contact: Karen Mantel, editor

Gifts & Tablewares
1450 Don Mills Road, Don Mills, Ont. M3B 2X7
(416) 445-6641
Contact: Elena Opasini, editor

Jewellery World
1491 Yonge Street, 4th Floor, Toronto, Ont. M4T 1Z4
(416) 968-3560
Contact: Stoney McCart, editor

Luggage & Leathergoods News
501 Oakdale Road, Downsview, Ont. M3N 1W7
(416) 746-7360
Contact: Janet McGee, editor

Men's Wear of Canada
501 Oakdale Road, Downsview, Ont. M3N 1W7
(416) 746-7360
Contact: Jim Panousis, editor

Style
85 Scarsdale Road, Suite 300, Don Mills, Ont. M3B 2R2
(416) 447-2263
Contact: Vivian Wilcox, editor

Tabletop Plus
55 Nugget Avenue, Suite 209, Scarborough, Ont. M1S 3L1
(416) 298-5800
Contact: Steve Lewis, editor

DATA PROCESSING

Canadian Datasystems
777 Bay Street, Toronto, Ont. M5W 1A7
(416) 596-5907
Contact: Tom Weissmann, editor

Computek
P.O. Box 91760, West Vancouver, B.C. V7V 4S1
(604) 986-9501
Contact: John Mulvihill, editor

ComputerData
501 Oakdale Road, Downsview, Ont. M3N 1W7
(416) 746-7360
Contact: Steve Wexler, editor

Computer Dealer News
2 Lansing Square, Suite 703, Willowdale, Ont. M2J 4P8
(416) 497-9562
Contact: Jerry Zeidenberg, editor

Computing Canada
2 Lansing Square, Suite 703, Willowdale, Ont. M2J 4P8
(416) 497-9562
Contact: David Paddon, editor

Data Product News
777 Bay Street, Toronto, Ont. M5W 1A7
(416) 596-5916
Contact: Ron Glen, editor

Software Canada
777 Bay Street, Toronto, Ont. M5W 1A7
(416) 596-5916
Contact: Ron Glen, editor

EDUCATION

The ATA Magazine
11010 - 142nd Street, Edmonton, Alta. T5N 2R1
(413) 453-2411
Contact: Timothy Johnston, editor

Bridges
2242 Lakeshore Boulevard W., Toronto, Ont. M8V 1A5
(416) 251-6571
Contact: Denny Peirce, editor

B.C. Teacher, The
2235 Burrard Street, Vancouver, B.C. V6J 3H9
(604) 731-8121
Contact: Nancy Flodin, editor

CAUT Bulletin
Published by the Canadian Association of University Teachers
75 Albert Street, Suite 1001, Ottawa, Ont. K1P 5E7
(613) 237-6885
Contact: Helen Baxter, editor

Canadian Vocational Journal
440 Albert Street, Suite 215, Ottawa, Ont. K1R 5B5
(613) 232-1028
Contact: Dr. Peter Findlay, editor

Classroom
123 Newkirk Road, Richmond Hill, Ont. L4C 3G5
(416) 883-5300
Contact: Sharon Brain, editor

College Canada
110 Eglinton Avenue W., 2nd Floor, Toronto, Ont. M4R 1A3
(416) 489-5925
Contact: Cornelia Schmitt, editor

Computers in Education
1300 Don Mills Road, Toronto, Ont. M3B 3M8
(416) 445-5600
Contact: Roger Allan, editor

Enseignants, Les
707 Demers Street, St-Jean-sur-Richelieu, Que. J3B 4W1
(514) 348-8718
Contact: Fernand Houde, editor

Forum
60 Mobile Drive, Toronto, Ont. M4A 2P3
(416) 751-8300
Contact: Paul Brandon, editor

Human Resource, The
2 Lansing Square, Suite 209, Willowdale, Ont. M2J 4P8
(416) 493-6686
Contact: Günter Ott, editor

Manitoba Teacher, The
191 Harcourt Street, Winnipeg, Man. R3J 3H2
(204) 888-7961
Contact: Miep van Raalte, editor

Quebec Home & School News
2535 Cavendish Boulevard, Suite 212, Montreal, Que. H4B 2Y5
(514) 481-5619
Contact: Dorothy Chant-Hannah, editor

Reporter, The
1260 Bay Street, Toronto, Ont. M5R 2B4
(416) 925-2493
Contact: Aleda O'Connor, editor

School Trustee, The
2222 - 13th Avenue, Suite 400, Regina, Sask. S4P 3M7
(306) 569-0750
Contact: Leslie Anderson, editor

Trustee, The
12310 - 105th Avenue, Edmonton, Alta. T5N 0Y4
(403) 482-7311
Contact: Tudor Williams, editor

ELECTRONICS AND ELECTRICAL

Canadian Electronics Engineering
777 Bay Street, Toronto, Ont. M5W 1A7
(416) 596-5729
Contact: Peter Thorne, editor

EIC-Electronique Industrielle & Commerciale
7063 St-Michel Boulevard, Montreal, Que. H2A 2Z6
(514) 374-7000
Contact: Ernest Bourgault, editor

Electronic Age
P.O. Box 160, Station H, Toronto, Ont. M4C 5H7
(416) 421-8969
Contact: Daphne Lavers, editor

Electronic Products and Technology
1200 Aerowood Drive, Unit 28, Mississauga, Ont. L4W 2S7
(416) 624-8100
Contact: David Kerfoot, editor

Electrical Business
501 Oakdale Road, Downsview, Ont. M3N 1W7
(416) 746-7360
Contact: Randolph Hurst, editor

Electrical Equipment News
1450 Don Mills Road, Don Mills, Ont. M3B 2X7
(416) 445-6641
Contact: Nancy Thomson, editor

Electronics Product News
777 Bay Street, Toronto, Ont. M5W 1A7
(416) 596-5731
Contact: Peter Thorne, editor

Electronics Times
2 Lansing Square, Suite 703, Willowdale, Ont. M2J 4P8
(416) 497-9562
Contact: Gordon Campbell, editor

Maître Electricien, Le
5925 Decarie Boulevard, Suite 100, Montreal, Que. H3W 3C9
(514) 738-2184, 1-800-361-9061
Contact: Joseph Patafie, editor

Monde de l'Electricité, Le
501 Oakdale Road, Willowdale, Ont. M3N 1W7
(416) 746-7360, and
7077 Beaubien Avenue E., Suite 208, Anjou, Que. H1M 2Y2
(514) 351-6320
Contact: Robert Bastin, editor

ENERGY, MINING, FORESTRY, LUMBER, AND PULP AND PAPER

Atlantic Energy News
192 Joseph Zatzman Drive, Unit 14, Dartmouth, N.S. B3B 1N4
(902) 463-2661
Contact: Adrienne Malloy, editor

British Columbia Lumberman
2000 W. 12th Avenue, Vancouver, B.C. V6J 2G2
(604) 731-1171
Contact: Paul MacDonald, editor

Canadian Forest Industries
1450 Don Mills Road, Don Mills, Ont. M3B 2X7
(416) 445-6641
Contact: Richard Holmes, editor

Canadian Mining Journal
1450 Don Mills Road, Don Mills, Ont. M3B 2X7
(416) 445-6641
Contact: John Hopkins, editor

Canadian Offshore Report
1015 Centre Street N., Suite 200, Calgary, Alta. T2E 2P8
(403) 276-7881
Contact: Jim Lyon, editor

Canadian Oil & Gas Handbook
7 Labatt Avenue, Toronto, Ont. M5A 3P2
(416) 368-3481
Contact: C.D. Gardiner, editor

CIM Bulletin
Published by the Canadian Institute of Mining

1130 Sherbrooke Street W., Suite 400, Montreal, Que. H3A 2M8
(514) 842-3461
Contact: Pierre Michaud, editor

Drillsite
1015 Centre Street N., Suite 200, Calgary, Alta. T2E 2P8
(403) 276-7881
Contact: Jim Lyon, editor

Energy Equipment News
1015 Centre Street N., Suite 200, Calgary, Alta. T2E 2P8
(403) 276-7881
Contact: Jim Lyon, editor

Energy Processing/Canada
205 - 9th Avenue S.E., Suite 503, Calgary, Alta. T2G 0R3
(403) 265-4750
Contact: Scott Jeffrey, editor

Financial Post Survey of Mines and Energy Resources, The
777 Bay Street, Toronto, Ont. M5W 1A7
(416) 596-5585
Contact: John Byrne, editor

Forestry Chronicle, The
151 Slater Street, Suite 815, Ottawa, Ont. K1P 5H3
(613) 234-2242
Contact: I.C.M. Place, editor

Forêt-Conservation
915 St-Cyrille Street W., Suite 210, Quebec, Que. G1S 1T8
(418) 681-3588
Contact: Jean-Pierre Drapeau, editor

Hiballer Forest Magazine
543 Seymour Street, Suite 117, Vancouver, B.C. V6C 3H6
(604) 669-7833
Contact: Paul Young, editor

Journal des Pâtes et Papiers
777 Bay Street, Toronto, Ont. M5W 1A7
(416) 596-5786
Contact: Jean-Guy Thibault, editor
(514) 332-4377, Montreal

Journal of Canadian Petroleum Technology
1130 Sherbrooke Street W., Suite 400, Montreal, Que. H3A 2M8
(514) 842-3461
Contact: Pierre Michaud, editor

Logging and Sawmilling Journal
1111 Melville Street, Suite 600, Vancouver, B.C. V6E 3V6
(604) 683-8254
Contact: Roman Hohol, editor

Mining Review
124 W. 8th Street, North Vancouver, B.C. V7M 3H2
(604) 985-8711
Contact: John Doyle, editor

Northern Miner, The
7 Labatt Avenue, Toronto, Ont. M5A 3P2
(416) 368-3481
Contact: Allan Jones, editor

Northern Miner Magazine
7 Labatt Avenue, Toronto, Ont. M5A 3P2
(416) 368-3481
Contact: Kerry Knoll, editor

Offshore Resources
1415 Welch Street, North Vancouver, B.C. V7V 4S1
(604) 986-9501
Contact: D. Cumming, editor

Oil & Gas Report
1415 Welch Street, North Vancouver, B.C. V7V 4S1
(604) 986-9501
Contact: D. Cumming, editor

Oil Patch
15740A Stony Plain Road, Edmonton, Alta. T5P 3Z5
(403) 486-2001
Contact: Donna Christensen, editor

Oilweek
1015 Centre Street N., Suite 200, Calgary, Alta. T2E 2P8
(403) 276-7881
Contact: Vic Humphreys, editor

Opérations Forestières et de Scierie
310 Victoria Avenue, Suite 201, Westmount, Que. H3Z 2M9
(514) 487-2302
Contact: Guy Fortin, editor

Propane/Canada
205 - 9th Avenue S.E., Suite 503, Calgary, Alta. T2G 0R3
(403) 265-4750
Contact: Scott Jeffrey, editor

Pulp & Paper Canada
310 Victoria Avenue, Suite 201, Westmount, Que. H3Z 2M9
(514) 487-2302
Contact: Peter Williamson, editor

Pulp & Paper Journal
777 Bay Street, Toronto, Ont. M5W 1A7
(416) 596-5829
Contact: Roman Hohol, editor

Roughneck, The
1305 - 11th Avenue S.W. Suite 204, Calgary, Alta. T3C 3P6
(403) 244-2221
Contact: David Yager, editor

Truck Logger, The
124 W. 8th Street, North Vancouver, B.C. V7M 3H2
(604) 985-8711
Contact: John Doyle, editor

FOOD, DRINK, AND HOSTELRY

L'Accommodeur
225 Roy Street E., Montreal, Que. H2W 2N6
(514) 282-9600
Contact: Margel Huguet, editor

Atlantic Fisherman
14 Main Street, Montague, P.E.I. C0A 1R0
(902) 838-2515
Contact: Sharon Fraser, editor

Bakers Journal
106 Lakeshore Road E., Suite 209, Port Credit, Ont. L5G 1E2
(416) 271-1366
Contact: Ernest Naef, editor

Barrique, La
5165 Sherbrooke Street W., Montreal, Que. H4A 1T6
(514) 481-5892
Contact: Nicole Barrette, editor

BC Hotelman
124 W. 8th Street, North Vancouver, B.C. V7M 3H2
(604) 985-8711
Contact: John Doyle, editor

BC Restaurant Roster
124 W. 8th Street, North Vancouver, B.C. V7M 3H2
(604) 985-8711
Contact: John Doyle, editor

Beverage Alcohol Reporter
178 Willowdale Avenue, North York, Ont. M2N 4Y8
(416) 222-2557
Contact: Lance Leray, editor

Beverage Canada
5200 Dixie Road, Suite 204, Mississauga, Ont. L4W 1E4
(416) 625-5277
Contact: Filomema Tamburri, editor

Canadian Beverage Review
106 Lakeshore Road E., Suite 209, Port Credit, Ont. L5G 1E2
(416) 271-1366
Contact: Ernest Naef, editor

Canadian Distributor & Retailer
8270 Mountain Sights Avenue, Suite 201, Montreal, Que. H4P 2B7
(514) 731-9517
Contact: Anthony Ross, editor

Canadian Food & Drug Product News
777 Bay Street, Toronto, Ont. M5W 1A7
(416) 596-5192
Contact: Robert Barratt, editor

Canadian Grocer
777 Bay Street, Toronto, Ont. M5W 1A7
(416) 596-5772
Contact: George Condon, editor

Canadian Hotel & Restaurant
777 Bay Street, Toronto, Ont. M5W 1A7
(416) 596-5782
Contact: Andrew Douglas, editor

Canadian Restaurant & Foodservice Assn. News
720 Spadina Avenue, Suite 419, Toronto, Ont. M5S 2T9
(416) 961-1028
Contact: Bob Bradford, editor

L'épicier
1001 de Maisonneuve Boulevard W., Suite 1000,
Montreal, Que. H3A 3E1

(514) 845-5141
Contact: Benoit Dutrisac, editor

Fisherman, The
111 Victoria Drive, Suite 160, Vancouver, B.C. V5L 4C4
(604) 255-1366
Contact: Geoff Meggs, editor

Food and Drug Product News
777 Bay Street, Toronto, Ont. M5W 1A7
(416) 596-5912
Contact: Bob Barratt, editor

Food in Canada
777 Bay Street, Toronto, Ont. M5W 1A7
(416) 596-5912
Contact: Bob Barratt, editor

Foodservice & Hospitality
980 Yonge Street, Suite 400, Toronto, Ont. M4W 2J8
(416) 923-8888
Contact: Steven Isherwood, editor

Food Store Magazine
236 King Street E., Suite 300, Toronto, Ont. M5A 1K1
(416) 368-1580
Contact: David Foley, editor

Fournée, La
6841 St. Hubert Street, Suite 201, Montreal, Que. H2S 2M7
(416) 273-7261
Contact: Mac Plourde, editor

L'Hospitalité
777 Bay Street, Toronto, Ont. M5W 1A7
(416) 596-5782
Contact: Basia Kielczewski, editor
Montreal office:
1001 de Maisonneuve Boulevard W., Suite 1000,
Montreal, Que. H3A 3E1
(514) 845-5141

Hospitality Product News
777 Bay Street, Toronto, Ont. M5W 1A7
(416) 596-5782
Contact: Andrew Douglas, editor

Hotel Amenities in Canada
176 Woolwich Street, P.O. Box 1747, Guelph, Ont. N1H 7A1

(519) 763-5058
Contact: Karen Mantel, editor

Inn Business
186 Main Street, Unionville, Ont. L3R 2G9
(416) 477-2922
Contact: Derek Suchard, editor

Modern Dairy
3269 Bloor Street W., Suite 205, Toronto, Ont. M8X 1E2
(416) 239-8423
Contact: I. Macnab, editor

Natural Healthproducts in Canada
176 Woolwich Street, P.O. Box 1747, Guelph, Ont. N1H 7A1
(519) 763-5058
Contact: Karen Mantel, editor

Ontario Innkeeper
720 Spadina Avenue, Suite 419, Toronto, Ont. M5S 2T9
(416) 961-1028
Contact: Janice Kray, editor

Ontario Restaurant & Foodservices Roster
720 Spadina Avenue, Suite 419, Toronto, Ont. M5S 2T9
(416) 961-1028
Contact: Janice Kray, editor

Prairie Hotelman
100 Sutherland Avenue W., Winnipeg, Man. R2W 3C7
(204) 947-0222
Contact: Will Oliver, editor

Sou'wester
P.O. Box 128, Yarmouth, N.S. B5A 4B1
(902) 742-7111
Contact: Alain Meuse, editor

Western Grocer
945 King Edward Street, Winnipeg, Man. R3H 0P8
(204) 775-0387
Contact: Gren Yeo, editor

HEALTH, DENTISTRY, MEDICINE, AND NURSING

L'Actualité Médicale
1425 Mountain Street, Suite 350, Montreal, Que. H3G 1Z3

(514) 288-3317
Contact: Jacques Lafontaine, editor

Canadian Clinical Laboratory
777 Bay Street, Toronto, Ont. M5W 1A7
(416) 596-5722
Contact: Earl Damude, editor

Canadian Dental Management
6420 Victoria Avenue, Unit 8, Montreal, Que. H3W 2S7
(514) 731-3523
Contact: Carole Clifford, editor

Canadian Doctor
1450 Don Mills Road, Don Mills, Ont. M3B 2X7
(416) 445-6641
Contact: Arthur Tan, editor

Canadian Family Physician
1200 Sheppard Avenue, Suite 507, Willowdale, Ont. M2K 2S5
(416) 442-0740
Contact: Dr. Reg Perkin, editor

Canadian Nurse, The
50 The Driveway, Ottawa, Ont. K2P 1E2
(613) 237-2133
Contact: Jane Wilson/Gertrude Pelletier, editors

Dental Practice Management
1450 Don Mills Road, Don Mills, Ont. M3B 2X7
(416) 445-6641
Contact: Janet Bonellie, editor

Diabetes Dialogue
78 Bond Street, Toronto, Ont. M5B 2J8
(416) 362-4440
Contact: Dr. Anne Kenshole, editor

Dimensions in Health Service
25 Imperial Street, Toronto, Ont. M5P 1C1
(416) 481-2244
Contact: Ruta Klicius, editor

Doctor's Review
640 St. Paul Street W., Suite 302, Montreal, Que. H3C 1L9
(514) 397-8833
Contact: David Elkins, editor

Geriatric Medicine
52 St. Clair Avenue E., Suite 210, Toronto, Ont. M4T 1M9

(416) 926-1038
Contact: Dr. Anthony Shellam, editor

Health Care
1450 Don Mills Road, Don Mills, Ont. M3B 2X7
(416) 445-6641
Contact: Keith Nickson, editor

Hospital Products & Technology
777 Bay Street, Toronto, Ont. M5W 1A7
(416) 596-5775
Contact: Tom Gale, editor

Medical Post, The
777 Bay Street, Toronto, Ont. M5W 1A7
(416) 596-5748
Contact: Derek Cassels, editor

Medicine North America
640 St. Paul Street W., Suite 302, Montreal, Que. H3C 1L9
(514) 397-9393
Contact: Dr. Ian R. Hart, editor

Ontario Medical Review
250 Bloor Street E., Suite 600, Toronto, Ont. M4W 3P8
(416) 963-9383
Contact: Ronald Brownridge, editor

Ontario Medicine
777 Bay Street, Toronto, Ont. M5W 1A7
(416) 596-2660
Contact: Elizabeth Watson, editor

Oral Health
1450 Don Mills Road, Don Mills, Ont. M3B 2X7
(416) 445-6641
Contact: Janet Bonellie, editor

Physician's Management Manuals
777 Bay Street, Toronto, Ont. M5W 1A7
(416) 596-5724
Contact: Olev Edur, editor

HOME IMPROVEMENT, FURNISHINGS, AND GARDEN EQUIPMENT

Alumi-News
P.O. Box 400, Victoria Station, Westmount, Que. H3Z 2V8

(514) 489-4941
Contact: Nachmi Artzi, editor

Bath & Kitchen Marketer
1450 Don Mills Road, Don Mills, Ont. M3B 2X7
(416) 445-6641
Contact: Ron Shuker, editor

Canadian Florist, Greenhouse & Nursery
1090 Aerowood Drive, Unit 1, Mississauga, Ont. L4W 1Y5
(416) 625-2730
Contact: Peter Heywood, editor

Canada's Furniture Magazine
7777 Keele Street, Unit 8, Concord, Ont. L4K 1Y7
(416) 669-6606
Contact: Rosalyn Wosnick, editor

Centre
2000 Ellesmere Road, Unit 1, Scarborough, Ont. M1H 2W4
(416) 438-1153
Contact: Laurie Merckel, editor

Floor Covering News
777 Bay Street, Toronto, Ont. M5W 1A7
(416) 596-5940
Contact: Helen Bahen, editor

Fleur Design
P.O. Box 554, Limoilou, Que. G1L 4W4
(418) 524-5471
Contact: François Bernatchez, editor

Furniture Product & Design
6420 Victoria Avenue, Unit 8, Montreal, Que. H3W 2S7
(514) 731-3523
Contact: Keith Fredericks, editor

Furniture Retailer
6420 Victoria Avenue, Unit 8, Montreal, Que. H3W 2S7
(514) 731-3523
Contact: Patricia Currie, editor

Greenhouse Canada
5 Caithness Avenue, Toronto, Ont. M4J 3X6
(416) 299-0365/299-0649
Contact: Jim Brown, editor

Hardware Merchandising
777 Bay Street, Toronto, Ont. M5W 1A7

(416) 596-5799
Contact: Sally Praskey, editor

Home Goods Retailing
777 Bay Street, Toronto, Ont. M5W 1A7
(416) 596-5940
Contact: Helen Bahen, editor

Housewares Canada
2000 Ellesmere Road, Unit 1, Scarborough, Ont. M1H 2W4
(416) 438-1153
Contact: Laurie Merckel, editor

Lawn & Garden Trade
3414 Park Avenue, Suite 221, Montreal, Que. H2X 2H5
(514) 282-0191
Contact: Peter Tasler, editor

Quincaillerie Matériaux
777 Bay Street, Toronto, Ont. M5W 1A7
(416) 596-5799
Contact: Sally Praskey, editor

INDUSTRIAL, PLASTICS, AND METAL WORK

Canadian Industrial Equipment News
1450 Don Mills Road, Don Mills, Ont. M3B 2X7
(416) 445-6641
Contact: Olga Markovich, editor

Canadian Machinery & Metalworking
777 Bay Street, Toronto, Ont. M5W 1A7
(416) 596-5720
Contact: Nick Hancock, editor

Canadian Occupational Safety
222 Argyle Avenue, Delhi, Ont. N4B 2Y2
(519) 582-2510
Contact: Donald Glendinning, editor

Canadian Plastics
1450 Don Mills Road, Don Mills, Ont. M3B 2X7
(416) 445-6641
Contact: Judith Nancekivell, editor

Canadian Welder & Fabricator
1077 St. James Street, P.O. Box 6900, Winnipeg, Man. R3C 3B1

(204) 775-0201
Contact: Dan Proudley, editor

Heating-Plumbing Air Conditioning
1450 Don Mills Road, Don Mills, Ont. M3B 2X7
(416) 445-6641
Contact: Ron Shuker, editor

Industrial Maintanance Repair and Overhaul News
777 Bay Street, Toronto, Ont. M5W 1A7
(416) 596-5802
Contact: Steve Gabhauer, editor

Industrial Management
277 Lakeshore Road E., Suite 209, Box 247, Oakville, Ont. L6J 6L9
(416) 842-2884
Contact: Carol Radford, editor

Industrial Product Ideas
777 Bay Street, Toronto, Ont. M5W 1A7
(416) 596-5231
Contact: Michael Shelley, editor

Industrial Surface Finishing
777 Bay Street, Toronto, Ont. M5E 1A7
(416) 596-5714
Contact: Nick Hancock, editor

Metalworking Production & Purchasing
7507 Kennedy Road, P.O. Box 460, Milliken, Ont. L0H 1K0
(416) 477-3222
Contact: Ronald Farrell, editor

New Equipment News
111 Peter Street, Suite 411, Toronto, Ont. M5V 2W2
(416) 596-1624
Contact: Barrie Lehman, editor

Ontario Industrial Magazine
801 York Mills Road, Suite 201, Don Mills, Ont. M3B 1X7
(416) 446-1404
Contact: Barry Shapiro, editor

L'Outilité
5 Chauvet, Quebec, Que. G2K 1L1
(418) 623-3383
Contact: André Pageau, editor

Plant Engineering & Maintenance
277 Lakeshore Road E., Suite 209, Box 247, Oakville, Ont. L6J 6L9

(416) 842-2884
Contact: Lee Scott, editor

Plant Management & Engineering
777 Bay Street, Toronto, Ont. M5W 1A7
(416) 596-5801
Contact: Ron Richardson, editor

Plomberie-Chauffage et Climatisation
310 Victoria Avenue, Suite 201, Westmount, Que. H3Z 2M9
(514) 487-2302
Contact: Guy Giasson, editor

Québec Industriel, Le
1001 de Maisonneuve Boulevard W., Suite 1000,
Montreal, Que. H3A 3E1
(514) 845-5141
Contact: Antoine Di Lillo, editor

Plastics Business
501 Oakdale Road, Downsview, Ont. M3N 1W7
(416) 746-7360
Contact: Karen Berlenbach, editor

Shop
1450 Don Mills Road, Don Mills, Ont. M3B 2X7
(416) 445-6641
Contact: Al Cairn, editor

MEDIA AND ADVERTISING

AV Business Communications
777 Bay Street, Toronto, Ont. M3W 1A7
(416) 596-5878
Contact: Don Long, editor

Broadcaster
7 Labatt Avenue, Toronto, Ont. M5A 3P2
(416) 363-6111
Contact: Colin Wright, editor

Broadcast Technology
P.O. Box 420, Bolton, Ont. L0P 1A0
(416) 857-6076
Contact: Doug Loney, editor

Marketing
777 Bay Street, Toronto, Ont. M5W 1A7
(416) 586-5835
Contact: Colin Muncie, editor

Media Magazine
643 Yonge Street, 3rd Floor, Toronto, Ont. M4Y 1Z9
(416) 927-7200
Contact: Sheri Craig, editor

Motivational Marketing
411 Richmond Street E., Toronto, Ont. M5A 3S5
(416) 362-8786
Contact: John Dunlop, editor

News Canada
121 Bloor Street E., Suite 300, Toronto, Ont. M4W 3M5
(416) 923-4000

Publicitaire, Le
1010 St. Catherine Street W., Suite 639, Montreal, Que. H3B 1G7
(514) 875-2565
Contact: Robert Bastin, editor

Press Review
P.O. Box 368, Station A, Toronto, Ont. M5W 1C2
(416) 368-0512
Contact: Sheila Johnston, editor

Sales & Marketing Management in Canada
3500 Dufferin Street, Suite 402, Downsview, Ont. M3K 1N2
(416) 633-2020
Contact: Ernie Spear, editor

MISCELLANEOUS PROFESSIONAL, BUSINESS, AND TRADE

Cable Communications Magazine
4 Smetana Drive, Kitchener, Ont. N2B 3B8
(519) 744-4111
Contact: Udo Salewsky, editor

Canadian Bar Review
130 Albert Street, Suite 1700, Ottawa, Ont. K1P 5L4
(613) 228-5400
Contact: A.J. McClean, editor

Canadian Cleaner & Launderer
1 Pacifique Street, Ste-Anne-de-Bellevue, Que. H9X 1C5
(514) 457-2347
Contact: Marcia Todd, editor

Canadian Coin Box Magazine
833 - 2nd Avenue E., Owen Sound, Ont. N4K 5P4
(519) 376-9680
Contact: Marion Walker, editor

Canadian Exporter
2000 Ellesmere Road, Unit 1, Scarborough, Ont. M1H 2W4
(416) 438-1153
Contact: Laurie Merckel, editor

Canadian Firefighter, The
P.O. Box 37, Sttion M, Toronto, Ont. M6S 4T2
(416) 233-2516
Contact: Lorne Campbell, editor

Canadian Funeral Director
174 Harwood Avenue S., Suite 206, Ajax, Ont. L1S 2H7
(416) 427-6121
Contact: Ray Halket, editor

Canadian Funeral News
2116 - 27th Avenue N.E., Suite 105, Calgary, Alta. T2E 7A6
(403) 250-5575
Contact: Randi Berting, editor

Canadian Home Economics Journal
151 Slater Street, Suite 805, Ottawa, Ont. K1P 5H3
(613) 238-8817
Contact: Barbara Baczynsky, editor

Canadian Journal of Applied Sport Sciences
P.O. Box 2274, Windsor, Ont. N8Y 4R9
(613) 748-5671
Contact: Dr. D. Cunningham, editor

Canadian Journal of Spectroscopy
1253 McGill College Avenue, Suite 111, Montreal, Que. H3B 2Y5
(514) 866-8236/866-6155
Contact: I. Butler, editor

Canadian Metallurgical Quarterly
150 Conumers Road, Suite 104, Willowdale, Ont. M2J 1P9
(416) 497-8337
Contact: J.M. Toguri, editor

Canadian Music Instruments & Supply Directory
6420 Victoria Avenue, Unit 8, Montreal, Que. H3W 2S7
(514) 731-3523
Contact: Keith Fredericks, editor

Canadian Music Trade
832 Mt. Pleasant Road, Toronto, Ont. M4P 2L3
(416) 485-8284
Contact: Ted Burley, editor

Canadian Packaging
777 Bay Street, Toronto, Ont. M5W 1A7
(416) 596-5745
Contact: Peter Cale, editor

Canadian Pool & Spa Marketing
P.O. Box 282, Station Q., Toronto, Ont. M4T 2M1
(416) 226-9885
Contact: Richard Hubbard, editor

Canadian Rental Service
145 Thames Road W., P.O. Box 1060, Exeter, Ont. N0M 1S0
(519) 235-2400
Contact: Peter Darbishire, editor

Canadian Research
777 Bay Street, Toronto, Ont. M5E 1A7
(416) 596-5722
Contact: Douglas Dingeldein, editor

Canadian RV Dealer
3414 Park Avenue, Suite 221, Montreal, Que. H2X 2H5
(514) 282-0191
Contact: Peter Tasler, editor

Canadian Security
46 Crockford Boulevard, Scarborough, Ont. M1R 3C3
(416) 755-4343
Contact: Jack Percival, editor

Canadian Vending
833 - 2nd Avenue E., Owen Sound, Ont. N4K 5P4
(519) 376-9680
Contact: Marion Walker, editor

Canadian Veterinary Journal, The
339 Booth Street, Ottawa, Ont. K1R 7K1
(613) 236-1162
Contact: Dr. W.T. Nagge, editor

Canadian Vet Supplies
1 Philipsburg Street, P.O. Box 1320, Bedford, Que. J0J 1A0
(514) 248-3356
Contact: Anne-Lise Brien, editor

Canadian Water Well
145 Thames Road W., P.O. Box 1060, Exeter, Ont. N0M 1S0
(519) 235-2400
Contact: Peter Darbishire, editor

CMAC Journal
Sponsored by the Cash Management Association of Canada
150 King Street W., 6th Floor, P.O. Box 112, Sun Life Centre, Toronto, Ont. M5H 1J9
(416) 979-6118
Contact: Jarl Kallberg, editor

Design Engineering
777 Bay Street, Toronto, Ont. M5W 1A7
(416) 596-583
Contact: James Barnes, editor

Design Product News
7507 Kennedy Road, P.O. Box 460, Milliken, Ont. L0H 1K0
(416) 477-3222
Contact: James Young, editor

Export Canada
P.O. Box 1048, Station A, Surrey, B.C. V3S 4P5
(604) 596-9426
Contact: Marjorie Butchard, editor

Farm Equipment Quarterly
145 Thames Road W., P.O. Box 1060, Exeter, Ont. N0M 1S0
(519) 235-2400
Contact: Peter Darbishire, editor

Feed & Farm Supply Dealer
1077 St. James Street, P.O. Box 6900, Winnipeg, Man. R3C 3B1
(204) 775-0201
Contact: James Buchok, editor

Fire Fighting in Canada Magazine
222 Argyle Avenue, Delhi, Ont. N4B 2Y2
(519) 582-2510
Contact: D.G. Glendinning, editor

Laboratory Product News
1450 Don Mills Road, Don Mills, Ont. M3B 2X7

(416) 445-6641
Contact: Rita Tate, editor

Laboratory Times
777 Bay Street, Toronto, Ont. M5W 1A7
(416) 596-5722
Contact: Douglas Dingeldein, editor

Machinery & Equipment Maintenance Repair & Overhaul
1560 Bayview Avenue, Suite 303, Toronto, Ont. M4G 3B8
(416) 488-8100
Contact: William Roebuck, editor

Marketnews
501 Oakdale Road, Downsview, Ont. M3N 1W7
(416) 746-7360
Contact: Robert Franner, editor

Materials Management & Distribution
777 Bay Street, Toronto, Ont. M5W 1A7
(416) 596-5709
Contact: Richard Rix, editor

Médecin Vétérinaire du Québec, Le
431 Alden Road, Unit 20, Markham, Ont. L3R 3L4
(416) 477-2030/477-2031
Contact: Patrick Guay, editor

Microscopical Society of Canada Bulletin, The
150 College Street, Room 79, Toronto, Ont. M5S 1A8
(416) 978-8896
Contact: F.W. Doane, editor

Modern Purchasing
777 Bay Street, Toronto, Ont. M5W 1A7
(416) 596-5955
Contact: Faye Bourgeois, editor

Motocycliste, Le
2021 Union Street, Suite 1150, Montreal, Que. H3A 2S9
(514) 284-9340
Contact: Normal Langelin, editor

Motorcycle Dealer & Trade
411 Richmond Street E., Suite 102, Toronto, Ont. M5A 3S5
(416) 362-7966
Contact: John Dunlop, editor

National
130 Albert Street, Suite 1700, Ottawa, Ont. K1P 5G4

(613) 237-2925
Contact: Hannah Bernstein, editor

Ontario Lawyers Weekly
2265 Midland Avenue, Scarborough, Ont. M1P 4S1
(416) 292-1421, or 292-1425 after 4 p.m.
Contact: Michael Fitz-James, editor

Optical Prism
31 Hastings Drive, Unionville, Ont. L3R 4Y5
(416) 475-9343
Contact: Allan Vezina, editor

Physics in Canada/La Physique au Canada
151 Slater Street, Suite 805, Ottawa, Ont. K1P 5H3
(613) 237-3392
Contact: J. Rolle, editor

Professional Musician
2817 Keele Street, Downsview, Ont. M3M 2G6
(416) 635-5530
Contact: Larry Wilson, editor

Purchasing Management Digest
277 Lakeshore Road E., Suite 209, Box 247, Oakville, Ont. L6J 6L9
(416) 842-2884
Contact: Rae Robb, editor

Québec Vert
P.O. Box 554, Limoilou, Que. G1L 4W4
(418) 524-5471
Contact: François Bernatchez, editor

Recreation Canada
333 River Road, Vanier, Ont. K1L 8H9
(613) 748-5651
Contact: Denny Neider, editor

RPM Weekly
6 Brentcliffe Road, Toronto, Ont. M4G 3Y2
(416) 425-0257
Contact: Walt Grealis, editor

Sciences & Techniques de l'Eau
6290 Perinault Street, Suite 102, Montreal, Que. H4K 1K5
(514) 337-4446
Contact: Raymond Larivee, editor

Shopping Centre Canada
777 Bay Street, Toronto, Ont. M5W 1A7

(416) 596-5915
Contact: Jamie Hubbard, editor

Sports Business
501 Oakdale Road, Downsview, Ont. M3N 1W7
(416) 746-7360
Contact: Jamie Howe, editor

Toys & Games
501 Oakdale Road, Downsview, Ont. M3N 1W7
(416) 746-7360
Contact: Janet McGee, editor

TradeAsia Magazine
P.O. Box 144, Station M, Toronto, Ont. M6S 3G8
(416) 762-4103
Contact: Richard Mann, editor

Volume Retail Merchandising
111 Peter Street, Suite 411, Toronto, Ont. M5V 2W2
(416) 596-1624
Contact: Doug Newman, editor

Water and Pollution Control
1450 Don Mills Road, Don Mills, Ont. M3B 2X7
(416) 445-6641
Contact: Leslie Burt, editor

Western Legal Publications
1 Alexander Street, Suite 301, Vancouver, B.C. V6A 1B2
(604) 687-5671
Contact: Phillip George, vice president

OFFICE EQUIPMENT AND INTERIOR DESIGN

Bureau, Le
777 Bay Street, Toronto, Ont. M5W 1A7
(416) 596-5251
Contact: Paul Saint-Pierre, editor

Canada's Contract Magazine
7777 Keele Street, Concord, Ont. L4K 1Y7
(416) 669-6606
Contact: Michael Knell, editor

Canadian Interiors
777 Bay Street, Toronto, Ont. M5W 1A7

(416) 596-5881
Contact: Dean Shalden, editor

Canadian Office
47 Lakeshore Road E., P.O. Box 190, Mississauga, Ont. L5G 4L7
(416) 271-1601
Contact: Bruce Glassford, editor

Canadian Office Products & Stationery
1450 Don Mills Road, Don Mills, Ont. M3B 2X7
(416) 445-6641
Contact: Lisa Sadowski, editor

COMDA Key
Published by the Canadian Office Machine Dealers' Association
3464 Kingston Road, Suite 214, Scarborough, Ont. M1M 1R5
(416) 261-1607
Contact: Donald Vickery, editor

Office Equipment & Methods
777 Bay Street, Toronto, Ont. M5W 1A7
(416) 596-5251
Contact: Tom Kelly, editor

Office Ergonomics
250 The Esplanade, Suite 100, Toronto, Ont. M5A 1J2
(416) 369-0080
Contact: Julian Zuckerbrot, editor

Office Product News
1450 Don Mills Road, Don Mills, Ont. M3B 2X7
(416) 445-6641
Contact: Elizabeth Schwartz, editor

PRINTING, GRAPHICS, AND PHOTOGRAPHY

Applied Arts
20 Holly Street, Suite 208, Toronto, Ont. M4S 3B1
(416) 488-1163
Contact: Tony Leighton, editor

Canadian Community Publisher
88 University Avenue, Suite 705, Toronto, Ont. M5J 1T6
(416) 598-4277
Contact: Ky Dills, editor

Canadian Printer & Publisher
777 Bay Street, Toronto, Ont. M5W 1A7
(416) 596-5884
Contact: Jack Homer, editor

Graphic Monthly, The
2065 Dundas Street E., Suite 205, Mississauga, Ont. L4W 2W1
(416) 625-7070
Contact: Alexander Donald, editor

Maître Imprimeur, Le
480 Mount Royal Avenue E., Montreal, Que. H2J 1W4
(514) 842-2751
Contact: Hélène Lagadec, editor

Photovideo
777 Bay Street, Toronto, Ont. M5W 1A7
(416) 596-5878
Contact: Don Long, editor

PrintAction
1865 Leslie Street, Suite 201, Don Mills, Ont. M3B 2M4
(416) 447-8536
Contact: Patricia Trusty, editor

Printing Product Guide
777 Bay Street, Toronto, Ont. M5W 1A7
(416) 596-5884
Contact: Jack Homer, editor

Professional Photographers of Canada
399 Berry Street, Suite 17, Winnipeg, Man. R3J 1N6
(204) 885-7798
Contact: Craig Kelman, editor

Studio
124 Galaxy Boulevard, Suite 102, Toronto, Ont. M9W 4Y6
(416) 675-1999
Contact: B.J. Murray, editor

TRANSPORTATION AND CARGO

Aerospace Canada International
777 Bay Street, Toronto, Ont. M5W 1A7
(416) 596-5794
Contact: Ted Hallas, editor

Airforce
424 Metcalfe Street, Ottawa, Ont. K2P 2C3
(613) 236-4673
Contact: Doug Stuebing, editor

Atlantic Trucking
920 Yonge Street, 6th Floor, Toronto, Ont. M4W 3C7
Contact: J.D. Corcoran, editor

Aviation Trade
2 Lansing Square, Suite 703, Willowdale, Ont. M2J 4P8
(416) 494-0745
Contact: Paul Plesman, editor

Boating Business
801 York Mills Road, Suite 301, Don Mills, Ont. M3B 1X7
(416) 443-8888
Contact: Penny Caldwell, editor

Calgary Airport Business Directory
1224 - 53rd Avenue N.E., Suite 158, Calgary, Alta. T2E 7E2
(403) 275-9457
Contact: Paul Skinner, publisher

Canadian Aircraft Operator, The
5200 Dixie Road, Suite 204, Mississauga, Ont. L4W 1E4
(416) 625-5277
Contact: R.G. Halford, editor

Canadian Aviation
777 Bay Street, Toronto, Ont. M5W 1A7
(416) 596-5791
Contact: Hugh Whittington, editor

Canadian Flight Magazine
P.O. Box 563, Station B, Ottawa, Ont. K1P 5P7
(613) 236-4901
Contact: W.N. Peppler, editor

Canadian General Aviation News
P.O. Box 563, Station B, Ottawa, Ont. K1P 5P7
(613) 236-4901
Contact: W.N. Peppler, editor

Canadian Ports & Seaway Directory
1450 Don Mills Road, Don Mills, Ont. M3B 2X7
(416) 445-6641
Contact: Lou Volpintesta, editor

Canadian Shipper, The
920 Yonge Street, 6th Floor, Toronto, Ont. M4W 3C7
Contact: J.D. Corcoran, editor

Canadian Shipping and Maine Engineering
5200 Dixie Road, Suite 204, Mississauga, Ont. L4W 1E4
(416) 625-5277
Contact: Patrick Brophy, editor

Canadian Transportation & Distribution Management
1450 Don Mills Road, Don Mills, Ont. M3B 2X7
(416) 445-6641
Contact: Robert Robinson, editor

Captain Lillie's Coast Guide and Radiotelephone Directory
355 Burrard Street, Suite C-310, Vancouver, B.C. V6C 2G6
(604) 685-4385
Contact: Murray D. McLellan, publisher

Cargo Exchange
P.O. Box 370, Station Q, Toronto, Ont. M4T 2M5
(416) 486-0516
Contact: Paul Rodney, editor

Corporate & Commercial Aviation
2 Lansing Square, Suite 703, Willowdale, Ont. M2J 5A1
(416) 494-0745
Contact: Paul Plesman, editor

Eastern Trucker
109 Vanderhoof Avenue, Toronto, Ont. M4G 2J2
(416) 425-9021
Contact: Barry Holmes, editor

L'Echo du Transport
7493 Trans-Canada Highway, Suite 102, St-Laurent, Que. H4T 1T3
(514) 337-9043
Contact: Pierre Gravel, editor

Great Lakes Navigation
1434 St. Catherine Street W., Suite 512, Montreal, Que. H3G 1R4
(514) 861-6715
Contact: O.J. Silva, editor

Harbour & Shipping
355 Burrard Street, Suite C-310, Vancouver, B.C. V6C 2G6
(604) 685-4385
Contact: Liz Bennett, editor

Helicopters in Canada
1224 - 53rd Avenue N.E., Suite 158, Calgary, Alta. T2E 7E2
(403) 275-9457
Contact: Paul Skinner, editor

ICAO Bulletin
Published by the International Civil Aviation Organization
1000 Sherbrooke Street W., Suite 327, Montreal, Que. H3A 2R2
(514) 285-8222
Contact: Charles LaFond, editor

Manitoba Highway News
25 Bunting Street, Winnipeg, Man. R2X 2P5
(204) 632-6600
Contact: Al Harris, editor

Marine Engineering Digest
116 Albert Street, Suite 706, Ottawa, Ont. K1P 5G3
(613) 234-3374
Contact: H. Arnsdorf, editor

Marine Trades
5200 Dixie Road, Suite 204, Mississauga, Ont. L4W 1E4
(416) 625-5277
Contact: Gary Arthurs, editor

Maritime Industries
P.O. Box 91760, West Vancouver, B.C. V7V 4S1
(604) 986-9501
Contact: D. Cumming, editor

Motor Truck
109 Vanderhoof Avenue, Toronto, Ont. M4G 2J2
(416) 425-9021
Contact: Barry Holmes, editor

Ontario Trucking Today
720 Spadina Avenue, Suite 419, Toronto, Ont. M5S 2S7
(416) 961-1028
Contact: Janice Kray, editor

Ports Annual
1434 St. Catherine Street W., Suite 512, Montreal, Que. H3G 1R4
(514) 861-6715
Contact: Megan Perkins, editor

Seaports & the Shipping World
4634 St. Catherine Street W., Montreal, Que. H3Z 1S3
(514) 934-0373
Contact: Brian Gallery, editor

Transport Routier du Québec
4837 Boyer Street, Suite 100, Montreal, Que. H2J 3E6
(514) 527-1359
Contact: Louis Fahndrich, editor

Transportation
P.O. Box 3835, Station B, Calgary, Alta. T2M 4N7
(403) 250-1876

Transportation Business
310 Dupont Street, Toronto, Ont. M5R 1V9
(416) 968-7252
Contact: Barrie Reynolds, editor

Truck Fleet
777 Bay Street, Toronto, Ont. M5W 1A7
(416) 596-5929
Contact: David Thompson, editor

Truck News
936-A Eastern Avenue, Toronto, Ont. M4L 1A4
(416) 461-0323
Contact: Pamela Light, editor

Trucking Canada
109 Vanderhoof Avenue, Suite 109, Toronto, Ont. M4G 2J2
(416) 425-9021
Contact: Rolf Lookwood, editor
Western Office:
4250 Dawson Street,
Burnaby, B.C. V5C 4B1
(604) 293-1275

Western Motor Fleet
945 King Edward Street, Winnipeg, Man. R3H 0P8
(204) 775-0387
Contact: Gren Yeo, editor

Wings Magazine
1224 - 53rd Avenue N.E., Suite 158, Calgary, Alta. T2E 7E2
(403) 275-9457
Contact: Paul Skinner, editor

TRAVEL

Agent Canada
1425 W. Pender Street, Vancouver, B.C. V6G 2S3

(604) 688-0481
Contact: Douglas Keough, editor

Bulletin Voyages
P.O. Box 85, Station E, Montreal, Que. H2T 3A5
(514) 287-9773
Contact: Etienne Ozan-Groulx, editor

Business Traveller
52 St. Clair Avenue E., Toronto, Ont. M4T 1M9
(416) 926-1038
Contact: Tin Thomas, editor

Canadian Travel Courier
777 Bay Street, Toronto, Ont. M5W 1A7
(416) 596-5806
Contact: Patrick Dineen, editor

Canadian Travel Press
310 Dupont Street, Toronto, Ont. M5R 1V9
(416) 968-7252
Contact: Edith Baxter, editor

Group Travel/Voyage en Groupe
425 Harris Street, St-Laurent, Que. H4N 2G8
(514) 744-3867
Contact: André Quesnel, editor

Journal des Voyages
133 de la Commune Street W., Suite 300, Montreal, Que. H2Y 2C7
(514) 288-6050
Contact: Patrick Verbeeck, editor

Marketing Voyages
674 Place Publique, Suite 215, Ste-Dorothée, Que. H7X 1G1
(514) 689-2543
Contact: Gérard Giguère, editor

On Target
310 Dupont Street, Toronto, Ont. M5R 1V9
(416) 968-7252
Contact: Edith Baxter, editor

Ontario Motor Coach Association Directory
720 Spadina Avenue, Suite 419, Toronto, Ont. M5S 2S7
(416) 961-1028
Contact: Robert Bradford, editor

Personnel Guide to Canada's Travel Industry
310 Dupont Street, Toronto, Ont. M5R 1V9

(416) 968-7252
Contact: Wendy Baxter-McClung, editor

Tourisme +
429 St. Vincent Street, Suite 304, Montreal, Que. H2Y 3A6
(514) 397-9535
Contact: Yves-Marie Belva, editor

Travel Destination Canada
310 Dupont Street, Toronto, Ont. M5R 1V9
(416) 968-7252
Contact: Edith Baxter, editor

Travelweek Bulletin
P.O. Box 575, Station F, Toronto, Ont. M4Y 2L8
(416) 924-0963
Contact: Jill Wykes, editor

FARM PUBLICATIONS

Most of these publications–some weekly tabloids, others monthly magazines–carry news of the latest developments in agriculture or dairy technology, as well as articles on animal health and nutrition, breeding, new agricultural machinery, and advice on farm management. Some feature profiles of innovative farmers; nearly all list and cover farm shows, ploughing matches, and country fairs.

Although they do not pay a lot, farm publications provide excellent opportunities for freelancers new to writing.

Agrologist
151 Slater Street, Suite 907, Ottawa, Ont. K1P 5H4
(613) 232-9459
Contact: John Watts, editor

Alberta Farm Life
1030 - 104th Street, Edmonton, Alta. T5J 1C2
(403) 425-1610
Contact: Chris Malcolm, editor

Breeder & Feeder
590 Keele Street, Toronto, Ont. M6N 3E3
(416) 766-9217
Contact: Jean Szkotnicki, editor

B.C. Orchardist
115 Gordon Drive, Suite 3, Kelowna, B.C. V1Y 3E3
(604) 763-1116/763-1544
Contact: Ted Noonan, editor

Bulletin des Agriculteurs, Le
110 Cremazie Boulevard W., Suite 422, Montreal, Que. H2P 1B9
(514) 382-4350
Contact: Claude Choquette, editor

Butter-Fat
P.O. Box 9100, Vancouver, B.C. V6G 4G4
(604) 420-6611
Contact: C.A. Paulson, editor

Canada Poultryman
605 Royal Avenue, New Westminster, B.C. V3M 1J4
(604) 526-8525
Contact: Tony Greaves, editor

Canadian Aberdeen Angus News
1201 - 3rd Avenue S., P.O. Box 1207, Lethbridge, Alta. T1J 4A4
(403) 381-7477
Contact: Dick Turner, editor

Canadian Ayrshire Review
1160 Carling Avenue, Ottawa, Ont. K1Z 7K6
(613) 728-8192
Contact: Réal Pelland, editor

Canadian Charolais Banner
1120 - 53rd Avenue N.E., Suite 101A, Calgary, Alta. T2E 6N9
(403) 295-2292
Contact: Mark Kihn, editor

Canadian Fruitgrower
222 Argyle Avenue, Delhi, Ont. N4B 2Y2
(519) 582-2510
Contact: Ben Steidman, editor

Canadian Guernsey Journal
368 Woolwich Street, Guelph, Ont. N1H 3W6
(519) 836-2141
Contact: Rosemary Peer, editor

Canadian Hereford Digest
5160 Skyline Way N.E., Calgary, Alta. T2E 6V1
(403) 274-1734
Contact: Kurt Gilmore, editor

Canadian Jersey Breeder
343 Waterloo Avenue, Guelph, Ont. N1H 3K1
(519) 821-9150
Contact: Russell Gammon, editor

Canadian Swine
R.R. 1, New Dundee, Ont. N0B 2E0

(519) 696-2535
Contact: D. Baltaz, editor

Canadian Tobacco Grower, The
222 Argyle Avenue, Delhi, Ont. N4B 2Y2
(519) 582-2510
Contact: David Maclaren, editor

Canadian Wool Grower
142 Franktown Road, P.O. Box 130, Carleton Place, Ont. K7C 3P3
(613) 257-2714
Contact: Eric Bjergso, editor

Cattlemen
1760 Ellice Avenue, Winnipeg, Man. R3H 0B6
(204) 774-1861
Contact: Gren Winslow, editor

Central Alberta Parkland News
Bag 5200, Red Deer, Alta. T4N 5G3
(403) 343-2400
Contact: Doug Brunton, editor

Coopérant Agricole, Le
1055 Marché Central Street, Montreal, Que. H4N 1K3
(514) 384-6450
Contact: Fernand Lecavlier, editor

Corn-Soy Guide
1760 Ellice Avenue, Winnipeg, Man. R3H 0B6
(204) 774-1861

Country Guide
1760 Ellice Avenue, Winnipeg, Man. R3H 0B6
(204) 774-1861
Contact: Dave Wreford, editor

Country Life in British Columbia
1345 Johnston Road, White Rock, B.C. V4B 3Z3
(604) 536-7622
Contact: Malcolm Young, editor

Crops Guide
1760 Ellice Avenue, Winnipeg, Man. R3H 0B6
(204) 774-1861

Crossroads
188 Wallace Avenue N., P.O. Box 188, Listowell, Ont. N4W 3H2
(519) 291-1660
Contact: Barry Wenger, editor

Dairy Contact
11802 - 124th Street, Suite 210, Edmonton, Alta. T5L 0M3
(403) 455-4173
Contact: Dr. Allen Parr, editor

Dairy Guide
1760 Ellice Avenue, Winnipeg, Man. R3H 0B6
(204) 774-1861
Contact: Gren Winslow, editor

Farm & Country
950 Yonge Street, Suite 700, Toronto, Ont. M4W 2J4
(416) 924-6209
Contact: John Phillips, editor

Farm Focus
2 Second Street, P.O. Box 128, Yarmouth, N.S. B5A 4B1
(902) 742-7111
Contact: Heather Jones, editor

Farm Gate, The
15 King Street, Elmira, Ont. N3B 2R1
(519) 893-8500
Contact: Bob Verdun, editor

Farm Light & Power
2352 Smith Street, Regina, Sask. S4P 2P6
(306) 525-3305
Contact: L.T. Bradley, editor

Farm Power Today
950 Yonge Street, Suite 700, Toronto, Ont. M4W 2J4
(416) 924-6209
Contact: John Phillips, editor

Farming Today
14 Victoria Street E., P.O. Box 280, Alliston, Ont. L0M 1A0
(705) 435-6228
Contact: Mariellen Venhola, editor

Feather Fancier
5 Lake Hill Road, Forest, Ont. N0N 1J0
(519) 899-2364
Contact: Jase Greinar, editor

Giant, The
Bag 5012, Main Post Office, Red Deer, Alta. T4N 6R4
(403) 346-3356
Contact: Ivan Mason, editor

Grainews
433 Main Street, Winnipeg, Man. R3C 3A7
(204) 944-5567
Contact: John Clark, editor

Grower, The
301 Ontario Food Terminal, 165 The Queensway, Toronto, Ont. M8Y 1H8
(416) 255-4473
Contact: John van der Zalm, editor

Hog Guide
1760 Ellice Avenue, Winnipeg, Man. R3H 0B6
(204) 774-1861
Contact: Dave Bates, editor

Hog Market Place Quarterly
950 Yonge Street, Suite 700, Toronto, Ont. M4W 2J4
(416) 924-6209
Contact: John Phillips, editor

Holstein Journal
335 Lesmill Road, Don Mills, Ont. M3B 2V1
(416) 441-3030
Contact: Bonnie Cooper, editor

Manitoba Co-Operator, The
P.O. Box 9800, Winnipeg, Man. R3C 3K7
(204) 943-0796
Contact: R.W. Hainstock, editor

Niagara Farmer's Monthly
P.O. Box 52, Smithville, Ont. L0R 2A0
(416) 957-3751
Contact: Ivan Carruthers, editor

North West Farmer-Rancher
P.O. Box 430, North Battleford, Sask. S9A 2Y5
(306) 445-4401
Contact: Lorne Cooper, editor

Ontario Corn Producer
222 Argyle Avenue, Delhi, Ont. N4B 2Y2
(519) 582-2510
Contact: Terry Daynard, editor

Ontario Farmer
P.O. Box 7400, Station E., London, Ont. N5Y 4X3
(519) 473-0010
Contact: Robert Way, editor

Ontario Milk Producer
6780 Campobello Road, Mississauga, Ont. L5N 2L8
(416) 821-8970
Contact: Karen Sample, editor

Producteur Agricole, Le
1 Philipsburg Street, P.O. Box 1320, Bedford, Que. J0J 1A0
(514) 248-3356
Contact: Anne-Lise Brien, editor

Producteur de Lait Québecois, Le
555 Roland Therrien Boulevard, Longueuil, Que. J4H 3Y9
(514) 679-0530
Contact: Evelyn Dumas, editor

Producteur Laitier, Le
1 Philipsburg Street, P.O. Box 1320, Bedford, Que. J0J 1A0
(514) 248-3356
Contact: Anne-Lise Brien, editor

Producteur de Porc Québecois, Le
1 Philipsburg Street, P.O. Box 1320, Bedford, Que. J0J 1A0
(514) 248-3356
Contact: Anne-Lise Brien, editor

Quebec Farmers' Advocate
P.O. Box 80, Ste-Anne-de-Bellevue, Que. H9X 3L4
(514) 457-2010
Contact: Steve Gruber, editor

Rabbits in Canada
Oak Street, Bewdley, Ont. K0L 1E0
(416) 797-2281
Contact: Charlotte Clay, editor

Richelieu Agricole, Le
84B Richelieu Street, St-Jean-sur-Richelieu, Que. J3B 6X3
(514) 861-4624
Contact: Robert Paradis, editor

Rural Voice, The
10A The Square, P.O. Box 37, Goderich, Ont. N7A 3Y5
(519) 524-7668
Contact: Sheila Gunby, editor

Saskatchewan Stockgrower, The
1170 - 8th Avenue, Regina, Sask. S4R 1C9
(306) 352-3445
Contact: Don Black, editor

Sheep Canada
P.O. Box 113, Moosehorn, Man. R0C 2E0
(204) 449-2302
Contact: Peter Schroedter, editor

Shorthorn News, The
P.O. Box 63, Qu'Appelle, Sask. S0G 4A0
(306) 699-7110
Contact: Craig Andrew

Simmental Country
4101 - 19th Street N.E., Suite 13, Calgary, Alta. T2E 7C4
(403) 250-7466
Contact: Ted Pritchett, editor

Stockman, The
P.O. Box 40, Clyde, Alta. T0G 0E0
(403) 348-5325
Contact: David Orey, editor

Terre de Chez Nous, La
555 Roland Thérrien Boulevard, Longueuil, Que. J4H 3Y9
(514) 679-0530, extension 276
Contact: Evelyn Dumas, editor

Union Farmer
250C - 2nd Avenue S., Saskatoon, Sask. S7K 2M1
(306) 652-9465
Contact: Terry Pugh, editor

Voice of the Elgin Farmer
254 Main Street, P.O. Box 490, Dresden, Ont. N0P 1M0
(519) 683-4485
Contact: Don Spearman, editor
"Voice of" editions are also published for the Ontario counties of Essex, Huron, Kent, Lambton, Middlesex, and Oxford.

Western Hog Journal
10319 Princess Elizabeth Avenue, Edmonton, Alta. T5G 0Y5
(403) 474-8288
Contact: W.L. Owen, editor

Western Producer, The
P.O. Box 2500, Saskatoon, Sask. S7K 2C4
(306) 665-3500
Contact: R.H.D. Phillips, editor

DAILY NEWSPAPERS

The easiest way to break into print is usually to write for a newspaper in a small community. Yet too many beginners try to penetrate the business by writing short stories or non-fiction articles for *Reader's Digest*, *Chatelaine*, or *Saturday Night*. They fail to realize that fiction and top-quality magazine pieces are among the most difficult of all literary forms, and that publications like these have very high standards. With each rejection slip discouragement mounts, often to the point where the idea of a writing career is abandoned.

Weekly papers are a good starting point. Because they usually have small staffs and low budgets, their editors are often only too pleased to accept outside contributions, particularly feature articles that cover the local scene. And since payment is modest, there is little competition from more experienced or established writers.

Always remember that news loses its value as briskly as it changes, and it is therefore usually gathered hurriedly – on large papers and small – by staff reporters. It is better, then, for freelance writers to concentrate on background stories about on-going issues, or write profiles of unusual or important area citizens and institutions.

For a well-written, well-researched article on an important or intriguing subject, many of the bigger city dailies pay as much, if not more, than the smaller journals and trade publications.

Stories about travel, hobbies, lifestyles, personal finance, and business are particularly welcome. So are strong human-interest pieces that point up a weakness in society. These are almost always among the best-read pieces in newspapers anywhere. Most editors like to build a bank of articles that are always timely and do not have to be used immediately.

Readable articles automatically find a market if they have been written in such a way that most "ordinary" people will understand them, and if they address *their* concerns – their jobs, the cost of living, hobbies, leisure time activities, health, or vacations.

Writers do not propose ideas to newspapers in the same way as they would for magazines. On newspapers, time is a much more crucial factor. So rather than craft a written story proposal, it is perfectly acceptable to solicit a go-ahead decision from the editor of one of the paper's sections with a quick telephone call.

Your best preparation if you are seriously considering this market, is to read critically several issues of the paper. Note the style, the story lengths preferred, how photographs are used, the paper's editorial policy, and how news stories and feature articles differ in content, construction, and tone.

If you have never studied journalism, you might need a reference book. Two that spring immediately to mind are *News Reporting and Writing* and *Basic News Writing*. Both are by Melvin Mencher, a professor at Columbia University's School of Journalism, and are published by William C. Brown of Iowa.

Naturally, it will take more experience to sell to the large, well-staffed metropolitan dailies, like *The Toronto Star* or *The Winnipeg Free Press*. But even here, the outside contributor has a chance, provided he or she has some specialized knowledge, can handle human-interest material with a deft hand, or can write full-bodied issue stories with conviction and authority.

Freelance writers submit their manuscripts to newspapers in much the same way as they would for magazines, and often write successfully for both. They meet deadlines even when to do so means losing a night's sleep. They are always aware that for the daily press, accuracy and reliability are two virtues worth cultivating, even under pressure. While the news story is essentially factual and must have a strong sense of immediacy, the feature article needs body and strength – as well as originality and freshness.

Timing is a key element. So keep a calendar of dates for seasonal stories based on anniversaries and read behind the news for feature ideas.

Besides writing for your city paper, you may be looking for an opportunity to act as a correspondent or stringer for one published elsewhere. In this case, it might be useful to have a list of all Canadian newspapers – dailies and suburban weeklies. The most complete is probably to be found in *Canadian Advertising Rates & Data*, published monthly for the advertising industry by Maclean Hunter. Canadian newspapers are also listed in such publications as *Canadian Almanac & Directory* and *Corpus Directory and Almanac of Canada*, both issued annually.

ALBERTA

Advocate
2950 Brenner Avenue, Bag 5200, P.O. Box 250,
Red Deer, Alta. T4N 5G3
(403) 343-2400

Calgary Herald
215 - 16th Street S.E., Calgary, Alta. T2P 0W8
(403) 235-7100

Calgary Sun
2615 - 12th Street N.E., Calgary, Alta. T2E 7W9
(403) 250-4200

Daily Herald Tribune
10604 - 100th Street, Grande Prairie, Alta. T8V 2M5
(403) 532-1110

Edmonton Journal
10006 - 101st Street, Edmonton, Alta. T5J 2S6
(403) 429-5400

Edmonton Sun
9405 - 50th Street, Edmonton, Alta. T6B 2Y2
(403) 468-5111

Fort McMurray Today
9701 Franklin Avenue, Bag 4008, Fort McMurray, Alta. T9H 3G1
(403) 743-8186

Lethbridge Herald
504 - 7th Street S., Lethbridge, Alta. T1J 3Z7
(403) 328-4411

Medicine Hat News
3257 Dunmore Road S.E., Medicine Hat, Alta. T1A 7E6
(403) 527-1101

BRITISH COLUMBIA

Alaska Highway News
9916 - 98th Street, Fort St. John, B.C. V1J 3T8
(604) 785-5631

Alberni Valley Times
4918 Napier Street, P.O. Box 400, Port Alberni, B.C. V9Y 7N1
(604) 723-8171

Chinese Canadian Bulletin
3289 Main Street, Vancouver, B.C. V5V 3M6
(604) 872-2810

Chinese Times
1 E. Pender Street, Vancouver, B.C. V6A 1S9
(604) 685-8575

Cranbrook Daily Townsman
822 Cranbrook Street W., Cranbrook, B.C. V1C 3R9
(604) 426-5201

Daily Bulletin
335 Spokane Street, Kimberley, B.C. V1A 1Y9
(604) 427-5333

Daily Courier
550 Doyle Avenue, Kelowna, B.C. V1Y 7V1
(604) 762-4445

Daily Free Press
223 Commercial Street, P.O. Box 69, Nanaimo, B.C. V9R 5K5
(604) 753-3451

Daily News
266 Baker Street, Nelson, B.C. V1L 4H3
(604) 352-3552

Kamloops News
63 W. Victoria Street, Kamloops, B.C. V2C 1A3
(604) 372-2331

Kamloops Sentinel
206 Seymour Street, Kamloops, B.C. V2C 2E6
(604) 372-7731

Peace River Block News
P.O. Box 180, Dawson Creek, B.C. V1G 4G6
(604) 782-4888

Penticton Herald
186 Nanaimo Avenue, Penticton, B.C. V2A 1N4
(604) 492-4002

Prince George Citizen
150 Brunswick Street, P.O. Box 5700, Prince George, B.C. V2L 5K9
(604) 562-2441

Price Rupert Daily News
P.O. Box 580, Prince Rupert, B.C. V8J 3R9
(604) 624-6781

Trail Times
1163 Cedar Avenue, Trail, B.C. V1R 4B8
(604) 368-8551

Vancouver Sun Province
2250 Granville Street, Vancouver, B.C. V6H 3G2
(604) 732-2515

Vernon Daily News
3309 - 31st Avenue, Vernon, B.C. V1T 6N8
(604) 545-0671

Victoria Times-Colonist
2621 Douglas Street, P.O. Box 300, Victoria, B.C. V8W 2N4
(604) 382-7211

MANITOBA

Brandon Sun
501 Rosser Avenue, Brandon, Man. R7A 5Z6
(204) 727-2451

Daily Bulletin
120 - 1st Avenue N.E., Dauphin, Man. R7N 1A5
(204) 638-4420

Daily Graphic
1941 Saskatchewan Avenue, P.O. Box 130, Portage La Prairie, Man. R1N 3B4
(204) 857-3427

Flin Flon Reminder
P.O. Box 727, Flin Flon, Man. R8A 1N5
(204) 687-3454

Swan River Report
120 Fifth Avenue, P.O. Box 1629, Swan River, Man. R0L 1Z0
(204) 734-2729

Thompson Citizen
P.O. Box 887, Thompson, Man. R8N 1N8
(204) 677-4534

Winnipeg Free Press
300 Carlton Street, Winnipeg, Man. R3C 3C1
(204) 943-9331

Winnipeg Sun
1700 Church Avenue, Winnipeg, Man. R2X 3A2
(204) 694-2022

NEW BRUNSWICK

Fredericton Gleaner
Prospect Street at Smythe, P.O. Box 3370,
Fredericton, N.B. E3B 5A2
(506) 455-6671

Telegraph-Journal & Evening Times-Globe
Crown Street, P.O. Box 2350, Saint John, N.B. E2L 3V8
(506) 632-8888

Times-Transcript
939 Main Street, P.O. Box 1001, Moncton, N.B. E1C 8P3
(506) 853-9321

NEWFOUNDLAND

Telegram
400 Topsail Road, St. John's, Nfld. A1E 2B8
(709) 364-6300

Western Star
West Street, P.O. Box 460, Cornerbrook, Nfld. A2H 6E7
(709) 634-4348

NOVA SCOTIA

Amherst Daily News
P.O. Box 280, Amherst, N.S. B4H 3Z2
(902) 667-5102

Cape Breton Post
255 George Street, Sydney, N.S. B1P 1J5
(902) 564-5451

Chronicle-Herald & Mail-Star
1650 Argyle Street, Halifax, N.S. B3J 2T2
(902) 426-2811

Daily News
6 Louise Street, Truro, N.S. B2N 5C3
(902) 893-9405

Evening News
352 E. River Road, New Glasgow, N.S. B2H 5E2
(902) 752-3000

ONTARIO

Barrie Examiner
16 Bayfield Street, Barrie, Ont. L4M 4T6
(705) 726-6537

Beacon Herald
108 Ontaio Street, P.O. Box 430, Stratford, Ont. N5A 6T6
(519) 271-2220

Brantford Expositor
53 Dalhousie Street, Brantford, Ont. N3T 5S8
(519) 756-2020

Brockville Recorder & Times
23 King Street W., P.O. Box 10, Brockville, Ont. K6V 5T8
(613) 342-4441

Cambridge Reporter
26 Ainslie Street S., Cambridge, Ont. N1K 3K1
(519) 621-3810

Citizen
1101 Baxter Road, P.O. Box 5020, Ottawa, Ont. K2C 3M4
(613) 829-9100

Coburg Daily Star
415 King Street W., P.O. Box 400, Coburg, Ont. K9A 4L1
(416) 372-0131

Daily Miner & News
33 Main Street, P.O. Box 1620, Kenora, Ont. P9N 3X7
(807) 468-5555

Daily News
45 Fourth Street, P.O. Box 2007, Chatham, Ont. N7M 2G4
(519) 354-2000

Daily Times
33 Queen Street W., Brampton, Ont. L6Y 1M1
(416) 451-2020

Globe and Mail
444 Front Street W., Toronto, Ont. M5V 2S9
(416) 585-5411

Guelph Mercury
14 Macdonnell Street, Suite 8, Guelph, Ont. N1H 6P7
(519) 822-4310

Hamilton Spectator
44 Frid Street, Hamilton, Ont. L8N 3G3
(416) 526-3333

Intelligencer
45 Bridge Street E., Belleville, Ont. K8N 1L5
(613) 962-9171

Kitchener-Waterloo Record
225 Fairway Road, Kitchener, Ont. N2G 4E5
(519) 894-2231

Le Droit
375 Rideau Street, Ottawa, Ont. K1N 5Y7
(613) 560-2747

Lindsay Post
15 William Street N., Lindsay, Ont. K9V 3Z9
(705) 324-2114

London Free Press
369 York Street, P.O. Box 2280, London, Ont. N6A 4G1
(519) 679-1111

Niagara Falls Review
4801 Valley Way, Niagara Falls, Ont. L2E 6T6
(416) 358-5711

North Bay Nugget
259 Worthington Street W., P.O. Box 570, North Bay, Ont. P1B 8J6
(705) 472-3200

Observer
186 Alexander Street, Pembroke, Ont. K8A 4L9
(613) 732-3691

Orillia Packet & Times
31 Colborne Street E., Orillia, Ont. L3V 1T4
(705) 325-1355

Oshawa Times
44 Richmond Street W., Oshawa, Ont. L1G 1C8
(416) 723-3474

Peterborough Examiner
400 Water Street, P.O. Box 389, Peterborough, Ont. K9J 6Z4
(705) 745-4641

Port Hope Guide
56 Walton Street, P.O. Box 296, Port Hope, Ont. L1A 3W4
(416) 885-2471

St. Catharines Standard
17 Queen Street, St. Catharines, Ont. L2R 5G5
(416) 684-7251

Sarnia Observer
140 S. Front Street, Sarnia, Ont. N7T 7M8
(519) 344-3641

Simcoe Reformer
105 Danly Drive, Simcoe, Ont. N3Y 4L2
(519) 426-5710

Star
145 Old Garden River Road, Sault Ste. Marie, Ont. P6A 5M5
(705) 253-1111

Sudbury Star
33 Mackenzie Street, Sudbury, Ont. P3C 4Y1
(705) 674-5271

Standard-Freeholder
44 Pitt Street, Cornwall, Ont. K6J 3P3
(613) 933-3160

Sun-Times
P.O. Box 200, Owen Sound, Ont. N4K 5P2
(519) 376-2250

Times-Journal
16 Hincks Street, St. Thomas, Ont. N5P 3W6
(519) 631-2790

Times-News/Chronical-Journal
75 S. Cumberland Street, Thunder Bay, Ont. P7B 1A3
(807) 344-3535

Timmins Daily Press
187 Cedar Street S., Timmins, Ont. P4N 2G9
(705) 268-5050

Toronto Star
1 Yonge Street, Toronto, Ont. M5E 1E6
(416) 367-2233

Toronto Sun
333 King Street E., Toronto, Ont. M5A 3X5
(416) 947-2333

Welland-Port Colborne Tribune
228 Main Street E., Welland, Ont. L3B 3W8
(416) 732-2411

Whig-Standard
306 King Street, Kingston, Ont. K7L 4Z7
(613) 544-5000

Windsor Star
167 Ferry Street, Windsor, Ont. N9A 4M5
(519) 255-5787

Woodstock-Ingersoll Daily Sentinel Review
16 Brock Street, Woodstock, Ont. N4S 8A5
(519) 537-2341

PRINCE EDWARD ISLAND

Guardian & Patriot
165 Prince Street., Charlottetown, P.E.I. C1A 4R7
(902) 894-8506

Journal-Pioneer
4 Queen Street, Summerside, P.E.I. C1N 4K5
(902) 436-2121

QUEBEC

Gazette, The
250 St. Antoine Street, Montreal, Que. H2Y 3R7
(514) 282-2222

La Presse
7 St. Jacques Street, Montreal, Que. H2Y 1K9
(514) 285-7306

La Tribune
1950 Roy Street, Sherbrooke, Que. J1K 2X8
(819) 569-9201

La Voix de l'Est
136 Main Street, Granby, Que. J2G 2V4
(514) 372-6433

Le Devoir
211 St. Sacrement Street, Montreal, Que. H2Y 1X1
(514) 844-3361

Le Journal de Montréal
4545 Frontenac Street, Montreal, Que. H2H 2R7
(514) 521-4545

Le Journal de Québec
450 Bechard Street, Ville-de-Vanier, Que. G1M 2E9
(418) 683-1573

Le Quotidien
1051 Talbot Boulevard, Chicoutimi, Que. G7H 5C1
(418) 545-4474

Le Soleil
390 St. Vallier Street, E., Quebec, Que G1K 7J6
(418) 647-3270

SASKATCHEWAN

Leader Post
1964 Park Street, Regina, Sask. S4P 3G4
(306) 565-8260

Lloydminster Daily Times
4828 - 44th Street, Lloydminster, Sask. S9V 0G8
(403) 825-5522

Prince Albert Herald
30 - 10th Street E., Prince Albert, Sask. S6V 5R9
(306) 764-4276

Star-Phoenix
204 - 5th Avenue N., Saskatoon, Sask. S7K 2P1
(306) 664-8340

Times-Herald
44 Fairford Street W., Moose Jaw, Sask. S6H 6E4
(306) 692-6441

BOOK PUBLISHERS

Unless they are crafting novels or writing on subjects deeply personal to them, which they feel must be written to feed their souls, professionals never produce books on speculation. The hard work involved, usually research and revisions stretched over many months, is always more safely invested after having secured a firm commitment from a publisher.

This usually follows a full proposal on how the book will be shaped, what each chapter will include, and how it will be written.

Professional writers will attest that writing books is somewhat easier after having consistently fed well-tailored articles to top Canadian magazines. Rather than being a long newspaper story, the magazine piece – in design, content, tone, and colour – is most certainly a short book, and a logical stepping-stone to the longer, more substantial works, which books really are.

Main considerations among book editors are obviously genre and quality, with length following closely behind. This applies, of course, to both fiction and non-fiction books, by far the easier product to market.

Fiction writers will be heartened to know that a rejection slip may only mean that the publishing house has filled its quota of novels for the next year. Books are normally "bought" well in advance of publication. A book for the fall season, for example, is usually required to be on an editor's desk by the previous January or February. The contract for it would have been signed a year or eighteen months prior to publication. It is also well to remember that a title rejected by a publisher one year could well be bought a couple of years later if editors think it fits their needs. You might also suggest a book and have it turned down because the publisher has a similar one – or maybe an import – already underway. If you study a publisher's list for one season, either for spring or for fall, you will note that it does not publish books so much as an editorial program of releases likely to satisfy many tastes. It never publishes two books on a similar subject in the same season.

There are all kinds of book publishers in Canada – from small, rural presses producing two or three titles a year, to large metropolitan houses which turn out as many as sixty. Most give authors an advance against royalties on acceptance of their proposal. This could range from $500 to $25,000 depending on the potential the book has in the marketplace. After publication, the author generally receives a royalty cheque every six months for the life of his or her book. An average royalty on a hardcover book is ten per cent of the selling price. At this rate, a 3,000-copy sale of a twenty-dollar book would yield the writer $6,000. Usually, authors can expect only an eight per cent royalty on a paperback version, but because this is cheaper than a hardcover, it is likely to sell more copies.

Acta Press
P.O. Box 3243, Station B, Calgary, Alta. T2M 4L8
(403) 270-3616
Contact: M.H. Hamza, president
Publishes manuscripts on business, education, and science, in English, and sometimes in French or German.

Addison-Wesley Publishers Ltd.
26 Prince Andrew Place, P.O. Box 580, Don Mills, Ont. M3C 2T8
(416) 447-5101
Contact: George Bryson, editor
Established 1965. Publishes manuscripts in all non-fiction categories, particularly elementary, high school and college text books, scholarly works, professional training books, education pamphlets and audio-visual material, and children's books.

Alcoholism and Drug Addiction Research Foundation
33 Russell Street, Toronto, Ont. M5S 2S1
(416) 595-6113
Contact: R.J. Hall, information and promotion
Established 1949. Publishes scientific and general works pertaining to many forms of addiction, primarily alcohol and drugs.

Thomas Allen & Son Ltd.
390 Steelcase Road E., Markham, Ont. L3R 1G2
(416) 475-9126
Contact: John Allen, publisher
Mostly publishes trade books in all categories: architecture, art, aviation, history, music, natural history, and sports. Also interested in children's books.

Allyn & Bacon Publishers
200 Steelcase Road E., Markham, Ont. L3R 1G2
(416) 477-3464

Contact: Gerald FitzGerald, editor
Specializes in college-level textbooks.

Altitude Publishing Ltd.
P.O. Box 490, Banff, Alta. T0L 0C0
(403) 762-4548
Contact: Kevin Tumback, manager
Established 1979. Publishes photographic and historic books about Canada and Alberta.

Anglican Book Centre, The
600 Jarvis Street, Toronto, Ont. M4Y 2J6
(416) 924-9122
Contact: The Rev. Michael Lloyd, publisher, or Robert Maclennan, managing editor
Publishes manuscripts on religion and social issues.

Annick Press Ltd.
5519 Yonge Street, Willowdale, Ont. M2N 5S3
(416) 221-4802
Contact: Rick Wilks or Anne Millyard, co-directors
Established 1975. Publishes children's literature, particularly picture books.

Aquila Communications Ltd.
2 Thorncliffe Park Drive, Suite 35, Toronto, Ont. M4H 1H2
(416) 425-9106
Contact: Sami Kelada, president
Established 1970. Publishes books that teach French as a second language, mostly high-interest, low vocabulary materials.

Arsenal Pulp Press Book Publishing Ltd.
986 Hunter Street, Suite 202, Vancouver, B.C. V6B 2W7
(604) 687-4233
Contact: Briam Lam or Steve Gunner, office managers
Established 1972. Publishes fiction, non-fiction, literary, trade, native art, politics, and children's books.

Asquith House Ltd.
94 Asquith Avenue, Toronto, Ont. M4W 1J8
(416) 925-3577
Contact: Michael Preston, acquisitions editor
Mostly publishes school education books.

Avon Books of Canada
2061 McCowan Road, Suite 201, Scarborough, Ont. M1S 3Y6
(416) 293-9404
Contact: Peter Austin, acquisitions editor
Publishes trade books in many categories, mostly non-fiction.

Aya Press
P.O. Box 1153, Station F, Toronto, Ont. M4Y 2T8
Contact: Beverley Daurio, publisher
Established 1978. Publishes high-quality trade editions of Canadian poetry, fiction, and children's literature.

Bantam Books Canada Inc.
60 St. Clair Avenue E., Suite 601, Toronto, Ont. M4T 1N5
(416) 922-4970
Publishes fiction and non-fiction aimed at a mass market. Will not accept unsolicited manuscripts.

Between the Lines
229 College Street, Toronto, Ont. M5T 1R4
(416) 597-0328
Contact: Robert Clarke, editor
Established 1977. Publishes non-fiction books on Canadian social and political issues, culture, and Third World development.

Black Moss Press
1939 Alsace Street, Windsor, Ont. N8W 1M5
(519) 252-2551
Contact: Marty Gervais, president
Established 1976. Publishes fiction, poetry, and children's books.

Black Rose Books
3981 St. Laurent Boulevard, 4th Floor, Montreal, Que. H2W 1Y5
(514) 844-4076
Contact: Josée Hershbain, promotions
Established 1970. Publishes critical studies of Canadian and other industrial societies.

Borealis Press Ltd.
9 Ashburn Drive, Ottawa, Ont. K2E 6N4
(613) 224-8837
Contact: Glen Clever, editor
Publishes poetry, fiction, and general material, preferably with Canadian authorship and interest.

Boston Mill Press, The
98 Main Street, Erin, Ont. N0B 1T0
(519) 833-2407
Contact: John Denison, president
Established 1974. Specializes in historical works, mostly local or regional.

Breakwater Books Ltd.
277 Duckworth Street, P.O. Box 2188, St. John's, Nfld. A1C 6E6
(709) 722-6680

Contact: Clyde Rose, president
Established 1973. Publishes educational materials and a wide selection of manuscripts about Atlantic Canada – plays, poetry, satire, biography, songbooks, cookbooks, fiction.

Brick Books
P.O. Box 219, Ilderton, Ont. N0M 2A0
(519) 666-0283
Contact: Don McKay, publisher
Established 1972. Publishes literary works, mainly poetry.

Brunswick Press
12 Prospect Street W., P.O. Box 3370, Fredericton, N.B. E3B 5A2
(506) 455-6671
Contact: Tom Crowther, publisher
Established 1951. Publishes Canadian works of interest to the Atlantic Provinces.

Butterworth and Company (Canada) Limited
2265 Midland Avenue, Scarborough, Ont. M1P 4S1
(416) 292-1421
Contact: Geoffrey Burn, acquisitions editor
Established 1912. Specializes in legal, business, and educational publishing.

Butterworth and Company (Western Canada) Limited
409 Granville Street, Suite 1455, Vancouver, B.C. V6C 1T2
(604) 684-4116
Contact: J. Michaud, editor
Established 1978 as a division of Butterworth and Company (Canada) Limited. Specializes in the fields of law and education. Also publishes in England, New Zealand, and South Africa.

Camden House Publishing Ltd.
7 Queen Victoria Road, Camden East, Ont. K0K 1J0
(613) 378-6661
Contact: Frank Edwards, managing editor
Established 1976. Publishes anthologies from *Harrowsmith* magazine and books on gardening, cooking, natural sciences, astronomy, wildlife, and history.

Canada Law Book Limited
240 Edward Street, Aurora, Ont. L4G 3S9
(416) 773-6300
Contact: A.D. Marks, editor
Publishes manuscripts dealing with the law.

Canadian Arctic Resources Committee
46 Elgin Street, Room 11, Ottawa, Ont. K1P 5K6
(613) 236-7379

Contact: Danna Leaman, editor
Established 1971. Publishes manuscripts pertaining to Canada's North: people, environment, and resource development.

Canadian Council of Social Development, The
55 Parkdale, P.O. Box 3505, Station C, Ottawa, Ont. K1Y 4G1
(613) 728-1865
Contact: Jean-Guy Carrier, editor
Established 1920. Publishes in English and in French on law, politics, housing, social policy, personal social services, healthcare, and income security.

Canadian Institute of International Affairs
15 King's College Circle, Toronto, Ont. M5S 2V9
(416) 979-1851
Contact: Clarence Shepard, president
Established 1928. Publishes Canadiana, education, literature, juvenile, and women's social issues, in English and in French.

Canadian Plains Research Centre
University of Regina, Regina, Sask. S4S 0A2
(306) 584-4795
Contact: Gillian Wadsworth Minifie, manager
Established 1973. Publishes scholarly material on all aspects of the Plains region.

Canterbury House
760 Somerset Street W., Ottawa, Ont. K1R 6P9
(613) 563-0565
Contact: Don Meakin, general manager
Established 1955. Specializes in religious books.

Carswell Legal Publications
2330 Midland Avenue, Agincourt, Ont. M1S 1P7
(416) 291-8421
Contact: J.A. Mullin, chairman
Toronto office:
120 York Street, Toronto, Ont. M5H 3P2
(416) 291-8421
Western office:
1520 4th Street S.W., Suite 280, Calgary, Alta. T2R 1H5
Established 1894. Publishes business, economics, and educational texts for primary and secondary schools and colleges. Also specializes in history, law, politics, science, and drama.

Centre Educatif et Culturel Inc.
8101 Metropolitan Boulevard E., Montreal, Que. H1J 1J9
(514) 351-6010
Specializes in French language children's books.

Choice Publications Ltd.
6 Denison Street, Markham, Ont. L3R 1B6
(416) 475-0211
Contact: C.W. Scheifele, editor
Established 1972. Publishes children's books, but is mainly a distributor.

Clare Educational Development Inc.
4188 Virginia Crescent, North Vancouver, B.C. V7R 3Z6
(604) 980-2598
Contact: William Clare, publisher
Mainly interested in manuscripts on education techniques.

Clock House Publications
P.O. Box 103, Peterborough, Ont. K9J 6Y5
(705) 742-6809
Contact: Peter Unitt, president
Established 1968. Specializes in books on antiques and collectables.

Coach House Press, The
401 (rear) Huron Street, Toronto, Ont. M5S 2G5
(416) 979-2217
Contact: Diane Martin, managing editor
Established 1965. Publishes fiction, photography, drama, and poetry.

Coles Publishing Company Ltd.
90 Ronson Drive, Rexdale, Ont. M9W 1C1
(416) 243-3132
Contact: Carol Hope, director of marketing
Established 1965. Publishes trade books, paperbacks, and educational reviews and critiques.

Collier Macmillan Canada Inc.
50 Gervais Drive, Don Mills, Ont. M3C 3K4
(416) 449-6030
Contact: Patrick Gallagher, managing editor
Publishes general, professional and reference books, medical books, and textbooks for the elementary, secondary school, college, and university levels.

Wm. Collins Sons & Co. Canada Ltd.
100 Lesmill Road, Don Mills, Ont. M3B 2T5
(416) 445-8221
Contact: Kathryn Schroeder, assistant editor
Established 1932. Publishes a wide assortment of reference and trade books, mostly non-fiction. Also publishes children's books.

David C. Cook Publishing (Canada) Ltd.
4141 Weston Road, Unit 15, Weston, Ont. M9L 1T4

(416) 749-1431
Contact: Robert West, business manager
Specializes in short stories on religious and life-related subjects.

Copp Clark Pitman Ltd.
2775 Matheson Boulevard E., Mississauga, Ont. L4W 4P7
(416) 238-5473
Contact: Stephen Mills, acquisitions editor
Publishes educational manuscripts for elementary and secondary schools, and colleges and universities.

Corpus Information Services Ltd.
1450 Don Mills Road, Don Mills, Ont. M3B 2X7
(416) 445-7101
Contact: Margot Fawcett, publisher
Specializes in works on business and the sciences, plus dictionaries and reference books.

Coteau Books/Thunder Creek Publishing Co-op.
2337 McIntyre Street, Regina, Sask. S4P 2S3
(306) 352-5346
Contact: Catherine Edwards, managing editor
Established 1975. Publishes poetry, short stories, novels, books on writers and writing, readers' guides, anthologies, children's stories, and drama.

Crabtree Publishing Co. Ltd.
102 Torbrick Road, Toronto, Ont. M4J 4Z5
(416) 463-8094/465-4120
Contact: Peter Crabtree, president
Established 1978. Publishes children's illustrated books, and elementary school and social studies textbooks.

Creative Publishers
803 Water Street, St. John's, Nfld. A1C 5M3
(709) 726-6590
Contact: Donald Morgan, publisher
Publishes books by Newfoundland writers.

Harry Cuff Publications Ltd.
1 Dorset Street, St. John's, Nfld. A1B 1W8
(709) 726-6590
Contact: Douglas Cuff, editor
Established 1981. Publishes books about Newfoundland by Newfoundlanders.

Deneau Publishers
760 Bathurst Street, Toronto, Ont. M5S 2R6
(416) 530-1035

Contact: Denis Deneau, publisher
Established 1977. Publishes fiction and non-fiction.

Detselig Enterprises Ltd.
P.O. Box G399, Calgary, Alta. T3A 2G3
(403) 283-0900
Contact: Ted Giles, president
Established 1976. Publishes college and university textbooks, and general-interest trade non-fiction.

Dominie Press Ltd.
1361 Huntingwood Drive, Unit 7, Agincourt, Ont. M1S 3J1
(416) 291-5857
Contact: Raymond Yuen, editor
Established 1975. Publishes educational textbooks and children's books.

Doubleday Canada Ltd.
105 Bond Street, Toronto, Ont. M5B 1Y3
(416) 977-7891
Contact: Peter Maik, president
Established 1944. Interested in Canadiana, children's books, adult fiction and non-fiction, and educational texts.

Douglas Gibson Books
c/o McClelland and Stewart Ltd.,
481 University Avenue, 9th Floor, Toronto, Ont. M5G 2E9
(416) 598-1114
Contact: Doug Gibson, publisher
General trade books. No unsolicited fiction. Query non-fiction.

Douglas & McIntyre (Educational) Ltd.
1615 Venables Street, Vancouver, B.C. V5L 2H1
(604) 255-7701
Contact: Linda Turnbull, sales and marketing manager
Established 1981. Specializes in elementary and high school learning materials.

Douglas & McIntyre Ltd.
1615 Venables Street, Vancouver, B.C. V5L 2H1
(604) 254-7191
Contact: Michael Scott, advertising and promotions
Toronto office:
26 Lennox Street, Toronto, Ont. M6G 1J4
(416) 537-2501
Contact: Kelly Mitchell, advertising and promotions
Established 1964. Publishes general trade books but specializes in Western Canadian biography, art, outdoors and recreation, and Northwest Coast anthropology.

Dreadnaught Co-operative Inc.
46 Harbord Street, Toronto, Ont. M5S 1G2
(416) 977-0769
Contact: Elizabeth Abraham, managing director
Established 1976. Publishes non-fiction for adults and children.

Dundurn Press Ltd.
1558 Queen Street E., Toronto, Ont. M4L 1E8
(416) 461-1881
Contact: Kirk Howard, president
Established 1974. Publishes Canadian history, biography, art, and literary criticism.

ECW Press
207 Coxwell Avenue, Toronto, Ont. M4L 3B5
(416) 694-3348
Contact: Jack David, publisher
Established 1974. Publishes reference books and literary criticism on Canadian writers and their works.

Eden Press
4626 Ste-Catherine Street W., Montreal, Que. H3Z 1S3
(514) 931-3910
Contact: Pamela Chichinskas, publisher
Established 1976. Publishes non-fiction trade books, scholarly, medical, and scientific works.

Encyclopedia Britannica Publications Ltd.
175 Holiday Inn Drive, P.O. Box 2249, Cambridge, Ont. N3C 3N4
(416) 691-1054
Contact: David Durnan, president
Produces textbooks, educational films, filmstrips, and other audio-visual material.

Ergo Productions
P.O. Box 4460, London, Ont. N5W 5J2
(519) 432-4357
Contact: Winston Schell, president
Established 1977. Publishes fiction, poetry, humour, and non-fiction, by writers from Southwestern Ontario.

Exile Editions Ltd.
69 Sullivan Street, Toronto, Ont. M5T 1C2
(416) 977-7937
Contact: Barry Callaghan, president
Established 1976. Publishes fiction, drama, poetry, and fiction and poetry in translation.

Fforbez Publications Ltd.
2133 Quebec Street, Vancouver, B.C. V5T 2Z9

(604) 534-2462
Contact: P.W. Zebroff, editor
Established 1971. Specializes in educational textbooks, mainly at the primary and secondary school levels. Also publishes health topics such as fitness and nutrition, and nutrition cookbooks.

Fiddlehead Poetry Books/Goose Lane Editions
132 Saunders Street, Fredericton, N.B. E3B 1N3
(506) 454-8319
Contact: Rebecca Leaman, managing editor
Established 1958. Publishes Canadian fiction, non-fiction, and poetry.

Fifth House
406 Clarence Avenue S., Saskatoon, Sask. S7H 2C7
(306) 242-4936
Contact: Caroline Heath, president
Established 1983. Publishes general trade material.

Fitzhenry & Whiteside Ltd.
195 Allstate Parkway, Markham, Ont. L3R 4T8
(416) 477-0030
Contact: Robert Read, vice-president
Established 1966. Publishes a wide selection of general trade books, audio visual materials, and elementary, high school, and college textbooks.

Formac Publishing Co. Ltd.
5359 Inglis Street, Halifax, N.S. B3H 1J4
(902) 421-7022
Contact: Carolyn MacGregor, publisher
Established 1977. Publishes regional titles including history, folklore, cookbooks, guidebooks, and Canadian biography.

Four East Publications
P.O. Box 29, Tantallon, Halifax County, N.S. B0J 3J0
(902) 923-2279
Contact: Richard Rogers, publisher
Established 1979. Publishes non-fiction about the Atlantic Provinces.

Fraser Institute, The
626 Bute Street, Vancouver, B.C. V6E 3M1
(604) 688-0221
Contact: Sally Pipes, assistant director
Established 1974. Publishes material on economic and public policy issues.

Frederick Harris Music Co. Ltd., The
529 Speers Road, Oakville, Ont. L6K 2G4

(416) 845-3487
Contact: W. Gilpin, general manager
Established 1904. Publishes music and books on music.

Gage Educational Publishing Corporation
164 Commander Boulevard, Agincourt, Ont. M1S 3C7
(416) 293-8141
Contact: Sylvia Gilchrist, vice-president, editorial
Established 1844. Publishes trade books and educational texts for elementary, secondary, and post-secondary schools, colleges and universities.

Garamond Press
67A Portland Street, Toronto, Ont. M5V 2M9
(416) 597-1527
Contact: Peter Saunders, director
Established 1981. Publishes academic and university texts.

General Publishing Co. Ltd.
30 Lesmill Road, Don Mills, Ont. M3B 2T6
(416) 445-3333
Contact: Carol Duffield, editorial department
Established 1957. Most releases are reprints of previously published material: art, business, economics, education (at the primary, secondary, and college levels), fiction, history, law, natural history, pets, photography, politics, science, sports, theatre. Also publishes reference books and mass-market paperbacks.

General Store Publishing House Inc.
1 Main Street, Burnstown, Ont. K0J 1G0
(613) 432-7697
Contact: Tim Gordon, president
Established 1980. Publishes history, cookbooks, children's books, and magazines.

Ginn & Company
3771 Victoria Park Avenue, Scarborough, Ont. M1W 2P9
(416) 497-4600
Contact: Richard Lee, president
Established 1867. Publishes books for elementary and high schools, particularly in the language arts, social sciences, and mathematics. Does not read unsolicited manuscripts.

GLC Publishers Ltd.
115 Nugget Avenue, Agincourt, Ont. M1S 3B1
(416) 291-2926
Contact: Doug Panasis, editor
Established 1970. Publishes children's books, educational texts at the primary and secondary school levels, reference works, audio-visual materials, and music.

Globe/Modern Curriculum Press
200 Steelcase Road E., Markham, Ont. L3R 1G2
(416) 497-4699
Contact: Mary Macchiusi, vice-president, editorial
Established 1975. Interested in manuscripts pertaining to education at the primary and secondary school levels. Also publishes college textbooks.

Gray's Publishing Ltd.
P.O. Box 2160, Sidney, B.C. V8L 3S6
(604) 656-4454
Contact: Gordon Cooper, president
Established 1962. Publishes books on Canadian history, natural history, biography, Métis culture, outdoor adventure, and seafaring. Also considers some regional fiction.

Greey de Pencier Books
56 The Esplanade, Suite 306, Toronto, Ont. M5E 1A7
(416) 868-6001
Contact: Sheba Meland, editorial director
Established 1968. Publishes general-interest trade books, how-to books and manuals, city guides, and texts about science, nature, and the environment for children.

Grolier Ltd.
16 Overlea Boulevard, Toronto, Ont. M4H 1A6
(416) 425-1924
Contact: Kenneth Pearson, vice-president
Publishes reference and single-title educational texts.

Grosvenor House Press Inc.
111 Queen Street E., Suite 375, Toronto, Ont. M5C 1S2
(416) 364-5510
Contact: Ian Burgham, president
Montreal office:
1456 Sherbrooke Street W., Suite 301, Montreal, Que. H3G 1K4
(514) 284-1138
Contact: Barry Schreiber, managing director
Established 1982. Publishes paperbacks for the general trade market.

Guidance Centre, The
Faculty of Education, University of Toronto, 252 Bloor Street W., Toronto, Ont. M5S 2Y3
(416) 978-3206
Contact: S.J. Totton, manager
Publishes manuscripts concerning guidance and counselling, educational administration, and general education.

Hancock House Publishers
19313 Zero Avenue, Surrey, B.C. V3S 5J9
(604) 538-1114
Contact: David Hancock, editor
Specializes in non-fiction adventures, popular natural history, anthropology, and human history. Also publishes academic reference books for trades and institutions.

Harbour Publishing Co. Ltd.
P.O. Box 219, Madeira Park, B.C. V0N 2H0
(604) 883-2730
Contact: Howard White, president
Established 1974. Publishes books on British Columbia regional history and culture, both literary and non-fiction. Specializes in B.C. authors.

Harcourt Brace Jovanovich, Canada
55 Barber Greene Road, Don Mills, Ont. M3C 2A1
(416) 444-7331
Contact: Anthony Craven, editor
Publishes school, college, and trade books.

Harlequin Enterprises Ltd.
225 Duncan Mill Road, Don Mills, Ont. M3B 1Z3
(416) 445-5860
Contact: Brian Hickey, editor
Established 1949. Interested in receiving outlines or manuscripts, particularly those with series potential in either fiction or non-fiction. Publishes mass-market paperback romances.

Hartley & Marks Ltd.
3663 West Broadway Street, Vancouver, B.C. V6R 2B8
(604) 738-0644
Contact: Victor Marks, president
Established 1973. Publishes architecture, building, fine wood-working, non-traditional medicine, country living, and technical manuscripts.

Harvest House Ltd.
2335 Sherbrooke Street W., Suite 206, Montreal, Que. H3H 1G6
(514) 932-0666
Contact: Maynard Gertler, editor
Established 1959. Publishes general trade books, with special interest in history, biography, science, and the social sciences.

Hayes Publishing Ltd.
3312 Mainway, Burlington, Ont. L7M 1A7
(416) 335-0393

Contact: Cyril Hayes, president
Specializes in children's books, and educational texts for primary and secondary schools and colleges.

D.C. Heath Canada Ltd.
100 Adelaide Street W., Suite 1600, Toronto, Ont. M5H 1S9
(416) 362-6483
Contact: Robert Ross, editor
Publishes college and school textbooks, and some general-interest trade books.

Herald Press
117 King Street W., Kitchener, Ont. N2G 4M5
(519) 743-9731
Contact: Paul Schrock, editor
Established 1908 in the U.S., and 1974 in Canada. Publishes works on family life, Christian community, peace, a disciplined Church, and programs of evangelistic and mission outreach. Specializes in books for children aged nine to fourteen, and Christian or religious fiction.

Henson College of Public Affairs and Continuing Education
Dalhousie University, Halifax, N.S. B3H 3J5
(902) 424-2526
Contact: Dr. Michael Cross, dean
Established 1936. Publishes manuscripts and discussion papers on public affairs, research, and community development.

Heritage House Publishing Co. Ltd.
5543 - 129th Street, Surrey, B.C. V3W 4H4
(604) 596-5245
Contact: Art Downs, president
Established 1969. Specializes in original works on genealogy, history, and travel in Western Canada.

Highway Book Shop
Cobalt, Ont. P0J 1C0
(705) 679-8375
Contact: Paul Bogart, general manager
Established 1970. Publishes adult trade, fiction, non-fiction and children's books–all by northern authors and with northern themes.

Holt, Rinehart & Winston of Canada Ltd.
55 Horner Avenue, Toronto, Ont. M8Z 4X6
(416) 255-4491
Contact: Mark Stewart, acquisitions editor
Established 1904. Publishes manuscripts on business and econo-

mics, and educational texts, primarily at the secondary school and college levels.

Horsdal & Schubart Publishers Ltd.
P.O. Box 1, Ganges, B.C. V0S 1E0
(604) 537-4334
Contact: Maralyn Horsdal, president
Established 1985. Specializes in Canadian non-fiction, with an emphasis on western history and biography.

Hosford Publishing Ltd.
17203 - 103rd Avenue, Edmonton, Alta. T5S 1J4
(403) 483-2683
Contact: Rick Checkland, editor
Publishes school books.

Houghton Mifflin, Canada Ltd.
150 Steelcase Road W., Markham, Ont. L3R 1B2
(416) 475-1755
Contact: John Champ, editor
Established in Canada in 1974. Publishes educational texts at the primary, secondary school, and college levels.

Hounslow Press
124 Parkview Avenue, Willowdale, Ont. M2N 3Y5
(416) 225-9176
Contact: Tony Hawke, president
Established 1972. Publishes picture books, cookbooks, popular non-fiction, some poetry, and novels.

House of Anansi Press Limited
35 Britain Street, Toronto, Ont. M5A 1R7
(416) 363-5444
Contact: Ann Wall, publisher
Established 1967. Specializes in non-fiction, contemporary social issues, literary criticism, fiction, and poetry by Canadian authors.

Hurtig Publishers
10560 - 105th Street, Edmonton, Alta. T5H 2W7
(403) 426-2359
Contact: Elizabeth Monroe, editor
Established 1961. Publishes Canadian non-fiction, particularly art, history, politics, biography, native culture, and nature.

Hyperion Press Ltd.
300 Wales Avenue, Winnipeg, Man. R2M 2S9
(204) 256-9204
Contact: Dr. Marvis Tutiah, president, or Arlene Osen, vice-president

Established 1978. Publishes non-fiction, social comment, politics, ethnic studies, how-to, and children's books.

International Self-Counsel Press Ltd.
306 W. 25th Street, North Vancouver, B.C. V7N 2G1
(604) 986-3366
Contact: Diana Douglas, president
Established 1971. Specializes in books on law, business, and personal health. Also publishes reference books.

IPI Publishing Ltd.
44 Charles Street W., Suite 2704, Toronto, Ont. M4Y 1R7
(416) 964-6662
Contact: Dr. Daniel Baum, editor
Established 1976. Publishes books – in English and in French – on business, education (primarily at the secondary school and college levels), history, law, medicine, and politics.

Irwin Publishing Company
180 West Beaver Creek Road, Richmond Hill, Ont. L4B 1B4
(416) 731-3838
Contact: Don Bastian, editor
Established 1945. Specializes in books for elementary and high schools, colleges, and trade. Also publishes some novels and biographies.

Is Five Press
467 Richmond Street E., Toronto, Ont. M5A 1R1
(416) 366-1518
Contact: Tom Scanlan, managing editor
Established 1976. Publishes manuscripts on social and educational concerns.

Jesperson Press
26A Flavin Street, St. John's, Nfld. A1C 3R9
(709) 753-5700
Contact: John Symonds, general manager
Established 1977. Specializes in trade and educational books.

Key Porter Books
70 The Esplanade, 2nd Floor, Toronto, Ont. M5E 1R2
(416) 862-7777
Contact: Gloria Goodman, assistant to the president
Established 1981. Publishes non-fiction books, primarily in architecture, art, business, history, natural history, photography, politics, sports, and theatre.

Kids Can Press Ltd.
585 Bloor Street W., Toronto, Ont. M6G 1K5
(416) 534-6389

Contact: Valerie Hussey, editor
Established 1973. Publishes picture books and non-fiction books for children, and adult books that relate to children. Prefers non-sexist, multicultural stories about city living.

Kosoy Travel Guides
112 Fairholme Avenue, Toronto, Ont. M6B 2W9
(416) 783-8578
Contact: Ted Kosoy, publisher
Established 1971. Specializes in travel guides.

Lancelot Press Ltd.
P.O. Box 425, Hantsport, N.S. B0P 1P0
(902) 684-9129
Contact: William Pope, president
Established 1966. Publishes non-fiction of particular interest to Atlantic Canada, and general trade books.

J.M. LeBel Enterprises Ltd.
6027 - 103A Street, Edmonton, Alta. T6H 2J7
(403) 436-8205
Contact: John LeBel, president, or K.C. Conroy, manager
Established 1972. Publishes Canadian children's books, children's historical fiction, educational and general books, and science and mathematics textbooks.

Lester & Orpen Dennys Ltd.
78 Sullivan Street, Toronto, Ont. M5T 1C1
(416) 593-9602
Contact: Gena Gorrell, senior editor
Established 1973. Publishes fiction, non-fiction, biography, history, art, young adult, politics, and social issues – a wide selection of adult general-trade books.

Lilith Publications Inc.
32 Lipton Street, Winnipeg, Man. R3G 2G5
(204) 774-7960
Contact: Adena Franz, president
Established 1984. Publishes books of any genre authored by women who write from a feminist perspective.

Log House Publishing Co. Ltd.
R.R. 1, Pender Island, B.C. V0N 2M0
(604) 629-6521
Contact: Mary Mackie, editor
Established 1977. Specializes in books about log construction.

Lone Pine Publishing
10357 - 109th Street, Suite 414, Edmonton, Alta. T5J 1N3
(403) 424-1278

Contact: Grant Kennedy, president
Established 1980. Publishes trade books with a particular emphasis on Canada's Northwest, its people and wildlife.

Longspoon Press
University of Alberta, Department of English,
Edmonton, Alta. T6G 2E5
(403) 432-9427
Contact: Shirley Neuman, vice-president
Established 1980. Primarily a poetry press, with special interest in modern experimental literature.

James Lorimer & Co. Ltd.
35 Britain Street, Toronto, Ont. M5A 1R7
(416) 362-4762
Contact: Curtis Fahey, editor
Established 1971. Specializes in general Canadian trade books on politics, history, economics, cooking, urban studies, and social issues. Also publishes some children's books.

Macmillan of Canada
146 Front Street W., Suite 685, Toronto, Ont. M5J 1G2
(416) 597-1060
Contact: Linda McKnight, publisher
Publishes a variety of general trade books, plus texts dealing with medicine and education at post-school levels.

McClelland and Stewart Ltd.
481 University Avenue, 9th Floor, Toronto, Ont. M5G 2E9
(416) 598-1114
Contact: Victoria Gruden, assistant editor
Established 1906. Publishes a wide selection of fiction, and non-fiction books on art, biography, economics, history, natural history, photography, poetry, religion, and sports. Also publishes reference books, and textbooks at the primary, secondary, and college levels.

McGill-Queen's University Press
McGill University, 849 Sherbrooke Street W.,
Montreal, Que. H3A 2T5
(514) 392-4421
Contact: Philip Cercone, editor
Queen's University office:
Watson Hall, Queen's University, Kingston, Ont. K7L 3N6
(613) 547-6614
Contact: Prof. Donald Akenson, or Prof. Peter Goheen, editors
Established 1969. Publishes scholarly books on Arctic and Northern studies and history, and political science with special emphasis on Canadian urban life, Commonwealth and Canadian literature, architecture, philosophy and religion, North American Native Peoples, anthropology, and sociology.

McGraw-Hill Ryerson Ltd.
330 Progress Avenue, Scarborough, Ont. M1P 2Z5
(416) 293-1911
Contact: Michael Richardson, editor
Established 1944. Specializes in reference and college and school books on many subjects. Also publishes general trade manuscripts, fiction and non-fiction.

P.D. Meany Publishers
P.O. Box 534, Port Credit, Ont. L5G 4M2
(416) 274-3049
Contact: Patrick Meany, editor
Established 1976. Specializes in scholarly publications.

Charles E. Merrill Publishing
230 Barmac Drive, Weston, Ont. M9L 2X5
(416) 746-2200
Contact: Linda Milne, editor
Publishes college and school textbooks.

Micromedia Ltd.
144 Front Street W., Toronto, Ont. M5J 2L7
(416) 593-5211
Contact: Robert Gibson, president
Established 1972. Publishes business and economics books, reference works, government documents, and Canadian patents.

Mika Publishing Company
200 Stanley Street, P.O. Box 536, Belleville, Ont. K8N 5B2
(613) 962-4022
Contact: Helma Mika, editor
Established 1962. Specializes in local Canadian histories: county, township, and city.

Milestone Publication Ltd.
P.O. Box 2248, Sidney, B.C. V6L 3S8
(604) 653-7312
Contact: Guy Chadsey, editor
Established 1973. Publishes travel books, and manuscripts on Western Canadian history, and natural history.

Mosaic Press
1252 Speer Road, Suite 10, P.O. Box 1032, Oakville, Ont. L6J 5E9
(416) 825-2130
Contact: Howard Aster, editor
Established 1974. Publishes literary and scholarly works–poetry, fiction, criticism, social sciences, humanities, and ethnic studies.

National Museums of Canada
Ottawa, Ont. K1A 0M8

(613) 993-0742/990-1447
Contact: Sharron Doyle, marketing officer
Established 1968. Publishes non-fiction books relating to the museums' collections.

NC Press Ltd.
31 Portland Street, Toronto, Ont. M5V 2V9
(416) 593-6284
Contact: Caroline Walker, editor
Primarily interested in children's books, and others on art, economics, history, poetry, politics, theatre, and cooking. Also publishes novels.

Nelson Canada
1120 Birchmount Road, Scarborough, Ont. M1K 5G4
(416) 752-9100
Contact: Martin Keast, vice-president, publishing
Established in Canada 1914. Publishes children's books, fiction, general non-fiction, and education texts at the elementary and secondary school levels.

Netherlandic Press
1176 Ouellette Avenue, Suite 1004, Windsor, Ont. N9A 6S9
(519) 252-2986
Contact: Joan Magee, editor
Established 1981. Specializes in the literature, history, art, and music of the Netherlandic culture, and in works by Dutch and Flemish immigrants.

New American Library of Canada Ltd.
81 Mack Avenue, Scarborough, Ont. M1L 1M8
(416) 699-7193
Established 1951. Publishes fiction with mass market appeal.

New Star Books
2504 York Avenue, Vancouver, B.C. V6K 1E3
(604) 738-9429
Contact: Lanny Beckman, publisher
Established 1974. Publishes manuscripts on feminism, socialism, labour, Canadian politics, and Third World issues.

NeWest Publishers Ltd.
8631 - 109th Street, Suite 204, Edmonton, Alta. T6G 1E8
(403) 432-9427
Contact: Jack Lewis, general manager
Established 1977. Publishes literature and non-fiction pertaining to Western Canada.

Nightwood Editions
P.O. Box 5432, Station A, Toronto, Ont. M5W 1N6

(416) 534-0392
Contact: Maureen Cochrane or David Lee, editors
Established 1965. Publishes literary books on music and cinema.

Nimbus Publishing Ltd.
6371 Lady Hammond Road, P.O. Box 9301, Station A,
Halifax, N.S. B3K 5N5
(902) 455-4286
Contact: Dan Sargeant, editor
Established 1978. Publishes general trade and educational material.

Oberon Press
401A Delta Ottawa, 350 Sparks Street, Ottawa, Ont. K1R 7S8
(603) 238-3275
Contact: Nicholas Macklem, general manager
Established 1966. Publishes Canadian fiction, poetry, history, biography, art, and children's books.

OISE Press
252 Bloor Street W., Toronto, Ont. M5S 1V6
(416) 923-6641
Contact: Hugh Oliver, editor
Established 1965 by the Ontario Institute for Studies in Education. Publishes educational texts for teachers, students, and educational researchers: curriculum materials, educational research, administrative planning, and professional development materials.

Oolichan Books
P.O. Box 10, Lantzville, B.C. V0R 2H0
(604) 390-4839
Contact: Ron Smith, editor
Established 1974. Publishes poetry, fiction, regional history, children's, and special limited editions.

Outcrop Ltd.
P.O. Box 1350, Yellowknife, N.W.T. X1A 2N9
(403) 920-4652
Contact: Ronne Heming, vice-president
Established 1975. Publishes general non-fiction about Canada's North.

Oxford University Press
70 Wynford Drive, Don Mills, Ont. M3C 1J9
(416) 441-2941
Contact: Michael Morrow, acquisitions editor
Publishes general Canadiana, children's books, and educational texts at the school and college levels.

PaperJacks Ltd.
330 Steelcase Road E., Markham, Ont. L3R 2M1

(416) 475-1261
Contact: Coleen Dimson, senior editor
Interested in all areas of mass-market publication, fiction, non-fiction, biography, and how-to books.

Peguis Publishers Ltd.
462 Hargrave Street, Winnipeg, Man. R3A 0X5
(204) 956-1486
Contact: Mary Scorer, editor
Regional publishers of trade books, and college and school texts.

Pemmican Publications Inc.
504 Main Street, Suite 411, Winnipeg, Man. R3B 1B8
(204) 942-0926
Contact: Beatrice Culleton, manager
Established 1980. Publishes books of concern or interest to Native people, particularly the Métis.

Pendragon House Limited
2525 Dunwin Drive, Mississauga, Ont. L5L 1T2
(416) 828-0400
Contact: John Badger, editor
Established 1962. Specializes in educational texts (primary, secondary school and college), history (Canadiana), and medical texts.

Penguin Books Canada Ltd.
2801 John Street, Markham, Ont. L3R 1B4
(416) 475-1571
Contact: Morton Mint, acquisitions editor
Publishes a wide selection of books, fiction, non-fiction, and educational. Always query before sending a manuscript.

Penumbra Press
P.O. Box 340, Moonbeam, Ont. P0L 1V0
(705) 335-2988
Contact: John Flood, president
Established 1979. Publishes literary, art, and children's books.

Pergamon Press Canada Ltd.
150 Consumers Road, Suite 104, Willowdale, Ont. M2J 1P9
(416) 497-8337
Contact: Donald Crawley, editor
Publishes manuscripts relating to the social sciences, particularly behaviour, and business.

Petheric Press Ltd.
P.O. Box 9310, Station A, Halifax, N.S. B3K 5N5
(902) 454-8381
Contact: Dan Sargeant, manager
Mostly publishes works on the history of the Maritimes.

Playwrights Union of Canada
8 York Street, 6th Floor, Toronto, Ont. M5J 1R2
(416) 947-0201
Contact: Jane Buss, executive director
Established 1972. Publishes Canadian plays in single editions, anthologies, and collections. Also publishes bibliographies, histories, translations, and drama criticism. All unsolicited manuscripts, to be accompanied by a reading fee, must have had professional theatre or media production.

Polestar Press Ltd.
R.R. 1, Winlaw, B.C. V0G 2J0
(604) 226-7670
Contact: T.W. Bluefield, editor
Established 1981. Publishes general trade books, with special emphasis on sports, business, current affairs, and children's non-fiction. Also publishes some novels.

Pontifical Institute of Mediaeval Studies
59 Queen's Park Crescent E., Toronto, Ont. M5S 2C4
(416) 926-7144
Contact: Ron Thomson, director of publications
Established 1939. Specializes in scholarly publications about the Middle Ages.

Porcupine's Quill Inc., The
68 Main Street, Erin, Ont. N0B 1T0
(519) 833-9158/(416) 454-2001
Contact: Ann Reatherford, general manager
Established 1974. Specializes in Canadian literature.

Potlatch Publications Ltd.
99 John Street S., Hamilton, Ont. L8N 2C2
(416) 528-2302
Contact: Robert Nielsen, president
Established 1972. Publishes the *Canadian Children's Annual*, which includes short stories, articles, poems, and activities for Canadian children aged from nine to thirteen.

Pottersfield Press
R.R. 2, Potters Lake, N.S. B0J 2S0
(902) 827-4517
Contact: Leslie Choyce, editor
Established 1979. Publishes short fiction, poetry, and books of interest to Atlantic Canada.

Prairie Publishing Company, The
P.O. Box 264, Station C, Winnipeg, Man. R3M 3S7
(204) 885-6469
Contact: Ralph Watkins, editor

Established 1969. Interested in manuscripts relating to the Prairies on architecture, art, and history. Also publishes children's books and biography.

Prentice-Hall Canada Inc.
1870 Birchmount Road, Scarborough, Ont. M1P 2J7
(416) 293-3621
Contact: Wallace Matheson, editor
Specializes in non-fiction manuscripts on history, natural history, politics, and sports, as well as education texts aimed at all levels of school and college.

Press Gang Publishers
603 Powell Street, Vancouver, B.C. V6A 1H2
(604) 253-2537
Contact: Barbara Kuhne, production coordinator
Established 1974. Specializes in Canadian women's writing.

Press Porcépic Ltd.
560 Johnson Street, Suite 235, Victoria, B.C. V8W 3C6
(604) 381-5502
Contact: Gerry Truscott, editor
Established 1971. Publishes new novelists and poets, particularly in translation from Québecois French. Also interested in children's literature, college-level education, theatre, literary criticism, humour, Canadian history, politics, computer technology, and business. Well known for publishing controversial works by Canadian authors.

Prise de Parole Inc.
P.O. Box 550, Station B, Sudbury, Ont. P3E 4R2
(705) 675-6491
Contact: Gaston Tremblay, editor
Established 1973. Publishes poetry, essays, novels, and educational texts in French.

Progress Books
71 Bathurst Street, 3rd Floor, Toronto, Ont. M5V 2P6
(416) 368-3550/368-5336
Contact: Anna Larson, manager
Established 1935. Publishes works on Canadian political and labour history, and on social commentary.

Quarry Press, The
P.O. Box 1061, Kingston, Ont. K7L 4Y5
(613) 376-3584
Contact: Bob Hilderley, president
Established 1965. Publishes poetry, fiction, educational texts, children's books, and manuscripts about theatre and drama.

Queenston House Publishing Company Ltd.
1584 Erin Street, Winnipeg, Man. R3E 2T1
(204) 775-1512
Contact: Joan Parr, editor
Established 1974. Publishes children's books, educational texts for all levels, novels, poetry, and books on history and architecture. Keenly interested in biographies and original views of local history. Encourages new writers.

Ragweed Press Inc.
145 Pownal Street, P.O. Box 2023, Charlottetown, P.E.I. C1A 7N7
(902) 566-5750
Contact: Libby Oughton, publisher
Established 1974. Publishes women's fiction and poetry, as well as books for juveniles and children, and educational texts.

Railfare Enterprises Ltd.
P.O. Box 33, West Hill, Ont. M1E 4R4
(416) 690-6963
Contact: D.R. Henderson, president
Established 1971. Publishes books on Canadian railways and electric transit systems.

Random House of Canada Ltd.
1265 Aerowood Drive, Mississauga, Ont. L4W 1B9
(416) 624-0672
Contact: Gordon Bain, editor
Publishes a wide selection of fiction and a general trade non-fiction list.

Red Deer College Press
P.O. Box 5005, Red Deer, Alta. T4N 5H5
(403) 342-3304
Contact: Dennis Johnson, editor
Established 1975. Publishes poetry, short fiction, illustrated children's books, and drama.

Royal Ontario Museum
100 Queen's Park, Toronto, Ont. M5S 2C6
(416) 586-5582
Contact: Hugh Porter, manager
Publishes manuscripts that relate to the museum's collection.

W.B. Saunders Company Canada Ltd.
1 Goldthorne Avenue, Toronto, Ont. M8Z 5T9
(416) 251-3787
Contact: Gerald Mungham, acquisitions editor
Established 1936. Specializes in books on medicine, nursing, dentistry, and veterinary science.

Saunders of Toronto Ltd.
250 Steelcase Road E., Markham, Ont. L3R 2S3
(416) 475-1926
Contact: J.D. Allen, president
An agency house with a limited publishing program.

Scholar's Choice
777 Douro Street, Stratford, Ont. N5A 6T9
(519) 271-3800
Contact: William Webster, president, or Linda Bell, product development
Publishes books for students aged between six and eight. Topics include arts, crafts, mathematics, music, natural history, science, sports, theatre, and games.

Scholastic-TAB Publications
123 Newkirk Road, Richmond Hill, Ont. L4C 3G5
(416) 883-5300
Contact: Larry Muller, manager
Specializes in educational materials, particularly children's reading aids. Also publishes short fiction and non-fiction books for teens.

Seal Books
60 St. Clair Avenue E., Suite 601, Toronto, Ont. M4T 1N5
(416) 922-4970
Contact: Susan Rutledge, editor
Established 1977. Publishes fiction and non-fiction paperbacks for mass market, and commercial reprints.

Simon & Pierre Publishing Co. Ltd.
P.O. Box 280, Adelaide Street Postal Station, Toronto, Ont. M5C 2J4
(416) 363-6767
Contact: Marian Wilson, president
Established 1972. Publishes Canadian drama and theatre-related titles, fiction, and the *Canadian Book Review Annual*. Keenly interested in art books, and good new Canadian authors able to write both fiction and non-fiction.

Sono Nis Press
1745 Blanshard Street, Victoria, B.C. V8W 2J8
(604) 382-1024
Contact: Richard Morriss, president, or Patricia Sloan, editor
Established 1968. Publishes works with a regional emphasis: biography, history, exploration, poetry, some maritime history, and literary criticism.

Special Interest Publications
1132 Hamilton Street, Suite 202, Vancouver, B.C. V6B 2S2
(604) 687-1581

Contact: Janet Genders, manager
Specializes in outdoor and sporting books and periodicals.

Steel Rail Publishing
P.O. Box 4357, Station E, Ottawa, Ont. K1S 5B3
(613) 233-2751
Contact: Terry Binnersley, general manager
Established 1976. Specializes in critical analyses of Canadian society.

Stoddart Publishing Co. Limited
30 Lesmill Road, Don Mills, Ont. M3B 2T6
(416) 445-3333
Contact: Jack Stoddart, publisher
Publishes general trade and education books.

Summerhill Press Ltd.
5 Clarence Square, Toronto, Ont. M5V 1H1
(416) 593-1899
Contact: James Williamson, president
Established 1981. Specializes in general trade.

Talon Books Ltd.
1019 E. Cordova Street, Suite 201, Vancouver, B.C. V6A 1M8
(604) 253-5261
Contact: David Robinson, editor
Established 1967. Specializes in drama, fiction, poetry, popular non-fiction, and women's literature.

Tantalus Research Ltd.
2405 Pine Street, P.O. Box 34248, Vancouver, B.C. V6J 4N8
(604) 876-6381
Contact: M.M. Hardwick, manager
Established 1964. Specializes in geographical monographs.

Theytus Books Ltd.
P.O. Box 218, Penticton, B.C. V2A 6K3
(604) 493-7181
Contact: Joe Terbasket, manager
Established 1981. Publishes Native Indian literature, fiction and non-fiction, art, and music.

Thistledown Press
668 East Place, Saskatoon, Sask. S7J 2Z5
(306) 477-0556
Contact: Glen Sorestad, president, or Caroline Walker, general manager
Established 1975. Specializes in Canadian poetry and fiction, particularly by Prairie writers.

Three Trees Press, The
2 Silver Avenue, Toronto, Ont. M6R 3A2
(416) 534-4456
Contact: Wence Horak, publisher
Established 1976. Specializes in children's books – fairy tales and short stories.

Tree Frog Press Ltd.
10144 - 89th Street, Edmonton, Alta. T5H 1P7
(403) 429-1947
Contact: Katherine Shute, manager
Established 1971. Publishes children's books.

Tundra Books Inc.
1434 St. Catherine Street W., Suite 308, Montreal, Que. H3G 1R4
(514) 932-5434
Contact: May Cutler, publisher
Established 1967. Specializes in books for young people, but also publishes books on art and architecture, and some adult fiction. Does not accept unsolicited manuscripts.

Turnstone Press Ltd.
99 King Street, Suite 607, Winnipeg, Man. R3B 1H7
(204) 947-1555
Contact: Patricia Sanders, editor
Established 1976. Publishes poetry, fiction, and literary criticism.

University of Alberta Press, The
141 Athabasca Hall, Edmonton, Alta. T6G 2E8
(403) 432-3662
Contact: Norma Gutteridge, director
Established 1969. Specializes in scholarly manuscripts: university-level textbooks, history, politics, and science. Mainly publishes original research that has a strong Western Canadian interest.

University of British Columbia Press, The
6344 Memorial Road, Suite 303, Vancouver, B.C. V6T 1W5
(604) 228-3259/228-5959
Contact: James Anderson, executive director
Established 1971. Publishes non-fiction for scholarly, educational and general audiences in the humanities, social sciences, and natural sciences.

University of Calgary Press, The
Library Tower, 2500 University Drive N.W.,
Calgary, Alta. T2N 1N4
(403) 220-7578
Contact: Linda Cameron, assistant director

Established 1981. Publishes scholarly works in the humanities and social sciences, and in such fields as engineering, earth sciences, and energy research.

University of Manitoba Press
106 Curry Place, Suite 244, Winnipeg, Man. R3T 2N2
(204) 474-9495/474-9242
Contact: Patricia Dowdall, director
Established 1967. Publishes scholarly books in the humanities and social sciences, and general interest books about the Prairie region.

University of Ottawa Press
603 Cumberland Street, Ottawa, Ont. K1N 6N5
(613) 564-2270
Contact: Ralph Hodgson, director
Established 1936. Publishes scholarly works in English and in French.

University of Toronto Press
63A St. George Street, Toronto, Ont. M5S 1A6
(416) 978-2239
Contact: Ian Montagnes, editor
Established 1901. Publishes scholarly and general works, and academic journals.

Véhicule Press
P.O. Box 125, Place du Parc Station, Montreal, Que. H2W 2M9
(514) 844-6073
Contact: Simon Dardick, editor
Established 1973. Publishes fiction, poetry, literary criticism, books on archives and records management and on social history. Also publishes memoirs.

Vesta Publications
P.O. Box 1641, Cornwall, Ont. K6H 5V6
(613) 938-8804/932-2135
Contact: Stephen Gill, editor
Mainly interested in fiction and poetry.

R.J. Watts & Associates Ltd.
4010 Bayridge Crescent, West Vancouver, B.C. V7V 3K4
(604) 926-7684
Contact: Reg Watts, president
Established 1972. Publishes educational and children's books.

Weigl Educational Publishers Ltd.
2114 College Avenue, Regina, Sask. S4P 1C5
(306) 569-0766

Contact: Linda Weigl, president
Established 1979. Publishes educational texts aimed at all school levels, as well as books on social studies and on the environment.

G.R. Welch Company Ltd.
960 Gateway, Burlington, Ont. L7L 5K7
(416) 681-2760
Contact: Dr. Ian McPhee, editor
Established 1940. Publishes children's books, educational texts, and manuscripts on history, religion, and science – all with a religious outlook.

Western Producer Prairie Books
P.O. Box 2500, Saskatoon, Sask. S7K 2C4
(306) 665-3548
Contact: Rob Sanders, manager
Established 1954. Publishes books on history, biography, and natural history, all with a strong regional flavour.

Whitecap Books Ltd.
1086 W. 3rd Street, North Vancouver, B.C. V7P 3J6
(604) 980-9852
Contact: Michael Burch, publisher
Established 1977. Publishes local guides and historical books. Also interested in books on cooking, nature, and railways.

John Wiley & Sons Canada Limited
22 Worcester Road, Rexdale, Ont. M9W 1L1
(416) 675-3580
Contact: John Dill, editor
Established 1968. Specializes in educational books on a wide variety of topics and at all levels. Also publishes some general-interest non-fiction.

Wilfrid Laurier University Press
75 University Avenue W., Waterloo, Ont. N2L 3C5
(519) 884-1970
Contact: Linda Holmberg, administrative assistant
Established 1974. Publishes scholarly books and journals.

Williams-Wallace Publishers
2 Silver Avenue, Toronto, Ont. M6R 3A2
(416) 532-4222
Contact: Ann Wallace, publisher
Established 1979. Publishes multicultural fiction, non-fiction, and poetry.

Women's Educational Press
229 College Street, Suite 204, Toronto, Ont. M5T 1R4

(416) 598-0082
Contact: Margie Wolfe, promotions
Established 1972. Interested in trade and college/university fiction and non-fiction from a socialist-feminist perspective. Also publishes non-sexist children's books and the *Everywoman's Almanac*.

York Press Ltd.
P.O. Box 1172, Fredericton, N.B. E3B 5C8
(506) 455-6501
Contact: Dr. Saad Elkhadem, editor
Established 1975. Publishes dictionaries, educational texts at the college level, scholarly publications, reference books, and manuscripts on literary criticism and comparative literature. Strong emphasis on high-quality creative writing.

LITERARY AGENTS

More and more books published in Canada are being placed not by authors, but by their agents. While it is true that most Canadian publishing houses act honourably as agents for their authors, especially when trying to sell their works to foreign markets, a lot of experienced or "name" authors are finding that they need expert counsel and sales help long before they actually begin writing a particular book.

Experienced agents are good at advising writers how a certain subject needs to be approached and covered. They are also often highly successful in finding a suitable publisher for a book purely on the basis of a good proposal.

Because fiction is considerably harder to sell than non-fiction, it is understandable that fiction writers depend heavily on agents. But they are also being used increasingly by non-fiction writers, who have concluded that the agent who fully understands the marketplace, copyright, and the broader sales possibilities of a book can negotiate a better contract with a bigger advance against royalties and including clauses that stipulate what rights the author should sell or, conversely, keep.

Agents like to attract a stable of competent non-fiction writers because they know that their works usually pull in bigger advances than novels, and that they will therefore be entitled to more of what the writer receives in royalties.

Agents charge a commission – usually between 15 and 20 per cent – on all material sold. But they earn every penny of it. They keep in close contact with editors, with whom they can exchange both their ideas, and those of their writers. In so doing, they become expert at guaging the commercial possibilities of an author's proposal. It goes without saying, then, that if an agent is chosen wisely, his or her relationship with the author will pay for itself many times over.

Typically, one agent says, "While our main business, and our only income, is derived from the sale of publication rights, we provide the writer with counsel, guidance, and encouragement. The fiduciary relationship between us is a unique and mutually rewarding professional bond." Says another: "We can be more aware of the markets in all areas since that is what we spend our time researching. We are also aware of the standard pitfalls in so-called standard contracts, and can work out the best possible contract from our specialized knowledge and experience."

The need for an agent is pressing for the short-story writer who hopes to sell his or her work to those national consumer magazines that print fiction. Magazine editors quite often reject short stories received directly from the author – "over the transom," as they say in the business – even those that may easily meet their editorial standards. Understandably, some editors are afraid to take chances in dealing with an unknown contributor in case their work has been plagiarized. When material is submitted to them through a reputable agent, however, the chance of a rejection on this basis is diminished considerably.

Canadian Speakers' and Writers' Service Ltd.
44 Douglas Crescent, Toronto, Ont. M4W 2E7
(416) 921-4443
Contact: Matie Molinaro

Colbert Agency, The
303 Davenport Road, Toronto, Ont. M5R 1K5
(416) 964-3302
Contact: Nancy Colbert/Stanley Colbert

Deutsch and Swan
633 Huron Street, Toronto, Ont. M3R 2R8
(416) 960-4713

Goodman and Goodman
20 Queen Street W., Toronto, Ont. M5H 1V5
(416) 979-2211

J. Kellock and Associates Ltd.
11017 - 80th Avenue, Edmonton, Alta. T6G 0R2
(403) 433-7477
Contact: Joanne Kellock

Peter Livingston Associates Inc.
143 Collier Street, Toronto, Ont. M4W 1M2
(416) 928-1019
Contact: Peter Livingston
New York office:
465 Park Avenue, New York, NY 10022
(212) 755-5000

Montreal-Contacts/The Rights Agency
P.O. Box 696, Station N, Montreal, Que. H2X 3M6

(514) 348-3236
Contact: Claude Choquette

Mary Novik, Literary Agent
5519 Deerhorn Lane, North Vancouver, B.C. V7R 4S8
(604) 987-4982
Contact: Mary Novik

Pacific Publishing Support Services Ltd.
1733 Kitchener Street, Vancouver, B.C. V5L 2W4
(604) 254-9640
Contact: Denise Bukowski

Sara Parker & Associates
85 Hogarth Avenue, Apartment 1, Toronto, Ont. M4K 1K5
(416) 466-3902
Contact: Sara Parker

Bella Pomer Agency Inc.
22 Shallmar Boulevard, P.H. 2, Toronto, Ont. M5N 2Z8
(416) 781-8597
Contact: Bella Pomer

Beverley Slopen Agency
131 Bloor Street W., Suite 711, Toronto, Ont. M5S 1S3
(416) 964-9598
Contact: Beverley Slopen

Van Veeren Writers' Consulting Service
5660 Monkland Avenue, Montreal, Que. H4A 1E4
(514) 487-6060
Contact: Janet Adams

Lucinda Vardey Agency
297 Seaton Street, Toronto, Ont. M5A 2T6
(416) 922-0250
Contact: Lucinda Vardey

Writers' Services and Seminars
5 - 48th Avenue, Lachine, Que. H8T 2R5
(514) 486-0778/486-6561
Contact: Allan Stoneham

PRIZES AND AWARDS

The following list contains nearly every award or prize available to the Canadian writer. There are, however, new ones being offered every year, and the latest information on them can be found in such well-known publications as *Quill & Quire*, the book publisher's bible, *The Book Trade in Canada*, *Canadian Author and Bookman*, and *Literary Market Place*, all available in most large municipal libraries.

Alberta New Novelist Competition
An award of $2,500, plus a publishing contract and an advance of $1,500 against royalties, is given every second year for an unpublished first novel by an Albertan with a minimum of eighteen months' residence. The manuscript must be between 60,000 and 100,000 publishable words. A further $1,000 and an advance of $500 may be given to the same author for any other publishable manuscript. Deadline: December 31. Contact: Alberta Culture, Film and Literary Arts, 12th floor, CN Tower, Edmonton, Alta. T5J 0K5

Alberta Non-Fiction Book Award
A prize of $1,000 and a publishing contract is awarded each year for the best non-fiction book of general interest written by an Albertan. Deadline: December 31. Contact: Alberta Culture, Film and Literary Arts, 12th Floor, CN Tower, Edmonton, Alta. T5J 0K5

Alberta Playwriting Competition
Awards of up to $1,000 are given annually to Alberta playwrights. Deadline: February 15. Contact: Alberta Culture Playwriting Competition, 11th Floor, CN Tower, Edmonton, Alta. T5J 0K5

Alberta Poetry Yearbook Competition
Awards totalling nearly $1,000 are given in eight categories annually to Canadian poets. Entries must be mailed between May 1 and September 30. Contact: Canadian Authors Association (Edmonton Branch), R.R. 1, Winterburn, Alta. T0E 2N0

Alberta Regional History Competition
A prize of $650 is given for an historic work of no less than 25,000 words. Deadline: December 31. Contact: Regional History Awards Committee, Alberta Culture, Film and Literary Arts, 12th Floor, CN Tower, Edmonton, Alta. T5J 0K5

Alberta Writing for Young People Competition
A prize of $2,500 is awarded annually for an outstanding manuscript designed to entertain readers aged between eight and sixteen. Deadline: December 31. Contact: Alberta Culture, Film and Literary Arts, 12th Floor, CN Tower, Edmonton, Alta. T5J 0K5

American Society of Newspaper Editors Writing Awards
Prizes of $1,000 in each of four categories – commentary, news, non-deadline writing, and editorials – are offered annually. Emphasis is on style. Deadline: February 1. Contact: Poynter Institute for Media Studies, 556 Central Avenue, St. Petersburg, Fla. 33701

Annual Adult Playwriting Competition
Prizes of up to $1,200 are offered to all Alberta residents in one-act, full-length, and teleplay categories. Deadline: February 15. Contact: Alberta Culture, Performing Arts Branch, Playwriting Competition, 11th Floor, CN Tower, Edmonton, Alta. T5J 0K5

Author's Awards
Awards totalling nearly $7,000 are given annually for outstanding fiction and non-fiction published in Canada for mass market magazines and paperbacks. Sponsored by the Foundation for the Advancement of Canadian Letters. Deadline: June 15. Contact: Argyle Communications Inc., 220 King Street W., 4th Floor, Toronto, Ont. M5H 1K4

Aviation/Space Writers Association Awards
Awards totalling $2,500 are distributed annually for outstanding non-fiction about achievements in aviation or space. Deadline: January 5. Contact: William Kaiser, Cliffwood Road, Chester, N.J. 07930

Book-of-the-Year Award for Children
A medal is presented each year to the Canadian author of the best Canadian children's book published in English. Deadline: February 1. Contact: Canadian Library Association, 151 Sparks Street, Ottawa, Ont. K1P 5E3

Books in Canada Award
A prize of $1,000 is awarded to a Canadian citizen or landed immigrant who writes in English, or translates into English from French, the year's most outstanding first novel. Deadline: December 31. Contact: *Books in Canada*, 366 Adelaide Street E., Toronto, Ont. M5A 1N4

B.C. Book Awards
A cash award and publicity tour is given to a British Columbia author who writes the year's most outstanding non-fiction book that contributes to a greater understanding of his/her province. Entry fee: $10.00. Contact: B.C. Books Awards, 1622 West 7th Avenue, Vancouver, B.C. V6J 1S5

Heywood Broun Award
A $1,000 award acknowledges a piece of journalism judged to be "in the spirit of Heywood Broun," who fought for the disadvantaged and underprivileged. Deadline: January 12. Contact: The Newspaper Guild, 1125 - 15th Street N.W., Washington, D.C. 20005

Canada Council Children's Literature Prizes
An award of $5,000 is presented to both a French and English Canadian author of the year's best children's book published either in Canada or abroad. Contact: The Canada Council, 99 Metcalfe Street, Ottawa, Ont. K1P 5V8

Canada Council Translation Prize, The
Awards of $5,000 each go for the year's best translations – one from English to French, the other from French to English. Contact: The Canada Council, 99 Metcalfe Street, Ottawa, Ont. K1P 5V8

Canadian Author and Bookman Awards
Prizes and scholarships totalling $800 are awarded to post-secondary students for work in non-fiction, fiction and poetry. Deadline: February 18. Contact: Creative Writing Contest, *Canadian Author and Bookman*, 24 Ryerson Avenue, Toronto, Ont. M5P 2P3

Canadian Authors Association Literary Awards
Prizes totalling $20,000 and silver medals are awarded for the year's best fiction, non-fiction, poetry and drama. Deadline: December 31. Contact: Canadian Authors Association, 24 Ryerson Avenue, Toronto, Ont. M5P 2P3

Canadian Booksellers' Author Award
A $500 prize is awarded for the year's best novel. Contact: The Canadian Booksellers' Association, 56 The Esplanade, Suite 400, Toronto, Ont. M5E 1A7

Canadian Broadcasting Corporation Annual Awards
Awards totalling more than $25,000 are distributed for short stories, poems, and autobiographies. Deadline: January 15. Contact: CBC Awards, P.O,. Box 500, Station A, Toronto, Ont. M5W 1E6

Canadian Fiction Magazine Prize
A prize is offered for original Canadian fiction in French or English and awarded to the writer whose work is selected as most outstand-

ing among the year's contributors. Contact: The Editor, Canadian Fiction Magazine, P.O. Box 946, Station F, Toronto, Ont. M4Y 2N9

Canadian Library Association
Medals are given annually for an outstanding children's book by a Canadian or resident of Canada, and for outstanding illustrations in a children's book published in Canada. Contact: 200 Elgin Street, Ottawa, Ont. K2P 1L5

Canadian Petroleum Association National Journalism Award
Awards totalling nearly $20,000 are distributed annually for outstanding reporting and/or commentary on oil subjects in Canada. Contact: Calgary Press Club, 633 Sixth Avenue S.W., Suite 1500, Calgary, Alta. T2P 2Y5

Canadian Young Writers' Award
Young Manitobans aged between thirteen and eighteen vie annually, with unpublished works of between 1,000 and 3,500 words long, for $225 in prizes given by the Manitoba Branch of the Canadian Authors Association. Deadline: March 15. Contact: Manitoba Branch of the C.A.A., 177 Lombard Avenue, 4th Floor, Winnipeg, Man. R3B 0W5

Chalmers Award
An award of $5,000 is given annually for a piece of drama by a Canadian playwright. Contact: The Ontario Arts Council, Theatre Section, 151 Bloor Street W., 5th Floor, Toronto, Ont. M5S 1T6

Children's Literature Prizes
Annual awards of $5,000 are given by the Canada Council to aid and encourage Canadian writers and illustrators of books for young people. Two English and two French books are selected each year. No formal application required. Contact: The Canada Council, 99 Metcalfe Street, Ottawa, Ont. K1P 5V8

City of Toronto Book Award
A $3,000 prize is given annually to the author of any book, fiction or non-fiction, will deals particularly well with any aspect of Toronto life. Contact: Lightwaves, 134 Peter Street, Toronto, Ont. M5V 2H2

Greg Clark Award
A $450 award is given for outstanding reporting of outdoor subjects in Ontario newspapers and magazines. Deadline: February 20. Contact: Communications Services, Ontario Ministry of Natural Resources, 99 Wellesley Street W., Room 5340, Whitney Block, Queens Park, Toronto, Ont. M5S 2C7

Columbia University Awards, Mario Moors Cabot Prizes
These annual awards, the oldest in international journalism,

comprise a gold medal, a $1,000 honorarium, and the round-trip air fare to New York City for the presentation ceremonies. Two medalists are selected each year, one or more from Latin America or Canada. Contact: Adelaide Katz, Director of the Cabot Prize Program, Room 706, Graduate School of Journalism, Columbia University, N.Y. 10027

Albert B. Corey Prize in Canadian-American Relations
An award of $2,000 is given for a history of Canadian-American relations or the history of both countries. Contact: Canadian Historical Association Secretariat, Public Archives of Canada, 395 Wellington Street, Ottawa, Ont. K1A 0N3

Eaton/Manitoba Branch C.A.A. Short Story Contest
Awards totalling $400 are given to Manitoba residents eighteen and older for an original, unpublished short story no longer than 3,500 words. Deadline: March 15. Contact: Eaton's Book Department, 320 Portage Avenue, Winnipeg, Man. R3C 0C2

Edmonton Journal Award
Four prizes of $400 each are given in the categories of short fiction (up to 3,000 words), short fiction for juvenile audience (up to 2,000 words), short poetry (up to twenty-five lines per poem), and long poetry (up to 100 lines per poem). The contest is open to all novice writers, excluding students, in the Journal's circulation area. Deadline: April 15. Contact: Community Journal, Edmonton, Alta. T5J 2S6

Arthur Ellis Award
A prize is given annually for a fiction or non-fiction book in the crime genre. Deadline: December 7. Contact: Crime Writers of Canada, 65 Gormley Avenue, Toronto, Ont. M4V 1Y9

Golden Carnation Awards
Awards totalling $2,000 are given for reporting on nutrition subjects. Deadline: September 1. Contact: George Wilkins, Carnation Company, 5054 Wilshire Boulevard, Los Angeles, Cal. 90036

Government of Newfoundland and Labrador Arts and Letters Competition
Awards totalling $400 are given for original work on Newfoundland history, in short story, poem, or drama form, by residents of Newfoundland and Labrador. A gold medal may also be awarded for outstanding achievement in any category. Contact: Arts and Letters Competition, Arts and Culture Centre, P.O. Box 1854, St. John's, Nfld. A1C 5S7

Governor General's Literary Awards
Administered by The Canada Council, these awards of $5,000 each are given annually to the authors of the best English-language and French-language works in the categories of poetry, drama, fiction,

and non-fiction. No formal application from the publishers or the author is required. Contact: The Canada Council, 99 Metcalfe Street, Ottawa, Ont. K1P 5V8

Grand Prize for Literature of the City of Montreal
A $300 prize for a literary work – fiction, short story, poetry, history, or essays – published in book form for the first time, is given annually. Entries must contain the word "Montreal" on the title page or overleaf. Contact: Greater Montreal Council of Arts, 700 St-Antoine Street E., Suite 112, Montreal, Que. H2Y 1A6

International Association of Fire Fighters Media Awards
Awards totalling $5,000 are presented annually in six categories, for stories and pictures depicting fire losses and firefighting professionalism. Deadline: March 15. Contact: International Association of Fire Fighters, 1750 New York Avenue N.W., Washington, D.C. 20006

Francis H. Kortright Awards
Prizes totalling $3,000 are presented annually for articles on outdoor recreation in Canada. Contact: Grant Mulholland, Outdoor Writers of Canada, 20 Wesley Avenue, Mississauga, Ont. L5H 2M5

Gerald Lampert Memorial Award
A $300 cash award for the best new Canadian writer alternates annually between poetry and prose. Contact: The League of Canadian Poets, 24 Ryerson Avenue, Toronto, Ont. M5P 2P3

La Pluma de Plata Mexicana
Prizes comprising $2,750, silver trophies, and trips are offered for articles promoting travel to Mexico. Deadline: March 15. Contact: Mexican National Tourist Council, 405 Park Avenue, New York, N.Y. 10022

Stephen Leacock Medal for Humour
A sterling silver medal and a cash prize are given for the best humorous work in verse, drama, or prose. Contact: Stephen Leacock Associates, P.O. Box 854, Orillia, Ont. L3V 6K8

Little, Brown Children's Book Award
A $1,000 prize, plus a $3,500 advance against royalties, rewards an original children's book by a Canadian citizen or resident. Awarded intermittently. Contact: Little, Brown & Co. (Canada) Ltd., 164 Commander Boulevard, Agincourt, Ont. M1S 3C7

Pat Lowther Memorial Award
An annual cash award of $300 is offered for the best book of poetry by a woman. Contact: The League of Canadian Poets, 24 Ryerson Avenue, Toronto, Ont. M5P 2P3

MacMillan Bloedel Awards
Prizes totalling $4,000 for quality in writing, journalistic initiative, and public service in British Columbia's daily newspapers are awarded annually. Deadline: July 3. Contact: MacMillan Bloedel Ltd., 1075 W. Georgia Street, Vancouver, B.C. V6E 3R9

McLuhan Teleglobe Canada Award
Award of $50,000 given biennially to an individual or group making an exceptional contribution to the better understanding of the influence of communications media and technology on society in general and on cultural, artistic, and scientific life. Contact: UNESCO, Ottawa, Ont.

Howard R. Marraro Award
A $500 award for a book, and a smaller amount for an article, are given annually for a published work dealing with Italian history or Italo-American history. Deadline: June 15. Contact: The American Historical Association, 400 A Street S.E., Washington, D.C. 20003

Vicky Metcalf Award
A $2,000 annual cash prize recognizes a body of work, fiction or non-fiction, of interest to youth, by a Canadian. Deadline: December 31. Contact: Canadian Authors Association, 24 Ryerson Avenue, Toronto, Ont. M5T 2P3

Vicky Metcalf Short Story Award
Cash award of $1,000 goes annually to a Canadian author for the best children's short story published in a Canadian magazine. Deadline: December 31. Contact: Canadian Authors Association, 24 Ryerson Avenue, Toronto, Ont. M5T 2P3

Roland Michener Award
Given for public service journalism. Deadline: February 15. Contact: Michener Award Foundation, The National Press Club, 150 Wellington Street, Ottawa, Ont. K1P 5A4

Molson Prizes
Three $20,000 prizes are given annually by The Canada Council to recognize and encourage outstanding contributions to the arts, social sciences, or humanities. Contact: The Canada Council, 99 Metcalfe Street, Ottawa, Ont. K1P 5V8

Mount Royal College Contest
Prizes of $100 each are awarded in three creative writing categories– short story, drama, and poetry. As well, the Edith Park Prize, also worth $100, is awarded for the best essay on a literary topic during the academic year. Contact: Mount Royal College, 4835 Richmond Road S.W., Calgary, Alta. T3E 6K6

Moyse Travelling Scholarship
Two scholarships of $4,000 each are awarded to distinguished graduating students – one from the Faculty of Arts, one from the Faculty of Science – for advanced studies in a British or European university. Contact: Faculty of Arts and Science, McGill University, 853 Sherbrooke Street W., Montreal, Que. H3A 2T6

National Business Writing Awards
Awards totalling $2,700 are given for reporting by a newspaper, a magazine, a news service writer, or a freelancer. Contact: Toronto Press Club, 73 Richmond Street W., Toronto, Ont. M5H 1Z4

National Education Reporting Awards
Awards totalling $4,000 recognize excellence in reporting on education issues. Deadline: January 18. Contact: College of Journalism, University of Maryland, College Park, Md. 20742

National Jewish Book Awards
Ten awards of $500 each are given annually for published books of literary merit and Jewish interest – fiction, poetry, juvenile, Jewish thought, and Jewish history. Candidates are nominated. Deadline: December 31. Contact: Jewish Book Council, 15 E. 26th Street, New York, N.Y. 10010

National Magazine Awards
Prizes of $1,500 are awarded in each of nineteen categories, including general articles, political writing, sports, business, science, photo journalism, fiction, humour, illustrations, fashion, art direction, magazine covers. Deadline: January. Contact: National Magazine Awards Foundation, 44 Laird Drive, Toronto, Ont. M4G 3T2

National Multicultural Theatre Association Prizes
Prizes totalling $2,000 annually recognize plays aimed at young people aged between twelve and seventeen. All works must be more than thirty minutes long, and less than ninety minutes, and reflect Canada's cultural diversity. Deadline: January 30. Contact: National Multicultural Theatre Association, 8 York Street, 6th Floor, Toronto, Ont. M5J 1R2

Nova Scotia Government Literary Contest
Awards totalling $2,000 are given annually for unpublished books (fiction or non-fiction), or articles up to 50,000 words. Contact: Canadian Authors Association, P.O. Box 2902, Armdale, N.S. B3L 4M7

Okanagan Short Fiction Award
An award of $125 and a promise of publication in *Canadian Author & Bookman* goes to a previously unpublished author with a manuscript of fewer than 3,500 words. The emphasis must be on quality writing. Contact: Canadian Author & Bookman, 70 Champlain Avenue, Welland, Ont. L3C 2L7

Eve Orpen Award for Publishing and Literary Excellence
An award of $1,000 goes to a publisher or a writer for excellence in publishing in Canada. Contact: Malcolm Lester, Lester & Orpen Dennys Ltd., 78 Sullivan Street, Toronto, Ont. M5T 1C1

Evelyn Richardson Memorial Literary Trust Award
A $700 prize and a trophy are given annually for the best book of non-fiction prose by a Nova Scotian. Deadline: April 15. Contact: Writers' Federation of Nova Scotia, P.O. Box 3608, Halifax South Post Office, Halifax, N.S. B3J 3K6

Saskatchewan Native Writers' Contest
A cash award of $200 is given annually by the IODE for a manuscript with appeal to native children or teenagers, written in English, Inuktitut or Indian, by a native author, on aspects of native life. Deadline: October 31. Contact: Provincial Library, Regina, Sask. S4R 1J0

Ruth Schwartz Memorial Award
A cash prize of $2,000 is awarded for the year's best children's book in English or in French. Contact: Ontario Arts Council, 151 Bloor Street W., 5th Floor, Toronto, Ont. M5S 1T6

Smolar Awards
An annual award honours the outstanding commentary of Jewish affairs. Deadline: September 1. Contact: Council of Jewish Federations, 575 Lexington Avenue, New York, N.Y. 10022

Southam Fellowships for Journalists
One year's tuition at a university for working journalists who have at least five years' experience and are under forty years of age is offered for prolonged outstanding work. Contact: Southam Fellowships, President's Office, Room 107, Simcoe Hall, University of Toronto, Toronto, Ont. M5S 1A1

Toronto Star Short Story Contest, The
Awards totalling $5,000 are given annually for the best original short story of between 1,500 and 2,500 words. The first prize is usually a word-processor or typewriter, the second $500 in cash, the third prize $250. Consolation prizes of $50 are offered for those stories selected for publication. Deadline: April 15. Contact: Short Story Contest, *The Sunday Star*, 1 Yonge Street, Toronto, Ont. M5E 1E6

Trillium Book Award/Prix Trillium
A prize of $10,000 is presented by the Ontario Ministry of Citizenship and Culture to honour the author of a book of "literary excellence," which contributes to a better understanding of Ontario and Ontario society. A further $2,000 is presented to the publisher, to encourage promotion of the winning book. Deadline: December 15. Contact: Ontario Ministry of Citizenship and Culture, Libraries

and Community Information Branch, 77 Bloor Street W., Toronto, Ont. M7A 2R9

University of British Columbia Medal
Given for popular Canadian biography. Contact: Selection Committee, Department of English, University of British Columbia, Vancouver, B.C. V6T 1W5

University of Regina Drama Award
A biennial award of $1,000 goes to an unpublished work of less than ninety minutes'. Deadline: September 30. Contact: Drama Department, University of Regina, Regina, Sask. S4S 0A2

University of Western Ontario Presidents Medals
These awards recognize outstanding Canadian literature in specific areas – the general article, scholarly article, single poem, and the short story. The Associataion of Canadian Magazine Editors has added cash awards totalling $250 for the best short story and article. Contact: Department of English, University of Western Ontario, London, Ont. N6A 3K7

Winnipeg Free Press Non-Fiction Contest
Prizes totalling $250 are awarded, in co-operation with the Winnipeg Branch of the Canadian Authors Association, for English manuscripts between 1,500 and 2,000 words long. Contact: Non-Fiction Contest, Winnipeg Free Press, 300 Carlton Street, Winnipeg, Man. R3C 3C1

Writer's Digest Awards
A prize of $500 and a silver cup is awarded annually to the grand prize-winner of the contest. Division first prize winners – in short stories, articles, poems, and scriptwriting – receive a plaque and a gift. Second- and third-prize winners receive plaques. Those who place fourth to one-hundredth receive certificates. Deadline: June 30. Contact: Writer's Digest Magazine, 9933 Alliance Road, Cincinnati, Oh. 45252

Writers' Federation of Nova Scotia
An award of $700 and a trophy is offered annually to a resident or native Nova Scotia author of a non-fiction book. Deadline: April 15. Contact: The Evelyn Richardson Award Selection Committee, Writers' Federation of Nova Scotia, P.O. Box 3608, Halifax, N.S. B3J 3K6

COURSES IN CREATIVE WRITING AND JOURNALISM

No professor can turn an ordinary soul into a successful wordsmith because writing cannot really be taught. Paradoxically, however, it *can* be learned – according to a set of principles and rules explained in all manner of courses, workshops, and seminars.

Creative writing is perhaps best fostered in the university or college environment, by working with a good professor who understands literary devices and the power of language. Non-fiction writing, however, which is generally considered more of a craft than an art, is nearly always learned by listening to those writers who have been successful in the field and therefore know not only how to refine ideas, but research them, transform them into workable structures, craft saleable words, and, finally, market them.

Acadia University
Wolfville, N.S. B0P 1X0
Academic: One creative writing course.
Extension: A half-course, An Introduction to Creative Writing, is offered.
Extra-Curricular: Publishes *The Athenaeum and Alpha*, a student literary magazine, and *Atlantis*, an interdisciplinary magazine on women's studies which carries poetry and scholarly articles.

University of Alberta
Edmonton, Alta. T6G 2M7
Academic: English Department offers four half-year and two full-year undergraduate courses in poetry and fiction for credit towards a BA. Sustained piece of creative writing accepted in lieu of MA thesis.

Algonquin College of Applied Arts and Technology
1385 Woodroffe Avenue, Ottawa, Ont. K2G 1V8
Academic: Two one-year journalism programs, one English and one French. Offers a two-year creative advertising program, also in both languages.

Assiniboine Community College
1430 Victoria Avenue, Brandon, Man. R7A 5Z9
Continuing Education: Journalism and creative writing courses.

Athabasca University
15015 - 123rd Avenue, Edmonton, Alta. T6C 0V2
Continuing Education: Sponsors writers' conferences.
Extra-Curricular: Publishes the *Athabasca University Magazine*. Occasionally accepts manuscripts from outside contributors.

Banff Centre School of Fine Arts, The
P.O. Box 1020, Banff, Alta. T0L 0C0
Continuing Education: Journalism and creative writing courses offered, but not for degree or diploma. Nonetheless, these are part of a highly acclaimed writing program that draws its teachers from publishing and literary circles. Does not accept beginning writers.
Extra-Curricular: Publishes *Free-Fall*, a creative writing magazine, and *The Banff Letters*, an arts journal that buys manuscripts from outside contributors.

Brandon University
Brandon, Man. R7A 6A9
Academic: Offers an introduction to journalism course worth six credits towards a bachelor's degree.
Extension: The creative writing workshop publishes *Pierian Spring*, a magazine of mainstream poetry and fiction.

University of British Columbia
2075 Westbrook Mall, Vancouver, B.C. V6T 1W5
Studio: Offers BFA degree course with a major in creative writing. MFA degree programs include creative writing concentrating on translation and creative writing for the theatre.
Extra-Curricular: Literary journal, *Prism International*, is edited by Creative Writing Department graduate students.

University of Calgary
2920 - 24th Avenue N.W., Calgary, Alta. T2N 1N4
Academic: Creative writing courses at the senior level.
Extension: Non-degree courses in both journalism and creative writing.

Cambrian College of Applied Arts and Technology
1400 Barrydowne Road, Sudbury, Ont. P3A 3V8
Academic: Diploma courses offering a journalism major.
Extra-Curricular: Publishes *The Shield*, a bi-weekly journalism lab paper.

Camosun College
3100 Foul Bay, Victoria, B.C. V8P 4X8

Academic: A one-semester course in creative writing with university transfer credit.
Career: Courses in writing for the print and electronic media are offered as components of the two-year Applied Communications program. Students write and produce *Camas*, a college news magazine, and some radio and cable television programs.
Continuing Education: Occasional journalism courses.
Extra-Curricular: Students are encouraged to submit material to *Camas* and *Camosun Review*, another on-campus journal.

Canadore College of Applied Arts and Technology
P.O. Box 5001, North Bay, Ont. P1B 8K9
Academic: A two-year print journalism diploma program which includes courses in news gathering, interviewing, libel and contempt, municipal reporting, court reporting, headline writing, news photography, darkroom techniques, and selected liberal arts subjects.

Capilano College
2055 Purcell Way, North Vancouver, B.C. V7J 3H5
Academic: Four courses in creative writing, plus one in magazine writing.
Continuing Education: Courses in script writing (film and television), and publishing.
Extra-Curricular: Publishes *The Capilano Courier*, the student newspaper, and *The Capilano Review*, a quarterly journal of literature, art, and science.

Cariboo College
900 McGill Road, Kamloops, B.C. V2C 5N3
Academic: Two courses in creative writing – one fiction and one poetry – both carrying credit towards BA. Diploma course offered in media communications.
Continuing Education: A creative writing course.
Extra-Curricular: Publishes *210 Express*, the student newspaper, and *Mag*, a creative writing magazine.

Carleton University
Ottawa, Ont. K1S 5B6
Academic: Offers a four-year program leading to an honours Bachelor of Journalism, and a one-year program – also leading to an honours BJ – for students who have completed a first degree. A one-year Master's degree program is available for students with a BJ and journalists with substantial working experience. Some creative writing courses are also given.

Centennial College of Applied Arts and Technology
651 Warden Avenue, Scarborough, Ont. M1L 3Z6
Academic: Three-year diploma programs in print and electronic media journalism and creative advertising are offered. So are

two-year diploma programs in book editing and design and in organizational communication. Programs include courses in reporting, editing, scriptwriting for radio and television, documentary writing, photography, cinematography, magazine writing, public relations, and newspaper feature writing.

Champlain Regional College
900 Riverside Drive, St-Lambert, Que. J4P 3P2
Academic: Journalism and creative writing courses offered as part of Humanities and English programs.
Continuing Education: Journalism and creative writing.
Extra-Curricular: Poetry reading and seminars are sponsored.

Concordia Lutheran College
7128 Ada Boulevard, Edmonton, Alta. T5B 4E4
Academic: Offers one creative writing credit course.

Concordia University (Loyola Campus)
7141 Sherbrooke Street W., Montreal, Que. H4B 1R6
Academic: English Department offers workshops in playwriting, poetry, and fiction, and gives courses in advanced composition and non-fiction. The Journalism Department has degree programs offering courses in writing and reporting, feature and magazine writing, editing, writing for radio and television news, and public affairs. Undergraduate and graduate programs have quotas, so students are screened for admission.

Concordia University (Sir George Williams Campus)
1455 de Maisonneuve Boulevard, Montreal, Que. H3G 1M8
Academic: Courses in creative writing (prose, poetry, and drama) at introductory and advanced levels are offered, as are credit courses in non-fiction and creative writing.
Extension: Full evening program in creative writing is open to those students not necessarily working toward a degree. Non-credit evening courses in journalism comprise advertising copywriting, magazine graphics and production, newspaper and magazine writing, and public relations.

Conestoga College of Applied Arts and Technology
299 Doon Valley Drive, Kitchener, Ont. N2G 4M4
Academic: Eighty-week program prepares graduates to work as reporter-photographers in newspapers or magazines, or as story editors and reporters for radio or television stations. Graduates are equipped with such editing skills as headline writing, design, and layout. Each student spends a minimum of two months working on a local newspaper or magazine. Public relations courses are also offered.
Continuing Education: Non-fiction and creative writing courses.

Dalhousie University
Halifax, N.S. B3H 3J5
Extension: An informal, non-credit course in creative writing.
Extra-Curricular: Publishes *The Dalhousie Gazette*, the student newspaper, and *University News*, a weekly paper devoted to university affairs. *The Dalhousie Review*, a long-established quarterly, publishes articles, reviews, and some short stories and poems.

David Thompson University Centre/Selkirk College
820 Tenth Street, Nelson, B.C. V1L 3C7
Academic: Offers a unique degree or diploma program in either creative or professional writing and a two-year diploma program transferable to a university that has courses in poetry, fiction, scriptwriting for stage and film, book and magazine production or written journalism.
Extra-Curricular: Shares visual and performing arts facilities with Selkirk College and the University of Victoria. The emphasis is interdisciplinary. Thus writing students work with those who are studying music, theatre, painting, sculpture, design, graphics, and photography. The writing program coordinates a Canadian writers' series, short-term residences with Canadian writers co-sponsored with the Canada Council, a literary magazine called *Writing*, and a summer writing school.

Dawson College
350 Selby Street, Westmount, Que. H3Z 1W7
Academic: Diploma courses in journalism and creative writing.
Continuing Education: Journalism and creative writing courses.
Extra-Curricular: Publishes a newspaper, *The Plant*, and runs four campus radio stations: CFKS, CHUV, CVIC, and CLAF.

Douglas College
P.O. Box 2503, New Westminster, B.C. V3L 5B2
Academic: University transfer and college credit course in creative writing. Courses in film, communications, and journalism.
Continuing Education: Creative writing course.
Extra-Curricular: Publishes a literary journal called *Event* twice yearly.

Durham College of Applied Arts and Technology
Simcoe Street N., Oshawa, Ont. L1H 7L7
Academic: Communication arts program leading to a two-year diploma in journalism, publics relations, or advertising. Graduates of other colleges and universities may qualify for direct entry into a special one-year program concentrating on practical subjects.
Extra-Curricular: Publishes *The Chronicle*, a college newspaper

which provides students with experience in writing, editing, design, layout, art, photography, and production.

Fanshawe College of Applied Arts and Technology
P.O. Box 4005, Terminal C, London, Ont. N5W 5H1
Academic: Creative writing is offered as an English elective credit.
Extra-Curricular: Non-credit creative writing courses.

George Brown College of Applied Arts and Technology
P.O. Box 1015, Station B, Toronto, Ont. M5T 2T9
Academic: Non-degree and non-credit courses in creative writing.

Georgian College of Applied Arts and Technology
401 Duckworth Street, Barrie, Ont. L4M 3X9
Academic: A journalism program provides training in what the college calls "academic, ethical, and procedural skills required" for finding news media jobs. The first semester offers a common curriculum covering journalism's basic tools and techniques. Students who successfully complete the first semester may take courses in newswriting, photography, media graphics, and production.
Extra-Curricular: Students publish a newspaper, *The Georgian*, and produce a radio program.

University of Guelph
Guelph, Ont. N1G 2W1
Academic: The English Department occasionally offers two-semester courses in creative writing, poetry, and drama. Department of Agriculture Economy offers two-semester courses in communications at the third-year level. These include some tuition in agricultural journalism.
Continuing Education: Special evening courses in creative writing are usually offered in fall and winter.

Holland College
P.O. Box 878, Charlottetown, P.E.I. C1A 4Z1
Academic: Diploma courses in journalism are offered.
Extra-Curricular: Publishes *The Surveyer.*

Humber College of Applied Arts and Technology
Humber College Boulevard, P.O. Box 1900, Rexdale, Ont. M9W 5L2
Academic: A three-year diploma course in print and broadcast journalism also includes creative writing.
Continuing Education: Certificate program in professional writing, including journalism and creative writing.

Huron College
London, Ont. N6G 1H3
Academic: Four undergraduate half-courses in journalism at the

University of Western Ontario are open to Huron College students in lieu of social science credits.

John Abbott College
P.O. Box 2000, Ste-Anne-de-Bellevue, Que. H9X 3L9
Academic: Journalism and creative writing courses offered occasionally. A three-week summer arts program includes a creative writing workshop.
Extra-Curricular: Staff and students collaborate with Deluge Press to publish the *Montreal Review.*

Keyano College
8115 Franklin Avenue, Fort McMurray, Alta. T9H 2H7
Continuing Education: A creative writing course is offered.
Extra-Curricular: Sponsors writers' conferences and publishes *Portage* for neophyte authors.

University of King's College, School of Journalism
Halifax, N.S. B3H 2A1
Academic: Two journalism programs are offered. The first is a four-year program, leading directly to an honours BJ degree, for students entering directly from high school. The second is an intensive one-year program, also leading to a BJ, for students who already have a BA or a BSc. Students in the four-year honours program are offered courses in broadcast journalism, interpretive and analytical reporting, magazine writing, television, radio and newspaper production, copy editing, and Canadian diplomacy techniques and operations. The intensive one-year program offers courses that include basic writing and reporting, legal issues, government operations, and newspaper production.

Lakehead University
Oliver Road, Thunder Bay, Ont. P7B 2E1
Academic: One degree course in creative writing.
Extension: One creative writing course.
Extra-Curricular: Publishes *The Argus.*

Lakeland College
4420 - 50th Avenue, Lloydminster, Alta. T9V 0W2
Academic: Creative writing diploma course.

Lambton College of Applied Arts and Technology, The
P.O. Box 969, Sarnia, Ont. N7T 7K4
Academic: Several courses are included in a two-year radio and television journalism arts program.
Continuing Education: Evening courses in journalism and creative writing.
Extra-Curricular: Publishes poetry and fiction and organizes seminars on contemporary authors.

Laurentian University
Ramsey Lake Road, Sudbury, Ont. P3E 2C6
Academic: Creative writing course.
Extra-Curricular: Publishes Lambda, a student newspaper, and Laurentian University Review, a literary journal.

Lethbridge Community College
3000 College Drive S., Lethbridge, Alta. T1K 1L6
Academic: Diploma courses in journalism. Creative writing is offered in conjunction with English literature and language courses.
Extra-Curricular: Publishes *The Endeavour*, a semi-monthly newspaper.

University of Lethbridge
4401 University Drive, Lethbridge, Alta. T1K 3M4
Academic: Two degree courses in creative writing.
Extension: Credit courses in creative writing.
Extra-Curricular: Students' union publishes *Meliorist*. Department of English publishes *Whetstone*, a poetry magazine.

Loyalist College of Applied Arts and Technology
P.O. Box 4200, Belleville, Ont. K8N 5B9
Academic: Two-year journalism program includes courses in newspaper production, feature writing, and script writing. Creative writing included in English courses.
Continuing Education: Creative writing courses.

Malaspina College
900 Fifth Street, Nanaimo, B.C. V9R 5S5
Academic: First- and second-year degree courses in creative writing. To major in creative writing a student must transfer to a university.
Continuing Education: Journalism and creative writing courses.
Extra-Curricular: Publishes *The Navigator*, a student newspaper, and *The Stump*, a creative writing journal. Sponsors writing conferences on a rotating basis with other colleges.

University of Manitoba
Winnipeg, Man. R3T 2N2
Academic: Offers courses in creative writing and advanced exposition.
Extra-Curricular: Publishes a creative writing magazine, *Northern Lights*, and journals for the comparative study of literature and ideas: *Mosaic, The Journal of Canadian Fiction*, *CV/II*, and *Canadian Review of American Studies*. Also publishes *Alumni Journal* and *The Manitoban*.

Marianopolis College
3880 Côte-des-Neiges Road, Montreal, Que. H3Y 1W1

Academic: One optional creative writing course gives one credit towards diploma.

McGill University
845 Sherbrooke Street W., Montreal, Que. H3A 2T5
Extension: Occasional non-degree, non-diploma courses in journalism and creative writing.

McMaster University
Hamilton, Ont. L8S 4L8
Academic: Courses in practical criticism and creative writing.
Extension: Journalism and writing courses.

Memorial University of Newfoundland
St. John's, Nfld. A1C 5S7
Extension: Occasional non-degree, non-diploma journalism and creative writing courses.

Mohawk College
135 Fennell Avenue W., Hamilton, Ont. L8N 3T2
Academic: A three-year diploma course in communication arts covering newspaper, radio and television journalism, advertising, and public relations. An elective course in creative writing is also offered.
Continuing Education: A writers' workshop.

Mount Allison University
Sackville, N.B. E0A 3C0
Academic: One degree credit course in advanced writing.

Mount Royal College
4825 Richard Road S.W., Calgary, Alta. T3E 6K6
Academic: A creative writing course covers fiction and poetry. An advanced composition course deals with semantics, style, and aesthetics.
Extra-Curricular: A journal of creative writing and art called *Skylines* is published three, sometimes four times a year.

Mount Saint Vincent University
166 Bedford Highway, Halifax, N.S. B3M 2J6
Academic: One creative writing course.

New Brunswick Community College
P.O. Box 6000, Fredericton, N.B. E3B 5H1
Continuing Education: Self-interest creative writing courses are sometimes offered, depending on demand. Journalism courses and writers' conferences are also being considered.

University of New Brunswick
P.O. Box 4400, Fredericton, N.B. E3B 6L3

Academic: A creative writing course with a BA credit is offered, as is an MA degree with a creative writing option (i.e. one third of course work, plus thesis). The MA degree also honours credit courses in expository writing, two at the introductory level and one at the more advanced level.
Extension: A non-credit creative writing course.
Extra-Curricular: Has a writer-in-residence and sponsors *Fiddlehead Poetry Books/Goose Lane Editions*, writers' conferences, plus a drama and radio workshop. Also publishes *The Brunswickan.*

College of New Caledonia
3330 - 22nd Avenue, Prince George, B.C. V2N 1P8
Academic: Liberal Arts and Science divisions offer an evening course in creative writing.
Continuing Education: A series of eight poetry readings are sponsored yearly.

Niagara College of Applied Arts and Technology
Woodlawn Road, Welland, Ont. L3B 5S2
Academic: Two-year journalism diploma course is offered.
Continuing Education: Credit coures in creative writing.
Extra-Curricular: Publishes a bi-weekly newspaper, *Niagara News.*

Northern College of Applied Arts and Technology
P.O. Box 2002, South Porcupine, Ont. P0N 1H0
Academic: Report writing included in all diploma courses.

Okanagan College
P.O. Box 1799, Oliver, B.C. V0H 1T0
Academic: One diploma course in creative writing has been proposed.
Continuing Education: Occasional courses in journalism and creative writing organized according to demand.

University of Ottawa
Ottawa, Ont. K1N 6N5
Academic: Undergraduate course in creative writing. BA, MA, and PhD courses in practical and speculative criticism are offered by day and in the evening.
Extra-Curricular: Publishes *Fulcrum*, the student newspaper, *Thalis*, a tri-annual scholarly journal, and a quarterly journal called *Alumni news/Revue de l'Université d'Ottawa.* Also publishes *The Canadian Short Story Series* to include representative stories by Canadian authors, and *Re-Appraisals of Canadian Literature*, a journal of criticism sponsored by the English Department.

Parkland Community College
317 Main Street, Melville, Sask. S0A 2P0

Continuing Education: Courses offered are requested by people living in nearby Esterhazy, Invermay, Ituna, Kamsack, Melville, Neudorf, Sturgis, Yorkton City, and Yorkton Rural. They are mostly non-credit courses involving some writing. A variety of junior and senior degree-credit English courses contracted from the University of Saskatchewan are offered in Yorkton.

University of Prince Edward Island
550 University Avenue, Charlottetown, P.E.I. C1A 4P3
Academic: One creative writing credit may be applied towards a bachelor's degree.
Extension: Creative writing courses.

Queen's University
Kingston, Ont. K7L 3N6
Academic: Creative writing courses.
Extra-Curricular: Publishes *Queen's Quarterly*, a journal of criticism and creative writing, and *Quarry*, a literary magazine containing poetry, prose and reviews.

Red Deer College
P.O. Box 5005, Red Deer, Alta. T4N 5H5
Academic: Diploma and degree course in creative writing. Students may major in writing with English Department courses.
Continuing Education: Writers' conferences are sponsored.
Extra-Curricular: Publishes *New Thursday* and *The Bricklayer*.

Red River Community College
2055 Notre Dame Avenue, Winnipeg, Man. R3H 0J9
Academic: A two-year diploma course in creative communications prepares students to work in print and electronic journalism, advertising, and public relations.
Continuing Education: Journalism and creative writing courses.
Extra-Curricular: Students in the Creative Communications program write for the college newspaper, *Projector*, and get on-the-job training as the Students' Association's communications director and/or the Athletic Department's information officer.

University of Regina
Regina, Sask. S4S 0A2
Academic: Four-year BA degree program in journalism is offered, as well as many creative writing courses. Although a student cannot major in creative writing, three or four courses may be applied to an English major.
Extension: Journalism and creative writing courses are offered and writers'conferences sponsored.
Extra-Curricular: The English Department publishes *Wascana Review*, a journal of poetry, short fiction, and scholarly articles. The university aso publishes *Canadian Plains Studies*.

Ryerson Polytechnical Institute
350 Victoria Street, Toronto, Ont. M5B 2K3
Academic: Three-year journalism degree program also includes courses in English literature and the humanities. A well-known school of journalism.
Extension: Copy editing, graphics and design, broadcast reporting.
Extra-Curricular: Publishes *The Ryersonian*, a daily newspaper, as well as *The Weekly* and *The Ryerson Magazine*, a monthly.

Saint Clair College
2000 Talbot Road, Windsor, Ont. N9A 6S4
Academic: Offers diploma courses in journalism and non-degree, non-diploma courses and workshops in creative writing.
Continuing Education: Creative writing courses.

Saint Francis Xavier University
Antigonish, N.S. B2G 1C0
Extra-Curricular: Publishes *The Antigonish Review.*

Saint Mary's University
Halifax, N.S. B3H 3C3
Academic: Two half-credits in creative writing.
Extension: Journalism and creative writing courses. Writers' conferences may be considered.
Extra-Curricular: Publishes *Sift*, a literary journal, and *The Atlantic Provinces Book Review.*

Saint Thomas University
Fredericton, N.B. E3B 5G3
Academic: Provides both freshmen and advanced students with degree courses in creative writing.
Extension: Journalism and creative writing courses.
Extra-Curricular: Writers' conferences. A fiction writing weekend is held each year. Publishes *Aquinian*, a newspaper, and *Revelations*, a literary journal. Accepts manuscripts from outside contributors.

University of Saskatchewan
Saskatoon, Sask. S7N 0W0
Academic: Creative writing courses.
Extra-Curricular: Publishes *The Sheaf*, the student newspaper.

Sault College of Applied Arts and Technology, The
443 Northern Avenue, P.O. Box 443, Sault Ste. Marie, Ont. P6A 5L3
Continuing Education: Occasional journalism and creative writing courses.

Seneca College of Applied Arts and Technology
1750 Finch Avenue E., Willowdale, Ont. M2N 5T7

Academic: Options offered to day students by the English and Communications divisions for television and radio scripting, playwriting, and journalism.
Continuing Education: Courses offered in various creative writing subjects. These change each semester according to demand and the availability of suitable instructors. A two-year diploma course in applied communications offers pre-professional training in print, broadcast, and film, including five writing courses in those media.

Sheridan College of Applied Arts and Technology
1430 Trafalgar Road N., Oakville, Ont. L6H 2L1
Academic: Offers a two-year diploma course in community journalism, plus a one-year journalism diploma course for university and community college graduates.

Simon Fraser University
Burnaby, B.C. V5A 1S6
Academic: A creative writing course.
Extra-Curricular: The English Department, like those in some other universities, has a writer-in-residence for one semester each year. The writer is available for consultation. University publishes *West Coast Review*, a creative writing journal.

Sir Sandford Fleming College
P.O. Box 653, Peterborough, Ont. K9J 7B1
Academic: Journalism and creative writing courses are under review.
Continuing Education: A general-interest non-credit course in creative writing is offered.

University of Toronto
Toronto, Ont. M5S 1A1
Academic: Creative writing courses are offered regularly by the English Department.
Continuing Education: Occasional creative writing and journalism courses are sponsored.
Extra-Curricular: Publishes *U of T Quarterly*, an academic journal which includes *Letters in Canada*, a critical survey of major Canadian books published in French and English, each summer. The various colleges – University, Victoria, Trinity, Saint Michael's – publish their own student newspapers and student literary magazines of which University's *Gargoyle*, Victoria's *Acta Victoriana*, and Trinity's *Salterra* are noteworthy. The Students' Union underwrites *The Varsity*, a student newspaper. A second student newspaper called *The Newspaper* was established in 1977.

University of Toronto (Erindale College)
3359 Mississauga Road, Mississauga, Ont. L5L 1C6

Academic: Two degree courses in creative writing are offered.
Continuing Education: Journalism and creative writing courses.
Extra-Curricular: Publishes the student newspaper, *Medium II*, and the student-edited *Erindale Review*, which accepts manuscripts from outside contributors.

University of Toronto (Victoria College)
73 Queen's Park, Toronto, Ont. M5S 1K7
Academic: One degree course in creative writing.
Extra-Curricular: Publishes a newspaper, *The Strand*, and a literary journal, *Acta Victoriana*. Accepts manuscripts from outside contributors.

Trent University
Peterborough, Ont. K9J 7B8
Extra-Curricular: Publishes *Catalyst*, a journal of theory and criticism, and *Park News*, which contains wilderness news, issues, publications, equipment, conferences, and expeditions.

Trinity Western University
7600 Glover Road, Langley, B.C. V3A 4R9
Academic: Credit courses in creative writing.
Extra-Curricular: Publishes a student paper, *Trinity Western Today*.

Vancouver Community College
100 W. 49th Street, Vancouver, B.C. V5Y 2Z6
Academic: Diploma courses in journalism. Transfer courses in creative writing lead to a degree from a nearby university.
Extension: Creative writing courses.
Extra-Curricular: Publishes *VCC Voice*, a newspaper.

University of Victoria
P.O. Box 2200, Victoria, B.C. V8W 2Y2
Academic: General and majors programs are offered in creative writing, both towards BA and BFA degrees.
Extra-Curricular: The Alma Mater Society publishes *The Martlet*, a student newspaper.

University of Waterloo
Waterloo, Ont. N2L 3G1
Academic: Arts elective courses in creative writing.
Extra-Curricular: Publishes *The Imprint*.

University of Western Ontario
London, Ont. N6A 3K7
Academic: A four-year BA course in journalism is offered, as well as a one-year diploma course.
Extension: Several journalism courses.
Extra-Curricular: A writer-in-residence, appointed by the English Department, advises students and helps them publish *Pom Seed*.

Wilfrid Laurier University
Waterloo, Ont. N2L 3C5
Academic: Courses in advanced writing, written communications, research techniques, media and society, creative writing, oral communication, and film are offered.

University of Windsor
Windsor, Ont. N9B 3P4
Academic: Four writing courses at both the general and honours level. The university grants an MA in English and creative writing at the graduate level.
Extension: Creative writing courses offered as the demand warrants.
Extra-Curricular: Publishes *The University of Windsor Review*, *Alumni Times*, *The Ambassador*, and *The Lance Generation*.

University of Winnipeg
515 Portage Avenue, Winnipeg, Man. R3B 2E9
Academic: Degree courses in creative writing and playwriting are offered to those students whose aptitude is obvious in written samples of their work. Two half-courses in composition (basic and advanced) are open to students wanting to improve their writing. Students may not major in writing but may include any of these courses in a major or honours program.
Extension: From time to time, according to demand and rotation of offerings, courses in creative writing and composition are available.
Extra-Curricular: Regularly invites writers to visit the campus to give readings and lectures, and hold informal discussions with students. Publishes *The Uniter*, a weekly undergraduate newspaper, and *Mandala*, a literary annual.

York University (Main Campus)
4700 Keele Street, Downsview, Ont. M3J 1P3
Academic: Offers students the chance to major in creative writing with workshop courses in poetry, prose, fiction, screen writing, playwriting, and other related subjects.
Extra-Curricular: Publishes *Excalibur*, *Open Letter*, *Waves*, *Direction*, and occasional anthologies of workshop poems.

York University (Glendon College)
2275 Bayview Avenue, Toronto, Ont. M4N 3M6
Academic: One course in both media and creative writing is offered by English Department. Special topics and honours theses in these areas are also possible.

WRITERS' ORGANIZATIONS

The Alberta Publishers' Association,
10022 - 103rd Street, Room 102,
Edmonton, Alberta
T5J 0X2

Association of Book Publishers of British Columbia,
1622 West 7th Avenue,
Vancouver, British Columbia
V6J 1S5

Association of Canadian Publishers,
70 The Esplanade, 3rd Floor,
Toronto, Ontario
M5E 2R2

Atlantic Publishers Association,
Killam Library,
Dalhousie University,
Halifax, Nova Scotia
B3H 4H8

Canadian Authors Association,
24 Ryerson Avenue,
Toronto, Ontario
M5T 2P3

Canadian Book Information Centre,
260 King Street E.,
Toronto, Ontario
M5A 1K3

Canadian Book Information Centre (West),
1622 West 7th Avenue,
Vancouver, British Columbia
VJ6 1B5

Canadian Book Information Centre (East),
Killam Library,
Dalhousie University,
Halifax, Nova Scotia
B3H 4H8

Canadian Book Information Centre (Prairies),
374 Donald Street, 3rd Floor,
Winnipeg, Manitoba
R3B 2J2

Canadian Book Publishers' Council,
45 Charles Street E., 7th Floor,
Toronto, Ontario
M4Y 1S2

Canadian Copyright Institute,
34 Ross Street, Suite 200,
Toronto, Ontario
M5T 1Z9

Canadian Periodical Publishers' Association,
2 Stewart Street,
Toronto, Ontario
M5V 1H6

Freelance Editors' Association of Canada,
34 Ross Street, Suite 200,
Toronto, Ontario
M5T 1Z9

The League of Canadian Poets,
24 Ryerson Avenue
Toronto, Ontario
M5T 2P3

Literary Press Group,
70 The Esplanade, 3rd Floor,
Toronto, Ontario
M5E 1R2

Magazines Canada,
250 Bloor Street East,
Toronto, Ontario
M4W 1E6

Periodical Writers Association of Canada,
24 Ryerson Avenue,
Toronto, Ontario
M5T 2P3

Playwrights Union of Canada,
8 York Street, 6th Floor,
Toronto, Ontario
M5J 1R2

Prairie Publishers Group,
374 Donald Street, 3rd Floor,
Winnipeg, Manitoba
R3B 2J2

The Writers' Federation of Nova Scotia,
P.O. Box 3608, South Post Office,
Halifax, Nova Scotia
B3J 3K6

The Writers' Development Trust,
24 Ryerson Avenue,
Toronto, Ontario
M5T 2P

The Writers' Union of Canada,
24 Ryerson Avenue,
Toronto, Ontario
M5T 2P3

USEFUL BOOKS

A Manual of Style, (12th edition, revised), University of Chicago Press, Chicago, 1974.

Burack, Sylvia K., ed. *The Writer's Handbook*, The Writer, Inc., Boston, 1982.

Bernstein, Theodore M. *Watch Your Language*, Atheneum, New York, 1976.

Bernstein, Theodore M. *Miss Thistlebottom's Hobgoblins: The Careful Writer's Guide to the Taboos, Bugbears and Outmoded Rules of English Usage*, Simon and Schuster, New York, 1971.

Bernstein, Theodore M. *The Careful Writer*, Atheneum, New York, 1965.

Kernaghan, E., Kernaghan, P., and Surridge, E. *The Upper Left-Hand Corner*, J.J. Douglas, Vancouver, 1979.

Messenger, William E. and de Bruyn, Jan. *The Canadian Writer's Handbook*, Prentice-Hall of Canada, Ltd., Toronto, 1980.

Miller, Casey and Swift, Kate. *The Handbook of Nonsexist Writing*, Lippincott & Crowell, New York, 1980.

Molinaro, M. and Wilson, M.C. *A Writer's Contract*, Canadian Speakers and Writers' Services, Toronto, 1979.

Peterson, Franklynn and Kesselman-Turkel, Judi. *The Magazine Writer's Handbook*, Prentice-Hall, Inc., Englewood Cliffs, N.J., 1982.

Shaw, Harry. *McGraw-Hill Handbook of English*, (2nd edition), McGraw-Hill Company of Canada Limited, Toronto, 1970.

Strunk, William Jr. and White, E.B. *The Elements of Style*, (3rd edition), Macmillan Publishing Co., Inc., New York, 1979.

The Canadian Style, A Guide to Writing and Editing, Dundurn Press Limited, Toronto, and the Canadian Government Publishing Centre, Ottawa, 1985.

Waller, Adrian. *Writing! An informal, anecdotal guide to the secrets of crafting and selling non-fiction*, McClelland and Stewart Limited, Toronto, 1987.

Woolfolk Cross, Donna. *Word Abuse*, Coward, McCann & Geoghegan, Inc., New York, 1979.

Zinsser, William. *On Writing Well*, Harper & Row, New York, 1980.

Zinsser, William. *Writing with a Word Processor*, Harper & Row, New York, 1983.

DICTIONARIES AND THESAURUSES

Chapman, Robert L., ed. *Roget's International Thesaurus*, (4th edition), T.Y. Crowell, New York; Fitzhenry & Whiteside Ltd., Toronto, 1977.

Copperud, Roy H. *A Dictionary of Usage and Style*, Hawthorn Books, Inc., New York, 1967.

Fowler, H.W. *Dictionary of Modern English Usage*, (2nd edition), edited by Sir E. Gowers, Oxford University Press, Oxford, 1965.

Hayakawa, S.I., ed. *Funk and Wagnalls Modern Guide to Synonyms*, Funk and Wagnalls, New York, 1986.

Funk and Wagnalls Standard College Dictionary, (Canadian edition), Fitzhenry & Whiteside, Toronto, 1976.

Oxford American Dictionary, Oxford University Press, New York, 1980.

Oxford Dictionary for Writers and Editors, Oxford University Press, Oxford, 1984.

REFERENCE BOOKS AND MAGAZINES

The Book Trade in Canada, published annually by Ampersand Publishing Services Inc.

Canadian Author and Bookman, published by the Canadian Authors Association, at 24 Ryerson Avenue, Toronto, Ont. M5T 2P3.

Literary Market Place, published annually by R.R. Bowker Publishing Co. Ltd.

Sources, The Directory of Contacts for Editors, Reporters and Researchers, published twice yearly at 9 St. Nicholas Street, Suite 402, Toronto, Ont. M4Y 1W5, as part of *Content Magazine*, and circulated to almost 12,000 newsmedia personnel.

The Writer, 120 Boylston Street, Boston, Massachusetts, 02116.

Writer's Digest, published by Writer's Digest, 9933 Alliance Road, Cincinnati, Ohio, 45242.

Writers' and Artists' Year Book, published annually by A. & C. Black.